NOCTURNAL ADMISSIONS

Behind the Scenes at Tunnel, Limelight, Avalon, and Other Legendary Nightclubs

BY STEVE ADELMAN

Foreword by ANTHONY HADEN-GUEST

SANTA
MONICA
PRESS

Published by: Santa Monica Press LLC
P.O. Box 850
Solana Beach, CA 92075
1-800-784-9553
www.santamonicapress.com
books@santamonicapress.com

Printed in the United States

Santa Monica Press books are available at special quantity discounts when purchased in bulk by corporations, organizations, or groups. Please call our Special Sales department at 1-800-784-9553.

ISBN-13   978-1-59580-114-2 (print)
ISBN-13   978-1-59580-780-9 (e-book)

Publisher's Cataloging-in-Publication data

Names: Adelman, Steve, 1962-, author. | Haden-Guest, Anthony, foreword author.
Title: Nocturnal admissions : behind the scenes at Tunnel , Limelight , Avalon , and other legendary nightclubs / by Steve Adelman; foreword by Anthony Haden-Guest.
Description: Solana Beach, CA: Santa Monica Press, 2022.
Identifiers: ISBN 978-1-59580-114-2 (print) | 978-1-59580-780-9 (e-book)
Subjects: LCSH Adelman, Steve, 1962-. | Nightlife--New York (State)--New York--History--20th century. | Nightclubs--New York (State)--New York--History--20th century. | Nightlife-- Boston (Mass.)--History--20th century. | Nightclubs-- Boston (Mass.)--History--20th century. | Celebrities--Anecdotes. | New York (N.Y.)--Biography. | BISAC BIOGRAPHY & AUTOBIOGRAPHY / Entertainment & Performing Arts | BIOGRAPHY & AUTOBIOGRAPHY / Personal Memoirs | MUSIC / Business Aspects | PERFORMING ARTS / Business Aspects
Classification: LCC F128.55 .A34 2022 | DDC 974.7/1/092--dc23

Cover and interior design and production by Future Studio
Cover photo: Drew Ressler/rukes.com

CONTENTS

This book is dedicated to my wife Michele,
who is always there beside me,
and to Mary and Mel, who touched the lives of so many
with their own unique ways of making us smile.

FOREWORD

BY ANTHONY HADEN-GUEST

Your life story must include a nightlife story.

Nightclubs were part of my growing up. Just walking into a good club was an upper, with high hopes of finding yourself in good company, whether familiar faces or promising new ones. So there was that, but there was also always keeping an eye open for the unexpected because the worlds that the clubs welcomed you into differed, somewhat or greatly, but they were all worlds apart from the overly known landscapes of home, college, workplace. That said, the nightworld of big cities has changed, hugely, and it is changing still. But we'll get to that. Right now, it's flashback time.

The London nightclubs of the late '50s and the '60s, which were my first clubs, were each the arena of a defined group. Annabel's in Berkeley Square was old-school posh. Indeed, ultra-posh. Queen Elizabeth II and most of the royals had made a night of it in Annabel's some time or other. But the emergent power, which was described by *Queen* magazine as the New Class and which included media hotshots and movie folk, would tend to go to Tramp in Jermyn Street. So it was naturally in Tramp that the debonair, late gossip columnist, Nigel Dempster, introduced me to his deceptively fragile looking protégé, Anna Wintour. Then there was Esmeralda's Barn in Knightsbridge, popular on the debutante circuit. Until it morphed into a gambling club and was taken over by the ultra-violent crime lords, the Kray Twins, who saw it as a way of extending their reach into London's posh West End.

There was also Raymond Nash's Condor Club in Soho, the name of which sounds just like the French for golden vagina, which was mostly for younger toffs, and in which I remember that witty singer, the late Jeremy Lloyd, delivering a King Arthur-themed ballad with the killer closing line: *And two dirty knights make one wonderful weekend.*

Also in Soho, there was the Ad Lib, which was given over to another emergent superpower, Pop, which was where the Beatles had their own private table. Indeed John Lennon appeared in a TV comedy, playing Dan the Doorman of the club, renamed the Ad Lav for the show. In 1971 they told *Rolling Stone* of going to a dinner at which their drinks had been spiked with LSD and tripping on their way to the club.

"We all thought there was a fire in the lift," Lennon said. "It was just a little red light, and we were all screaming, all hot and hysterical."

Within the club things improved. "I had such an overwhelming feeling of well-being, that there was a God, and I could see him in every blade of grass," George Harrison told the mag. "It was like gaining hundreds of years of experience in twelve hours."

When disco exploded in New York the sense that there was a special dimension to nightlife was yet stronger. Steve Rubell, partner in Studio 54 with Ian Schrager, was ultra-smart when he chose to disregard the social hierarchies which were foundational in the London clubs and instructed Mark Benecke, who was working the door, not to just focus on toffs, whether homegrown or Eurotrash, but upon getting a good mix, creating—Rubell's word—a "salad." This was a time of intense social curiosity, being also the time of Tom Wolfe's New Journalism, so at Studio clubbing was not the comfortable same old, same old, but unpredictable, exciting.

This was also the period when the tabloid-molded celebrity culture was in an early phase. It added to the zing of Studio-going that clubbers might easily spot a movie star, a singer, a sports star— Elizabeth Taylor, say, Dolly Parton, OJ Simpson—in the lobby but that nobody back then would bother them. The photographers did their thing at the door but Rubell seldom allowed them within and if the famous should elect to misbehave, well, that's what VIP rooms were for.

So to the Beatles' Ad Lib trip. This was way out there, yes, but extreme experiences may well be part of any regular clubgoer's memories, whether great or iffy. Such as the night in the mid-90s my date and I got privately close in the Club Liquid in Miami Beach. At least I had thought privately. Until I spotted the photographer.

Other extreme club experiences may not be things you undergo, but happenings, just things you see. Like the evening in the Pyramid in the East Village, the club where Nirvana did their first New York gig, which was where I first saw Karen Finley, writhing, emitting pure energies on the floor. Or the night I went at the invitation of the performer, Otter, and arrived in time to see her disrobe from her Little Bo Peep costume— *Alice in Wonderland* stockings, a plumed hat—while another woman was running around topless, screaming at a heckler "It's not that I like women. I hate men!"

A bald young man then stood there while a beer bottle was shattered on his head. No blood, though. The next two bottles just bounced. End of story. A fellow then came onstage, suit and skinny tie, salesman attire, much of which he took off while he created fire, and began first to swallow it, then embrace his body with it. It didn't look as if it was particularly hot though, more like the blue flame that lingers on a Christmas pudding, so it didn't seem terribly threatening when he breathed the flame onto Otter's not particularly private parts. The bald young man was standing outside with somebody as my date and I left.

"Are you alright?" I inquired, meaning it.

"Now you ask," he said.

"A little late," said his friend.

Such fragmentary memories don't, of course, begin to convey the wholeness of my clubbing experience in Manhattan. Studio and Xenon were unalike, but both were haute disco. Distinctly different nocturnal terrains were occupied by the Mudd Club, Arthur Weinstein's After Hours joint, The Jefferson, Jackie 60/Mother, where performers included Mikhail Baryshnikov, Debbie Harry, Kembra Pfahler, and Genesis P-Orridge. Or Eric Goode's Area, where art ruled, where Warhol presented his Invisible Sculpture and the Land artist, Michael Heizer, parked a boulder on the dance floor, and there was the Roxy, which took rap and graffiti mainstream, where I first met Steve Adelman, who was surveilling the daft bacchanal with enviable cool. Each of these nocturnal magnets had its peculiar magic, and each offered nightlifers a space to mingle with other hopefuls. Each allowed you to deposit rich material into your memory bank, perhaps sometimes fear that you have depleted your brain cells, to be yourself or to wear a mask and be somebody wildly, splendidly other.

Dreariness arrived with a thump. Mayor Rudy Giuliani's Quality of Life project was his unqualified attempt to purge New York of any kind of free-thinking fun, an enterprise which now seems like a training run for the clownish follies of the Trump years, though more effectively conducted.

The closing of these wildly popular and creative mega-clubs, which had defined the era, pulled NYC nightlife down to such an extent that some of the more imaginative entrepreneurs, like Steve, took their skills elsewhere, lighting up the nights in such promising hotspots as Boston and Hollywood.

Which brings us to the Now. What will be the future of the New York nightworld? Certain tech changes will not be helpful. No photographs of the Beatles tripping have come my way, neither have any of the Otter event, nor, come to that, have I seen any of myself in Liquid, though I was reassured at the time that the shot had excluded my head. But the iPhone premiered in January 2007. So much for the deliciously decadent action of the VIP rooms-that-were.

The clubs in which those VIP rooms were situated are, of course, mostly gone anyway. Annabel's survives in London, but all the New York places named above are no more, with the Pyramid closing this April, felled by COVID-19, after 41 years being the last to go. Clubs have always tended to have a short lifespan though. Club culture sprang back to life after AIDS, it will do so after the virus.

My story is told from the lens of one who has over-enjoyed countless nights out as a guest. In the pages ahead, we'll go behind-the-scenes and into the world of the host, a nightlife architect if you will, who creates the nocturnal playground that becomes a part of all our lives.

Yes, the light and the dark. It's sometimes just welcoming to the weary, comfortingly the same, then all of a sudden it's astonishing, enriching, even shocking. It's the nightlife.

INTRODUCTION

"No one looks back on their life and
remembers the nights they got plenty of sleep."

—UNKNOWN

I'm a believer that sometimes you find things in your life, and sometimes they find you. This has proven to be true for me in just about
everything of consequence: relationships, business endeavors, pas-
sions, love. Growing up in Essexville, Michigan, it seemed that not much
of consequence was destined to happen for me there, so at a young age I
decided my future was somewhere else. My hometown's main distinction
will depend on whom you ask. Speed skater Terry McDermott, the "Essexville Rocket" who won the gold medal in the Innsbruck 1964 Olym-
pics, grew up there, as did Madonna . . . well, sort of. As a pseudo suburb
of Bay City, where Madonna was born, Essexville adopted her as one of
its own. These rights were later relinquished after she called Bay City a
"smelly little town" in a Jane Pauley interview.

My introduction to nightlife came at the young age of six. Watching
episodes of *I Love Lucy*, I couldn't wait for the action to move to Ricky's
Tropicana Club. As band leader, then club owner, guitar player, and singer in both English and Spanish, Ricky was my idol from a far-off land.

Combined with Lucy's antics, for me, the show's nights at the Tropicana were not only entertaining, but fascinating as well. When asked what I wanted to be when I grew up, an astronaut or the president were not in my plans. I wanted to be Ricky Ricardo.

The first dance floor I ever stepped onto was at my eighth-grade graduation gala held in the school's gym. The most distinct recollection I have from that night was the feeling of dancing under the lone disco ball without a care in the world. Since my only how-to reference was a New Year's Eve party I'd attended with my parents earlier that year, my moves were a repertoire inspired by the over-forty suburban crowd.

As flawed a dancer as I was, it didn't matter. There we were various "John Hughes" types, along with the voluptuous Miss Sanderson, all in harmony absent any judgment or self-consciousness. The entire class had rallied as one, a swept-up collective where all that mattered was the next song. The night was magical, and as I look back, I realize how its impact helped shape my life.

By the time I was thirty years old, I had already become a director for New York City's five largest nightclubs, at a time considered by most as the "golden era" of NYC nightlife. Within another ten years, I would come to own Hollywood's hottest celebrity clubs and travel to Asia to build the most expensive nightlife venue ever, all during the nightlife heydays of Los Angeles and Singapore. As improbable as this path has been, considering my Essexville beginnings, the ability to develop a single skill—one that many overlook—has helped me greatly in my journey.

I've learned to observe.

This book is about those observations. The road from small town to big city, filled with a cast of characters I could never have imagined. The legendary venues I directed and storied venues I created, from Boston to Singapore. The experience of navigating city crackdowns, crazed partners, and cultural differences while still being able to look at it all for what it was: a winding road less traveled that, if taken too seriously, would lead to the end of a high cliff.

Of course, observation without action leaves you as a spectator on the sidelines. If I've learned anything, it's if you are going to jump out onto the dance floor, best take a good hard look before you leap.

Over time, I've adopted many of my observations into needed guidance (and a way to maintain sanity) that I call "learned axioms." These "laxioms," for lack of a better term, come from years of negotiating, absorbing, having bizarre encounters, and interacting with people in various stages of drunkenness, sexual frustration, self-denial, narcissism, depression, euphoria, and just about any other human condition you could think of.

These laxioms have become my code, never to be broken and constantly in use as a reference for anything life throws my way, from the urgent to the mundane to the ridiculous. Most importantly, they have helped me to both survive and thrive for over three decades in an industry where most last less than a year. I have chosen to include some of these laxioms in the book since, without them, the adventure ahead would have taken a different path.

The "world at night" I have lived in for almost my entire working life is unlike any other, continually transforming itself . . . and us. Whether it was the mainstream acceptance of gay culture, the influence of dance music on all facets of society, or the genesis of Kardashian culture, pop culture has always taken its cues from nightlife, which in turn serves as a mirror reflecting the culture at that moment in time. Nightlife's true history is one each of us creates for ourselves, recounted to longtime friends, family, loved ones, and new acquaintances throughout our lives.

Nightlife is critical to our well-being, a transcendent gathering place where people can become whomever they like; a world within itself where we are unbound by the restrictions and limits set forth by daytime responsibilities, income level, sexual orientation, race, or political beliefs. It has always filled the universal need for the ultimate escape, a place to forget your worries, fears, and problems while bonding with others, if only for a few short hours.

This has never been more evident than during the COVID-19 pandemic, during which, after months of insolation, salvation was initially found through TikTok dance videos and Zoom parties. However, while virtual connections filled a short-term void, the hard-wired desire for physical proximity soon led to dangerous non-social distancing activities in pop-up nightclubs, the most notable being the exposed, illegal house parties that raged in Los Angeles and the underground club nights in Brooklyn.

Think for a moment about a society without nightlife. It's hard to imagine.

Derived from our deepest form of self-expression, nightlife, in its many forms, is our permanent friend, always there when needed. Like most things of intrinsic value, it is rooted in simplicity, needing only a beat and a single disco ball to create magic and memories lasting a lifetime.

PART I
1989–1999

Roxy, Limelight, Palladium, Tunnel,
Club USA, Avalon, Axis, Embassy

CHAPTER 1

IN FULL SWING

"From my first days of my career as an entrepreneur,
I have always used my own and my team's
lack of experience to our advantage. . . .
Our inexperience fed our restless enthusiasm for trying
new things, which became the core of our mission."

—SIR RICHARD BRANSON

A rriving in New York City, I had no real sense of my way around. I'd only been there once before, two years earlier in 1987. As I hailed a taxi, my only guidance was a crumpled piece of paper with a street name and an indiscernible address scratched onto it.

"Take me to Eighteenth Street," I told the driver.

"Where on Eighteenth, buddy? Do you have an address? In Manhattan?"

"Manhattan, for sure. I think. Do you know where the Roxy is?"

"I know the Roxy Deli on Forty-Fourth."

"Just drop me on Eighteenth Street, and I'll find my way from there."

I was already on my way to becoming a true New Yorker.

As the cab drove, I peered out the half-frozen window, struck by the wintery chaos. Cabs, limos, and buses sprawled everywhere with seemingly no rules governing their comings and goings. A lone police officer appeared to be conducting an impromptu symphony, but it was clear that none of the strings, woodwind, or brass sections gave a damn. It was every oboe for itself, survival of the ready and opportunist. Little did I know, this would become a metaphor for my life in the City That Never Sleeps.

After being forced quickly out of the taxi, I began a "man on the street" interview process to determine my final destination. I always found that the best way to get directions was just to ask. This habit tended to drive some people crazy for either being unsafe or showing weakness and laziness. I could see those points, but for me it was a simple matter of practicality, tapping into others' knowledge and experience.

I realized years later that this trait came from my father, who, when visiting me in New York, would roam up to any random person and ask them just about anything. I was taken back to the times I'd witnessed this growing up. Fifth Avenue execs, gangbangers, the homeless, a mother with her child in the park—my father held no prejudices. "Hey, how are you today?" he'd inquire. Most times, this was met with a blank stare or a mumble. This didn't faze him, and he'd be on to the next person. My mother, Myrna, would soon become apoplectic. "Meellllvinnn!" she'd shout in her shrill voice. "Can you *please* just *stop*?"

Me, I loved him for it. Just imagine a world with millions of

---

LAXIOM #1
People care, just not that much.
During one of Mel's visits to New York, I watched as he made his rounds, struck by how he seemed to have no concern for others' perceptions of him. Asking if this was indeed the case, his response was: "Most people are really only concerned with themselves, so why should I be worried about what they think of me when they really don't care that much to begin with?"

---

open-hearted Mels.

Fifth time being a charm, I found an elderly, bundled-up man and asked him if he knew where the Roxy was.

"Oh, yeah, the roller-skating rink," he said. *Roller-skating rink?* "It's on Tenth and Eighteenth."

With snow fluttering down like New Year's Eve confetti in Times Square, I began walking down Eighteenth Street, where, within ten minutes, I dead-ended at Avenue D. I grabbed the first person I saw.

"Looking to get to Tenth and Eighteenth," I managed to spit out through trembling lips.

"You must mean Tenth Avenue and Eighteenth Street. Dude, you're on the wrong side of the city. It's fifteen blocks that way." He pointed in the direction from where I'd just come.

Then, just when I needed it most, it happened: a taxi drop-off ten feet in front of me. As I rushed toward my would-be ride, my mind easing somewhat, a black-clad version of the Flash appeared out of nowhere, cutting me off in a split second. The cab door slammed shut and it sped away, leaving me behind to enjoy what was now turning into a blizzard.

I set out on the thirteen-block trek. With six blocks down and frost-bite imminent, I found a parked taxi with its driver frantically eating from a Styrofoam container. He motioned me in without missing a mouthful.

When we arrived at Tenth and Eighteenth, I realized I was missing the one thing I'd be needing the most—my wallet. This, of course, didn't sit well with my "I'd rather be anywhere else than here" driver, who let me know that the only reason he took me on board was because his shift was ending and he was on his way to drop off his cab. Explaining that I needed to get money from someone inside the building elicited the ire of my already-on-edge companion.

"How long will that take? I need to get this car back *now*!"

"Ummm . . . I'm not even sure where I'm going yet . . . exactly."

"Just get out!" he yelled, throwing a "fuck you" tirade as he sped away.

Using the process of elimination, I took my chances on a black building with a barely visible "Mendon Trucking" sign scrawled across it. A large metal pull-down gate covered what appeared to be an entrance, adjacent to a lone black door. A handwritten sign that read "Ring for Deliveries" was taped to the small buzzer. Entering what appeared to be a large, sloped hallway, made to look even more expansive by the mirrors that lined both sides, I trod forward with barely enough light to make out anything around me. I ended up at a large counter with a "Rentals Here" sign hovering over it.

"Can I help you?" a woman asked as she seemingly glided across the floor like a Billie Eilish apparition.

"Is Gene in?" I asked.

Before she could answer, another voice came out of the semi-darkness: "I think he's in a meeting. Are you here to meet him?"

"I am," I answered, now able to put a face to the voice as a figure seemingly plucked from a Tom Ford runway emerged from the shadows. "I'm Steve . . . from Boston."

"Hello, Steve from Boston. I'm Gregory."

I didn't know it at the time, but this chance meeting was the beginning of a thirty-year friendship and professional collaboration across the United States and Asia.

"Looks like I made it to the right place, at least," I said, shaking his hand. "Not the easiest place to find."

"Only in New York can you find a roller rink and nightclub behind an unmarked door," Gregory replied with a chuckle.

Ghost Billie then led us into an unexpectedly vast space, defined by a football-field-sized dance floor, where she proceeded to perform an artful figure eight. As we walked, Gregory explained that the Roxy had been a roller rink since the late '70s. It was owned by Steven Greenberg, a sixty-something man-about-town whose flowing white hair gave him the appearance of a modern-day Benjamin Franklin. It now had a second act as a nightclub.

"So, what do you do here?" I asked Gregory.

"I'm the creative director, the marketing and branding designer. What do you think of these?" He took a folder out of his Gucci briefcase; it contained multiple Roxy logos in progress.

"I really like this one," I said, wowed by all I was seeing.

"Good call. Me too. Seems like you have a good eye for these things." Gregory gathered the pages back into his folder.

Wearing tight jeans that gave way to the latest designer sneakers, accentuated by a vintage Dior suit coat and trendsetting fade haircut, Gregory Homs looked every bit the part. He was a bit of a celebrity for his ingenious work at the World nightclub, the East Village converted theater famed for its diverse clientele (its actual name was the End of the World, which was derived by owner Arthur Weinstein based on its far-off-the-beaten-path location.)

On any night at the World, you might come across Keith Haring, Madonna, Prince, or Brooke Shields mixing with members of voguing houses, drag queens, and banjee boys. They danced to the sounds of house-music legend Frankie Knuckles, with cameo performances from the likes of David Bowie, the Beastie Boys, and Public Enemy, further adding to the club's cachet.

"And here we are," said Billie, stopping the tour at an inconspicuous room where Gene DiNino sat behind a small desk. The cramped office was making me feel claustrophobic. Uneven stacks of papers were strewn about, along with other random items like a mini disco ball and fabric swatches. Nightclub posters from Syracuse taped to each wall provided artwork.

"How can the fee be fifty percent of the actual job?" Gene sputtered into the phone. "Fuck you, this is just some designer fucking bullshit." He motioned for us to give him a minute. "Our meeting is here," he said, breaking away for a second before returning to the call.

Just then, two additional people packed themselves into the clown car of an office. None of us had enough space to sit. As I made awkward eye contact with the attendees, I soon recognized a "what the hell am I doing here" look on their faces, which no doubt mirrored my own expression.

Gene finished his call and turned to us. "Lee, David, meet Steve from Boston. He just got into town. You already know Gregory, of course. I wanted you all to meet as soon as possible, since Steve's going to be helping me out."

Before I could say anything, Lee, who appeared to be a big fan of vintage Vivienne Westwood with the styling of Tweedle Dee, beat me to the punch. "Help with what, exactly?" This brought a smirk from David, who, outfitted in full "hipster Liberace," brought his own unique presence to the proceedings.

After what seemed like ten minutes of frozen silence, I broke the awkwardness. "With anything I can," I stated with false bravado.

"Exactly," agreed Gene, who had already recommitted to his phone, dropping what were hopefully the only f-bombs left in his arsenal for the day.

An hour later, here's what I was able to ascertain: Gene had taken over the location four years earlier, and shortly thereafter began utilizing the skating rink as a mega dance floor on weekends, naming it the 1018 (for Tenth Avenue and Eighteenth Street). After a relatively short time, 1018 was closed for numerous violations, including purported drug sales and violence, putting Gene back at square one . . . operating a roller rink. The plan now was to restart as a nightclub, reverting back to the location's original name—minus the problems that had gotten it earmarked by the city as a public nuisance.

Months earlier, celebrated party promoter Susanne Bartsch used what was now the Roxy to host one of her gala spectacles, which incorporated the only-in-New-York, anything-goes energy of the World while upping the ante with the top echelons from the fashion and modeling industries, drawing the likes of Karl Lagerfeld, John Galliano, Helena Christensen, and Steven Meisel into the mix. The World had recently shut down for good after its latest owner, Steven Venizelos, described by the *New York Times* as a "corpulent man with a penchant for gold jewelry," was found shot to death at point-blank range on the club's balcony.

Lee and David, established promoters themselves, were regular attendees at Bartsch's events and were convinced that, after the success of her Roxy event, they could continue on in a similar manner every

Saturday night.

"She even left her swing here for us," David was quick to point out, referring to the large makeshift contraption over the dance floor that had been used by Bartsch's guests.

It was clear that Gene was taking issue with the entire idea, mainly based on his limited experience dealing with a New York City "fashion-fabulous" crowd, which fed his skepticism over replicating Susanne's one-time success.

"I really don't know about this, seems like a bit of a stretch," he said. "A weekly Saturday gay night for three thousand people? Steve, what do you think?"

Somewhat stunned, I felt pressure on my foot and, turning as best I could to Gregory, who was cozied up to me, I caught what I thought to be a small wink.

"Well," I mumbled, "this all does sound very interesting, to say the least." This was met by a small jab to my ribs. Gregory gave me a smile and a nod.

"As I see it, Gene has had some troubles in the past," I continued, "which makes opening the Roxy as a full-time nightclub . . . we'll say . . . challenging."

Blank stares all around. *Thanks for telling us what we already knew.*

"The idea on the table worked once before, so I think it's worth another try," I blurted, trying to hold the room.

This brought a pained look to Gene's face. "Maybe so, but Lee and David's proposal is very expensive," he said. "They want all new furniture and lighting—go-go boys, drag performers at three hundred dollars each, a two-thousand-dollar weekly theme design budget . . . four hundred for a doorman? A DJ at fifteen? Whatever happened to a three-hundred-dollar DJ and just open the doors? All the risk is on me, and if it doesn't work, I'm left holding the bag."

I hadn't yet considered this, and glanced quickly at Gregory. He maintained the same smile, nodding once again.

"Understood . . . but if it *does* work, you'll have no competition to speak of and a party that could continue for years," I blurted out, hoping I'd read my cue correctly. "I really think it's a good idea," I continued. "Something you should jump on."

"I think your instincts are right on," Gregory chimed in. "This could be groundbreaking for New York nightlife."

Lee and David turned out to be very right. Their weekly Saturday night event, named "Locomotion," quickly became a mecca not only for the fashion elite but for all those who wanted to experience nightlife as a theatrical art form. The scene became something to behold: a staff of up to twenty dressed-to-the-max drag queens lit up on podiums, along with a dozen or so thonged Chelsea muscle boys moving to the beats of such celebrated New York City DJs as Mark Kamins, Jellybean Benitez, and Sister Dimension.

Weekly theme concepts ranged from "Night of a Thousand Chers" to "Leather Daddies Christmas Spectacular," featuring a live performance from the Village People. A design crew of a dozen was brought in weekly to reimagine the look of the club, bringing the designated theme to life. The swing remained intact as a featured part of the festivities, becoming the ultimate photo op for frequent attendees Marc Jacobs and the Three Amigos: Linda, Naomi, and Kate.

Susanne Bartsch was furious, perceiving the whole phenomenon as a blatant act of plagiarism. I was proclaimed the director of the Roxy two days after that first meeting, a title I was ill prepared to deliver on. Any impressions Gene had about my experience were overly inflated—and that presented itself as potential for trouble in the weeks to follow.

CHAPTER 2

ON THE CASE

"The game is afoot."
—SHERLOCK HOLMES

I was twenty-four before I visited my first nightclub, putting me about five years behind the curve with my classmates at the Boston College Graduate School of Economics. I'd never considered nightlife as a career path, having determined that becoming an economic consultant was my way forward. How that was decided, I'm not quite sure, but it led to my being hired by a prestigious Boston firm, where I proceeded to dread every moment. I left after six months.

I had already discovered that if I didn't have a true emotional and vested interest in both the process and outcome of an event, I would lose focus and motivation at an alarmingly fast rate. If I didn't really *care* about something, I just shut down. Problem was, after years of predetermining what I cared about, economics turned out to be anything but, leaving me back at square one at the age of twenty-six with respect to career prospects.

As a result of an accidental meeting with Ira, the investor of a soon-to-be-opened nightclub in downtown Boston, I was asked to help run some numbers on a freelance basis. Not knowing what running numbers even entailed, I assured him that I could be of great assistance. I spent very little time crunching figures and instead became intrigued by how the business actually functioned, helping wherever I was needed. I quickly became a jack-of-all-trades, affording me my first (self-proclaimed) nightlife title: manager of stuff.

From ordering liquor to opening doors, I felt a strong desire to understand how it all worked. I could quickly see that in this world, one had opportunities to shape events and see the results on a daily basis, then begin the process anew the next morning. This served my constant bouts of ADD well and opened up the prospect of waking up on any given day with an idea, any idea—good, or even not so good—and turning it into reality.

After the club opened, I tried my hand at promotion, with the first party I organized being a night themed "Attack of the Killer Tomatoes," paying homage to the '70s camp film that had deemed itself "the funniest movie ever made." The theme consisted of blowing up fifty oversized, tomato-like beach balls, which I'd then toss into the crowd from my perch on the balcony.

To heighten the experience, the movie's theme song, along with the sound of the vicious vegetables approaching—a combination of dramatic *Jaws*-like music and comical gibberish—were played at full volume. The site of a completely desolate club, with only my trusted friend, Mary, batting beach balls into the air, might have been discouraging for some, but not for me. With some help from my ADD, I'd already adopted the nightlife adage of: You're only as good as your last party. The *"Attack of the Killer Tomatoes"* night may have bombed, but next month's "Seven Deadly Sins" party, hosted by RuPaul, would knock 'em dead. And it did.

Shortly thereafter, I received a call from Stacy, the assistant to the owner of the Roxy nightclub in NYC. She'd heard great things about me from RuPaul and was wondering if I'd be willing to come there. Hours later, I accepted the position with very little thought given to either planning or expectations for the future. I'd been in the nightlife business for all of five months and had never held an actual formal position. Two days later, after quickly scribbling down the club's address, I boarded a shuttle flight to NYC carrying only an old hockey-style duffle bag.

Now, it appeared that RuPaul, a charming, natural-born promoter and showman—skills that would serve him well as he became the face of drag culture in mainstream America—might have placed me on the edge of a double-edged sword. On any given night at Locomotion, I'd encounter a multitude of club-goers and celebrities who implicitly equated the night's success with the new guy in town—Steve from Boston. Jean Paul Gaultier spoke with me as if I were some sort of genius, as did both Dolce *and* Gabbana. I was quick to point out that all the credit belonged to Lee and David, who had created nothing short of a nightlife phenomenon. But this was mistaken for modesty, which only further enhanced my budding reputation.

As a result, I constantly suffered from imposter syndrome, heightened by my temporary residence on Gene's couch. As I saw it, the only way through this situation was to learn everything I could about my newly adopted world as quickly as possible.

In setting out to do so, it quickly became apparent that learning on the job would mean facing multiple challenges. I could ask as many questions as I wanted, hoping to not give myself away—but who could I ask? There were no *NYC Nightlife for Dummies* guides or academic courses available. If I was going to develop a keen understanding of the New York City club scene, this was going to have to be an on-the-ground, frontline initiative involving all-night legwork.

Clubs in NYC open at 10:00 PM, but beyond tourists, no one would be caught dead in one before midnight, when the true New Yorkers ventured out. This reverse Cinderella phenomenon created a scenario where 1:00 AM became prime time for me to glean information, putting me back home around 4:00 AM. On most nights, a small black notebook became my travel companion as I began a habit of writing down all I witnessed, sharpening my observation skills on a weekly basis.

"Are you a reporter?" a woman asked me one night at Nell's, a swanky hangout. Her strong London accent, dyed-green hair, and sequined red catsuit gave her the appearance of a glistening strawberry plucked right off Carnaby Street.

"No, just observing the scene and taking a few notes," I responded with a smile.

"Well, what are you then, a reporter?" she slurred. "Maybe some kind of detective? I know . . . you're Sherlock Holmes, and you're investigating a murder. Am I a suspect? Buy me a drink, and I'll confess to everything. Hi, I'm the Mysterious Shirley . . . as in *surely* you'll buy your star witness a cocktail." She extended her hand, barely remaining upright.

"Elementary," I exclaimed, in my best impromptu Sherlock Holmes voice. "You've had too much—"

But before I could complete the thought, Shirley Strawberry had toppled face-first to the floor.

Ms. Strawberry's comment stuck with me in the weeks to come, as I continued to carefully document my unfamiliar world. With my periodic ADD hampering my focus—not to mention long nights (and early mornings) of deafening music, blinding lights, and drunken ramblings—I employed an alter ego to help me cope.

LAXIOM #2
Be your own competition.

Frequently when I was out at night, I'd see the same rival club owner at the bar, chatting it up with a group of admirers. He seemed to be everywhere . . . except at his *own* club. When I asked him about this, he replied, "I have people I trust to tell me what goes on *there*. If I'm going to stay ahead, I need to know what my competitors are doing or, more importantly, what they're *thinking* of doing. You'd be surprised what people will tell you if you buy them a drink. I get most of my best ideas by stealing what other clubs are planning."

In romantic, Walter Mitty-like fashion, I began to imagine myself as a private eye of sorts, each evening venturing out to solve a different mystery. As a child, I'd been obsessed with detective mysteries, making weekly trips to the library for my latest *Hardy Boys* and *Encyclopedia Brown* hardcovers and taking it as a personal challenge to connect the clues before the clever boy-genius protagonists did. Years later, this reading passion transferred to the greatest fictional sleuth of all, Sherlock Holmes. Like Holmes, I would rely on the power of observation and become the greatest—and perhaps the *only*—nightlife detective.

My alter ego would begin to take over at around 10:00 PM, as I began the trek out of my apartment for dinner. I rarely, if ever, ate at home and would go months without ever using my stove or even entering my kitchen. Dinner was used as a tactical gathering where I could meet with various accomplices, many later accompanying me on adventures until sun-up. One night it could be the mysterious girl-about-town Evelyn, who would arrange entrance into the opening of a competitor's new Thursday night party. On another night, it was the promoter Johnny D. who had his ear to the ground, providing needed information on the nightlife world as we hopped to different East Village bars.

One of my favorite "cases" involved a trip to see a competitor who would unexpectedly later become a colleague. I called it "The Case of the Blabbering Deception." It took place on a Saturday night at the height of the Roxy's success.

The night began at the uber-trendy restaurant Indochine, where we met up with my trusted deputy, Alfredo. Tucked away behind two large, unassuming doors, with a small neon sign overhead denoting 430 Lafayette Street, the restaurant could easily be missed if one happened to be momentarily distracted when walking by, in true too-cool-for-school fashion. Alfredo entered and saw me seated alone in the booth adjacent to the six-stool bar.

I was dressed in what had become somewhat of my uniform: black newsboy cap, black button-up shirt, black jeans, and black Chuck Taylor sneakers, which I'd been told by Alfredo I had the distracting habit of displaying at table height as I sat with one leg crossed over the other.

"Thanks for joining me, right on time as always," I said, greeting him as I ushered him to sit.

"Expecting rain?" he asked, glancing at the umbrella on the seat next to me. "Seems like a clear night."

"Alfredo, you are indeed a master of the obvious—it's the obscure we need to flush out of you," I replied with one of my favorite Holmes quotes, while settling into my "other self."

"Is it always necessary to be eating this late? I mean, most people are in bed at eleven."

This brought a short laugh from me. "Since when are we like most people? Our workday is just starting."

I had already observed a few things before Alfredo arrived, which I took note of. First, for being one of the most popular dining experiences in NYC, the place was almost completely empty. I then noticed the full bottles of vodka lined up evenly on the shelf behind the bartender, as well as the neatly stacked cocktail napkins on the bartender's left. The hostess was dressed in the season's Margiela, and slung across her chair was a Kate Spade handbag. Our server was wearing Alexander McQueen sneakers. From this I determined that the crowd would be very late to arrive and comprised mainly of the fashion industry, making them "fashionably late." I had an ulterior motive for choosing Indochine that night: beyond their French Indonesian food being the talk of the town, it was also light cuisine.

Weeks earlier, I had learned a valuable lesson when joining an accomplice at the famed Brooklyn steakhouse Peter Luger. Dinner began at 11:00 PM, since the only reservation time available was 10:00 PM and we had to wait for our double-booked table. Anthony, our feeble, pushing-seventy waiter ordered the renowned porterhouse steak for me—no menu needed, he assured.

The sheer size of the one-and-a-half-inch-thick colossus that came to the table—which seemed to take every ounce of strength Anthony could muster to lift from his oversized serving tray—stirred feelings of amazement that quickly turned into ill-fated determination, egged on by the two dirty martinis with extra stuffed olives I had sipped on while waiting. Following the tradition established in 1887 by countless immigrants and native New Yorkers, to be truly a part of NYC one must consume an entire Peter Luger steak.

One hour later, after struggling to complete my initiation ritual, we headed to our destination: the third incarnation of the recently opened Danceteria on East Thirty-First Street, where, upon entering and settling into a chair, I proceeded to fall asleep in a meat-induced coma, the loud music and crowd around me quickly fading from my consciousness. I would learn later that although *visiting* Peter Luger was indeed a long-standing NYC tradition, finishing an entire porterhouse was not.

The ritual was explained to me by the owner of an after-hours club where I was sleuthing. Weighing around 350 pounds, sporting a thick Brooklyn accent, and resembling every guy ever named "Tiny" in a mob movie, "Mac" (full nickname being Big Mac, the origin of which seemed self-evident) seemed to know what he was talking about when it came to NYC eating customs.

Mac's place opened at 4:00 AM and stayed open until . . . well, I'm not really sure. Located in north Tribeca, it had no sign, nothing marking its location other than a metal door. A lone lookout security guard stood outside. When approaching him, protocol was to whisper the night's password, at which time the door would open and Mac would appear, sitting in a chair and waiting to take your $25 in his left hand, depositing the money in the cash register with his right hand.[1]

Walking through a small, dark room and overpowered by an incense of pot with a hint of cigarette and cigar, I could make out a group of Mac

---

1 The passwords were sometimes overly elaborate, in my opinion (like "Chitty, Chitty, Bang, Bang the drum") which made it critical that they be written down to be remembered, which in turn seemed to defeat the whole point of making them elaborate.

"Michelin Man" body doubles playing poker through the haze, using $5 bills instead of chips. A pool table sat in the corner with a single red light bulb overhead and, in the center, a dance floor able to accommodate up to fifty people was lit by what appeared to be a flashlight emanating from a raised DJ booth. Over the years, I have forgotten the actual name of the club, but not the three times that I visited.[2]

The cast of characters at Mac's was like nothing I could have imagined. There was Frankie Watches (best lookout security in town), Tina Tits (as in, "she's the tits"), Frankie the Clown (purveyor of bad jokes . . . and an occasional good one), strippers coming off their shifts and going by their requisite work names, Wall Street traders, card and pool sharks, impeccably dressed drag queens, nightclub staff looking to have *their* night out, professional athletes, and even Shirley Strawberry (real name Pam Notting, as I remember).

Mac's fashion sense leaned "sporty casual," encompassing mainly the Mets, Jets, Nets (who played in New Jersey at the time), and sweats. He donned a signed XXL jersey of one of his three favorite teams and gray, heavy cotton drawstring Champion sweatpants, pulled up "Lalanne style" over his girth to defy gravity. He would appear as he made his rounds, checking on his guests, all of whom he seemed to have some manner of business.

During my initial time at Mac's I was accompanied by Rae, the only female-born dancer at the Roxy. She assured me that the trip would be worth my while.

"What is this place?" I asked her as she dragged on her hand-rolled cigarette.

"If you really want to know what's going down in the clubs, dis is da place to find out, man," she replied in her heavy Russian accent. "Mock

---

2 I actually remember the name being Bassline, but was reminded by an ex-employee that Bassline was a different after-hours club founded by DJ Junior Vasquez and partner Christina Visca. The ex-employee also couldn't remember the official name of Big Mac's place, although he'd been there numerous times himself. It's amazing what you *can't* remember after 4:00 AM.

does za business with everyone."[3]

"Rae, so good to see you, and looking hot as always," said Mac, stopping by our table. "If your guys want any more Knicks tickets, just let them know I can get them on the floor for twenty-five hundred dollars apiece. Who's your friend?"

"This is Steve from Boston. He works at za Roxy. What was your job again?"

"Director."

"Yeah, director . . . he directs shit."

"Steve . . . from Boston, huh," said Mac, rubbing the stubble on his cantaloupe-sized chin. "I can get you tickets to Celtics games with one phone call. I'm talking right down in the fuckin' action."

"Thanks, Mac, I'll keep that in mind."

"And those gays have lots of money. Send them to me for Broadway tickets and shit like that and I'll give you fifteen percent."

"Give me twenty and I'm in."

"I like this guy," said Mac, cracking a wide smile highlighted by a gold front tooth, then spotting his next potential deal and moving on.

Mac was indeed a good source of information. He knew which clubs were having financial problems (Roxy, alarmingly, being one of them) and what every club owner in all five boroughs was planning. His insights weren't free; you paid your $25 and were expected to order at least two watered-down drinks at $15 apiece. Those were the rules.

"Boston Steve, can I get yo a drink?" Mac would ask. He seemed to always know if I was short of my quota. It became evident that Mac wasn't asking, but telling me.

When the Celtics played the Knicks at the Garden, old classmates from Boston College asked me if I could get tickets, which led me to Mac, who was thrilled that I had brought him customers from a potential

---

3 Rae would later let me in on one of Mac's lucrative ventures: staking one of the Michelin poker guys for a percentage of his winnings, which were substantial, given he was one of the Ukraine's best players.

new market to grow his enterprise.

"Tell them, that before the game they need to go to Peter Lugers," Mac told me. "They are booked six months in advance, but I can get them in. Let me tell you about Peter Lugers . . ."

"Fuckin' Mac told you what?" said one of the Roxy security guards when I asked him about the practice later. "Man, those steaks are supposed to be for at least *two* people. Didn't you read the menu? They're over thirty ounces. Man, that's some whack shit."

Apparently, Mac's personal traditions didn't translate to all New Yorkers, but it had taught me that heavy eating on work nights was off limits if I was going to be an agile nightlife detective.

A month after coming out of my beef slumber, I went back to Mac's for some clarification on the rumor that Red Zone, the mega disco of Fifty-Fourth Street, was closing. The heavy metal door was now a pull-down grate with "RIP" graffitied on it. But Big Mac's place was gone—and so was Big Mac.

After securing the table we needed in order to monitor the entire restaurant, I let Alfredo in on my plan.

"Tonight, there is something sinister afoot."

"Sinister afoot?" he said with an exaggerated eye roll. "Is that another one of your Sherlock Holmes quotes? What's up with that, anyway?"

"Indeed, it is," I replied. "I use them for inspiration."

I then ordered for the both of us: steamed Vietnamese ravioli and filet of sole cooked in coconut milk.

"I'm sure you're aware of the Palace de Beauté in Union Square?" I asked, taking a sip of the well-regarded infused vodka.

"Yup," Alfredo replied, sampling his own house version of a cosmopolitan. "Looks like we've got some real competition."

"I've been told they're going after the Saturday Roxy crowd. Apparently, their plan is to take our key VIPs." I explained. "And Indochine will be part of the plan."

"Here . . . how?

"All in good time," I replied. "Isn't the food here fantastic? We've got to leave room some dessert."

As our dinner came to an end, an increasing level of dread appeared to creep over Alfredo.

"You know what this means?" he asked solemnly. "Lewis."

Turning my head, I gave him an ever-so-slight nod, then continued on with my ginger crème brûlée.

Alfredo was referring to Steven Lewis, called simply "Lewis" by anyone who had met him. He'd risen to prominence as the director of the World nightclub, where his schemes and tactics against competitors became tales of legend. Loathed but tolerated by seemingly everyone in the New York City nightlife scene, he was atypical in every sense. While his rare combination of false bravado, intelligence, dry humor, frantic energy, knowledge, and insecurity made him a narcissistic pariah to others, I found him both fascinating and charming. One thing was certain: Lewis seemed to know everybody, and everybody seemed to know Lewis.

With the Roxy now holding the mantle as New York City's number-one club, Lewis and his current club, Palace de Beauté, the newly opened nightclub owned by New York City nightlife legend Maurice Brahms, were in the unfamiliar situation of *not* being the center of attention. Alfredo's last sighting of Lewis had been at the Palace, where he had taken up a position outside two weeks earlier and Lewis had also deemed himself head doorman. As Alfredo approached the red velvet ropes, an impromptu conversation began between Lewis and his sidekick, longtime sanctuary guardian and drag-queen-about-town Kenny Kenny, before Lewis disappeared inside.

"I just con't let you in," explained Kenny in his dramatic English accent. "Sorry . . . it's Lewis."

It was a long-standing tradition that, to avoid having staff and patrons solicited by another club, rival club staff was rarely allowed in, except for those who had reached a certain status. This ran from owners to promoters, who were notorious for flooding competitors with invitations and business cards. This was bad enough, but if the invites were for the same night of the week (a promoter hawking their Saturday party on a Saturday night at another club, for example), it was tantamount to warfare.

Clever competitors like Lewis had found a way around this nightlife NATO alliance by hiring attractive girls to stand outside, blocks away from rival clubs, and hand out complimentary entrance passes to those walking up and exiting.

"I chased them all away, but it's the city's sidewalk, so there's only so much I can do," our head of security would tell me, on what was now becoming a weekly basis. Given that they were on public property, it really couldn't be stopped—only temporarily halted.

These guns for hire were very good at their jobs, knowing where to lurk unseen and, when caught, turn on the charm to mitigate any damage. Often, this came off as what it was: a nefarious attempt to steal customers. But free is free, and oftentimes it had the desired effect. A phone call from owner to owner did little to stop the practice, so one's recourse was either to do the same to them or continue to chase the squad away. Unfortunately, this was the Wild West, with every man, woman, and those in-between for themselves.

After Alfredo encountered promoters in action inside the Roxy, they were quick to point out that it was Lewis who had sent them from the Palace.

"This was all Lewis's idea," said Michael Alig, the leader of the rival pack. "I would *never* do something like this on my own."

Alfredo pointed out to Michael that he was not even allowed to enter the Palace, with Michael quickly setting the record straight.

"Oh, that's just Lewis. Come by next week, and I'll get you in."

As we left Indochine, Alfredo turned to me.

"What *is* the plan here?" he asked. "Is there even one, or are we going to just roam around?" Excitement was overcoming his earlier dread.

"Just be yourself," I assured him. "Next stop, the Palace."

With that, Alfredo took off on a beeline toward Union Square, his walk turning into an almost-run, as if he was trying to lose me. As I arrived at our destination, two blocks behind Alfredo, the entrance was engulfed by a buzzing swarm.

"Just trying to beat the crowd," Alfredo explained, now slightly out of breath.

As we stood outside, we spotted Kenny approaching us with the bad news. He was quickly cut off by Michael, who was wearing a Bavaria-meets-Mugler ensemble, complete with full clown makeup.

"That's okay, Kenny, they are my guests," said Michael. He edged Kenny aside and opened the ropes, giving Alfredo a big kiss on the cheek and then holding his hand while skipping us past a furious Lewis.

Once inside, we were led to a balcony overlooking the subterranean dance floor. Turning to take it all in, we were met by the threatening stare of our antagonist standing less than a foot behind us.

"You're not allowed in here, Michael or no Michael," Lewis grumbled. But rather than forcing the issue by asking us to leave, the Dr. Jekyll braggadocio side of our would-be tormentor soon took over. "Isn't this place fabulous?" he gushed. "Like a Nell's for the future. It's the old Underground, you know. All these design ideas . . . mine. Here, let me give you the tour."

From there, Lewis led us around, never once pausing his running commentary. "Did you see the opening invites from David LaChapelle, with Grace Jones performing? I mean, how fabulous, right? We're open on weekends only for now, but we're adding a Wednesday and Thursday night next month."

"I'm really sorry I missed it! Must have really been something!" Alfredo shouted over the music. "This place is really great."

"I know," said Lewis. "Wait till you see my latest genius idea."

With that, he opened a door which, without close inspection, one would have taken to be part of the hallway artwork. We entered a room that could best be described as Victorian Pop, with ornately shaped couches and ottomans surrounded by neon-lit walls.

"I designed this myself," beamed Lewis. "You can put around three hundred people in here. We'll be ready to open in two weeks."

Our tour came to an end as Lewis reached into his pocket and handed us drink tickets, which was met by a tip of my cap. And with that, our wonderfully blustering foe was off.

"I have one thing to check," I told Alfredo, heading toward the exit. "Meet me at Pravda in forty-five minutes."

Pravda was one of my frequent meeting places where I preferred a secluded table in the back, a heavy contrast to the raucous bar scene the modern-day tavern had become known for. Though I wasn't much of a drinker, I enjoyed shots from their large selection of vodkas, many of which neither Alfredo nor I had ever tried before.

"Coming here makes sense," I'd told Alfredo once. "They serve not only alcohol, but a sense of discovery at the same time."

I sat down and, true to form, requested to try Zyr from Russia and Studer Gold from Sweden.

"A great night," I said, raising my shot glass.

"Sorry I couldn't be of more help," Alfredo said, seeming surprised by my exuberance.

"Alfredo, you were fabulous," I proclaimed, slapping him on the shoulder and causing him to choke on his own sample, Wyborowa from Poland. "Everything went exactly as planned."

"You're being patronizing," he said, reaching for another shot. "I did nothing."

I crossed my legs, my black sneaker popping into view. "Let me lead you through what *actually* happened tonight," I told him, "and after I'm done, if you still feel the same way I'll buy you a round of shots."

"Sounds like a no-brainer," he replied. "Let me have it, oh great Sherlock."

"Inviting you to dinner tonight was no coincidence," I began. "I overheard you talking with Michael Alig and knew he would make sure you were allowed into the Palace. It was my strong opinion that, given the right audience, Lewis would tell us everything we needed to know. Not that I needed him for help in getting what I wanted, mind you. But I did need him as a *decoy*."

"Decoy?"

"I knew you would be the perfect bait," I continued on, "because your greatest quality is that you are a world-class listener, to the point of being a magnet for confidential information. I already knew Lewis has a huge ego. When I arrived at Indochine, I immediately went to the bar and noticed what appeared to be undersized drink coasters behind the bartender, with the initials 'SLR' in Victorian-style lettering. When I had the bartender hand me one, the other side revealed that it was good for one complimentary drink at the Palace on Saturday night, in the soon-to-be-opened Steve Lewis Room. So I knew the name of the room and its design style."

I handed Alfred the ornately designed cardboard coaster and motioned to our waitress to bring another round.

"Why did you take off from the Palace in such a hurry?" Alfredo asked.

"I'll get to that in a minute," I replied. "I had already calculated the room's capacity before we met Lewis. If the purpose of this space was to steal key Roxy guests, they would need a space large enough to accomplish this but also small enough to not feel half empty. So, three hundred people. The only thing I needed to determine now was who Lewis had recruited to help him carry out his plan. This is where you, once again, were very helpful. As you listened intently to Lewis—not an easy feat—I was able to scan the room. I spotted Julie, our Saturday hostess who had conspicuously called in sick to work that morning. She was huddling with Palace staff members."

I paused and readjusted my legs, as I had reached a new phase in my observations of the night.

"Before arriving here, I returned to Indochine to get my umbrella, which I knew would be taken to the host stand. After a thank you and a short chat with our hostess, I confirmed what I had already expected—that she and Julie were roommates, and the bartender, Julie's boyfriend. As I looked around the restaurant, which was now filled to capacity, I noticed dozens of our VIP guests finishing dinner before venturing out."

"Are you saying Lewis has hired Julie to lure away the Roxy crowd?" Alfredo asked, grabbing for his last shot.

"That is exactly what I am saying," I replied, breaking out of my concentration long enough to take a sip. "Got to give it to Lewis, it was quite a clever plan actually. He targeted our crowd in one fell swoop from a single location before they could reach the Roxy."

"Wow, you've really got this observation thing down," said Alfredo. "The great nightlife private eye ... Obscure-Locks Roams ... what do you think of that name?"

"Very descriptive," I replied. "And that would make you ... Dr. Walk-Run."

Alfredo smiled as he raised his shot glass. "Roams and Walkrun. I'll drink to that. Sounds like a great name for the world's first nightclub detective agency."

Over the next few days, I reached out to a friend I'd made recently who, as it happened, had designed Indochine. He, in turn, contacted the owner, who was furious that his staff was promoting nightclubs out of his business. After that night, Julie was never allowed in either the Roxy or Indochine again—and the Saturday night Locomotion party continued on strong for years.

CHAPTER 3

DISCO GRANNY

"Nightlife is like a funhouse mirror for everyday life."
—UNKNOWN

Within three months, my investigative work started to pay off. Where Sherlock Holmes had his Baker Street Irregulars—a group of street boys who reported to him, undetected, on the comings and goings in London—I'd developed my own network of invisible spies. At the nightclub Danceteria, it was the unnoticed busboy, Jorge; at the after-hours club Save the Roberts, it was back-door security guard, Mario. In total, I had over two dozen eavesdroppers and emissaries on the lookout, tipping them $50 each for their work.

On one of my after-dark missions, I'd befriended a group responsible for the events at the Pyramid Club, the famed East Village gay club long known as an intimate home for struggling artists and actors. It was also a launching pad for a diverse group of performers that included Debbie Harry and Deee-Lite. Taking advantage of the Pyramid being dark on Mondays and Thursdays, I soon had the group promoting a weekly Thursday night party at the Roxy called "Disco Interruptus."

The night moved gay subculture to the big stage, with performances by drag icons like Lady Bunny and Lypsinka periodically "interrupting" the dance floor. With the addition of a Thursday night at Locomotion, on any given week more than five thousand people were making their way through the Roxy's doors.

As the club continued to garner success, I found myself increasingly in demand. At the same time, I realized that Gene was having some previously undisclosed problems. To renovate the space and purchase the necessary lights and sound system (while continuing to pay rent), he had taken out a "loan" from a man named Irving. You didn't *not* pay Irving. By Christmas Eve, Gene was almost out of money, asking me to lend him a few hundred dollars to get through the holidays.

Just a week earlier, I'd been offered a position by Maurice Brahms, the longtime owner of Infinity and Red Zone. Maurice was perhaps best known as the person Studio 54's Ian Schrager testified against to shorten his own prison sentence for tax evasion, subsequently sending Maurice to jail.

The offer was something I needed to at least consider, given the revelations at the Roxy. As for the job—it was to join Lewis as co-director of the Palace.

"I've almost had enough of this guy," Maurice told me, rubbing his head over dinner at his favorite Upper West Side Italian restaurant. "The only thing he understands about money is how to spend it."

Maurice was the first person I'd heard actually break down the real economics of a major nightclub. He introduced me to concepts such as a "loss leader," which meant hiring a promoter or paying for a personal appearance that technically loses money but attracts paying customers. For example, if a promoter who makes $1,500 a night brings in twenty people for free, *but* those twenty people include a Jennifer Lopez, a Mike Tyson, or an Uma Thurman, then you can bet you'd read about it the next day on Page Six of the *New York Post*.

This was guaranteed if the club's publicist called in the celebrity sighting, accompanied by an often-exaggerated (and sometimes fabricated) story behind it. If two celebrities were seen entering the club together, they were reported as "holding hands" or "getting close in a dark corner." Both celebrities *knew* it would be reported in this manner, and planned accordingly. After the fact, their publicist could deny the report, which would generate even more press.

"To these people, no press is bad press," explained Maurice. "The thing they fear most is not being covered by the press at all—death by irrelevance."

Both the celebrities and their publicists knew the promoter was profiting off their presence. But they counted on the promoter to make sure they were at the "right" club on the "right" night, adding to the story's cachet while also satisfying the person cutting the check. This was all a controlled process. The rules were implicitly understood by the celebrity, club, and press alike, down to the requisite "No Cameras Allowed" sign posted at the entrance to ensure those snapping photos were part of Team Illusion.

The recently divorced Donald Trump took this process to a new level. First he befriended promoters, who in turn gave him information on a night's hotspot. He would turn up with a young model type, then call it in himself to the tabloids under the guise of being a publicist, disguising his voice on the phone. This resulted in dozens of calls made by the likes of "John Miller" trying to establish Trump as a ladies' man.[4]

As Facebook—and later, Instagram—began encroaching on the process, the rules changed drastically. Now *everyone* was posting about what they saw, or didn't see, during their night out. This was a bonus for the club, whose free publicity grew exponentially, but it caused an issue for our celebrities, since they and their publicists had lost control of the

4 Trump actually began publicizing himself with pseudonyms in the 1980s, "John Barron" being the most notorious. For years, Barron spread rumors ranging from Trump buying the World Trade Centers to why he *didn't* buy the Cleveland Indians. In 2018, a Forbes reporter released the audio of a call with Barron two decades earlier, where Trump was attempting to inflate his wealth for the Forbes 400 list. Trump's effort to disguise his voice was so comical, the conversation became a viral sensation.

process. Responding to preordained bullshit is one thing; dealing with multiple stories written by unfriendly writers across multiple formats is something completely different. This trend would continue to the point where manipulating social media became a celebrity-maker in its own right. Using nightlife as a much-needed milieu, being famous for fame's sake was on its way to becoming part of pop culture, as the likes of Paris Hilton and Lindsay Lohan would soon take their places on the covers of *In Touch Weekly* and *Star*.

Was a loss leader worth it to the club? The actual costs could be traced back to the promoter. Promoter + cost of celebrity free drinks = Page Six story + Page Six denial. Are two Page Six stories worth $1,700? Let's say a hundred people read these stories and decide to go the club, perceiving it as a celebrity hotspot, each paying a $30 admission cost. Then, yes.

"I *never* pay for advertising," Maurice told me weeks before offering me the Palace job. "No one wants to hear you *say* how great you are. They want to be able to figure it out themselves through 'unbiased' accounts. Of course, everything comes with a price, but your customers don't need to know that."

After weeks of discussion, Maurice informed me that the Palace wasn't being granted a lease extension, and it would be closing within three months. We lost touch after that, speaking only one other time when, nine months later, I reached out to him with condolences. A Petco now stood where his club once was.

With the closing of the World, Mars, Red Zone, and now the Palace, New York City nightlife had become a one-club affair for discerning club-goers. That would all change with the awakening of a sleeping giant: Limelight.

Located on Twentieth Street and Sixth Avenue, Limelight opened with pronounced fanfare in 1983. The building itself was built in 1845 as the site of the Episcopal Church of the Holy Communion. For ten years prior to housing a nightclub, it was the location of a rehabilitation program as part of Odyssey House, a national organization for the treatment and prevention of drug abuse.

The first Limelight was opened in southern Florida by Canadian owner Peter Gatien, followed by locations in Atlanta, New York, Chicago, and London. By the end of the decade, "the church," as it had come to be known by New York City tourists, was the only location that remained. By then, native New Yorkers had all but stopped going there.

Out of a job after the Palace closed, Michael Alig convinced Peter to allow him to host his own weekly party at Limelight every Wednesday, dubbing it "Disco 2000." It became an immediate success, fueled by Alig's unique sense of creativity. After a few months, the party had its own magazine. "Hosts" for the evening included the likes of Edith Fore, the actress who had turned "I've fallen, and I can't get up" into a famous catchphrase on LifeCall's medical-alarm commercials. When she entered the empty stage at a sold-out Disco 2000 and pretended to faint, uttering the now-famed sentence, the crowd broke into mayhem. At a thousand dollars for the appearance, she had to be at the top of the all-time loss-leader board.

There was a psychedelic dinner for forty at the club with Timothy Leary, and a kissing booth with the then-fifty-eight-year-old Tina Louise, who had played Ginger on *Gilligan's Island*. Other classics included the *Beverly Hillbillies* hoedown hosted by Donna Douglas (aka Elly May Clampett); Rip Taylor's glitterati gathering where, toupee askew, the host joyously sprinkled tinsel on invited guests; and entertainment reporter Michael Musto's multiple annual birthday parties, attended by the likes of Roxanne Pulitzer and Sylvia Miles. Michael Alig resurrected more careers of retired actors and pseudo celebrities than the Hallmark Channel, if only for one glorious night.

Like a trip to an amusement park funhouse, you never knew what, or whom, you would encounter at Limelight. Outside, guests were enthusiastically welcomed by the Disco 2000 mascot, Clara the Carefree Chicken (Club Kid Ernie Glam dressed in a full whimsical chicken suit). Entering the Chapel, one of Limelight's many rooms (and indeed, the original church chapel) you could hitch a ride on the shoulder saddle of Danny the Wonder Pony, the strapping young taxi-in-waiting. He would then gallop you to the Shampoo Room, where you could have your nails done. All this while Georgia transplant drag-belle Lahoma Van Zandt—a cross between Reese Witherspoon and Lucille Ball—hosted a strip competition on the club's oversized main stage, where phrases like "she's spread out like a cold supper" were used with the utmost of Southern charm.

Capitalizing on its unearthed second act and opening its doors six nights a week, Limelight was set to expand when Michael approached me about coming on board. I attended a meeting he set up with Peter and longtime Limelight publicists John Carmen and Claire O'Conner. I quickly appreciated something in the veteran group that was far different from what I'd experienced since my fuck-you fest introductory seminar to New York City nightlife: these were people I could *learn from*. However, with his reserved nature, Peter didn't exactly appear to be one to impart wisdom as a manner of communication. As such, I'd need to become a covert grasshopper, expanding my observations to Peter and those around him to take in both the good and the wish-I-hadn't-seen-that.

LAXIOM #3
Never let them hear you pee.
During meetings Peter would, without warning, get up and go into the bathroom and start peeing without shutting the door, making his attendees wait as they listened to him relieve himself. This was so distracting and uncomfortable that, to this day, I flush the toilet *while* I'm going, to avoid any streaming sounds.

Unbeknownst to almost everyone (except Big Mac, of course), the financial situation at the Roxy was atrophying at an alarming rate, with Gene's penchant for purchasing antiques (an odd habit akin to Helen Mirren spending outrageously for used-car parts) throwing gas on the fire and my pay coming in at sporadic intervals. One month after my initial meeting with Peter, I was hired as a Limelight director, with an office directly above that of the also recently hired Steven Lewis.

On my first week on the job, I received an unexpected call from back home in Michigan. My eighty-one-year-old grandma, my dad's mother, was in town on a Broadway bus tour with her friends. She'd have called me earlier, but she knew how busy I was and didn't want to bother me. Could she take me out to dinner tonight? Of course.

After picking her up at her hotel, we headed down to the Tribeca Grill. While my father had no qualms talking to anyone about anything, Grandma Mary had turned it into an art form; she was a social Picasso. This, combined with her true zest for life, ornate hat collection, impeccable style, and unlimited energy of someone fifty years younger made anyone in Mary's orbit immediately drawn to her. By the time we finished dinner, complete with rounds of appetizers from the kitchen and a bottle of wine compliments of owner Robert DeNiro, we were escorted to a waiting town car as the maître d' planted kisses on both of her cheeks. "Please come again, Mademoiselle Mary," he requested passionately with both hands on his heart.

"They were so nice," said Mary, oblivious to the scene she'd just caused at one of Manhattan's swankiest restaurants. "Can't wait to go dancing."

I looked at her, surprised. *Huh?*

Mary arrived at the Limelight entrance with no plans to head back to her hotel. "I don't believe it, Stevie," she exclaimed. "Your club is in that big church ... I just don't believe it." For her seventy-fifth birthday, Mary had received a "I DONT B LEVE IT" custom license plate, which she proudly displayed on the back of her enormous lemon-yellow Cadillac Seville.[5] It was her own famous catchphrase.

It was a popular Wednesday night, and the outside of the club was already crowded. A two-block line was forming with the usual suspects,

---

5 As president of the local Salvation Army, Mary saw her duty as always being available to help people, filling the car's oversized trunk to the brim with sweaters, pants, shoes, and baked goods. "U NVR NO WEN SUM1 MITE NEED SUMPIN" would have been just as appropriate as her license plate, if the lettering would have fit.

ranging from downtown drag queens to Brooklyn tough guys. I'd called ahead for Chuck, our head of security who was otherwise known as "the Mountain," to help escort Mary in. Still, the commotion at the door threatened to injure my ninety-pound, four-foot-ten grandmother.

"Oh, is this my date for the evening?" she asked, reaching up to grab hold of Chuck's massive arm to steady herself. "Hope you can keep up with me."

I called for backup, and minutes later four more staff members appeared to assist in the mission, walking Mary through a designated VIP door. Once inside, the sight of an unknown person being walked in by security drew gawkers, who then began to follow behind in Pied Piper fashion.

As the entourage of twenty-five got closer to the dance floor, the heart-pounding music and strobing lights were overwhelming, causing me to panic as I imagined the untimely death of beloved Nana at my hands. My plan had been to take her to a quiet area on the balcony where she could survey the scene for a few minutes. But apparently she had other designs, redirecting her followers to the center of the action.

Now, out in the middle of the dance floor surrounded by a growing crowd of onlookers, cheers began to emanate, causing my anxiety to heighten. Unable to get near the group, I sprinted up to the balcony and peered down through the artificial smoke and rainbow of moving colors. The scene was surreal; I became an unwilling spectator of the "Mary and the Mountain" show, in sync as if they'd choreographed the routine for weeks. Helpless to intervene and surrounded by remnants of what was once a house of worship, I could only pray for the best.

When Mary finally decided it was time to leave, her departure caused more of a stir than her entrance. She'd already made quite a few friends, and her admirers had since doubled, causing a mini mob scene.

"Thank you, Stevie," she said, still looking as fresh as a daisy as she pretended to use Chuck's arm for balance. "All these nice, young people called me by my new nickname, 'Disco Granny.' I think they're just

Disco Granny   51

wonderful."

I spotted Michael Alig to my left, sporting a new look consisting of a bright plaid blazer, pressed white dress shirt, bow tie, and inch-long multicolored eyelashes.

"Genius," he blurted out. "I heard she's your grandmother. And the outfit, just fabulous. Can we book her to come again? We could pay her, like, fifteen hundred." You could almost see the dollar signs swirling around in his head, along with the envy of Mary's natural ability to attract devotees.

I'd never considered my grandma as a potential loss leader. I paused before answering. "I'll ask her, but I don't think she takes a lot of out-of-state gigs."

"Let me know," said Michael, skipping back inside. "I need to have Claire call this into Page Six right away."

I was able to catch a glimpse of Grandma Mary waving from the back window of her taxi before she disappeared into the sea of cars on Sixth Avenue. I realized it wasn't just me she was waving to, but also Clara and over two dozen club-goers of all types around me, who returned the favor. As I savored the smile she always seemed to leave behind, I could only think that Mary had created another one of her masterpiece appearances, and all those fortunate enough to experience it could hardly believe it.

I would also have never believed the tragic events that were about to transpire, with ruinous consequences for all involved.

CHAPTER 4

YERTLE SYNDROME

"All mine . . .
Oh, the things I now rule!"
—KING YERTLE

T he offices at Limelight consisted of a three-story maze of chambers designated by a separate entrance, dating back to 1845 when the area housed the church rectory. I arrived at 10:00 AM daily, working across from Michael Alig on the secluded third floor. This gave me until 3:00 PM, when the parade of nightlife oddities and anomalies began rolling in.

As the leader of a nightlife group calling themselves the Club Kids, Michael's idea of office work revolved around finding a place to hold court—and he had the perfect location from which to rule his domain. Out of sight from everyone but myself, his troupe planned their domination of the NYC club scene without interference or prying eyes.

It was here that I met the likes of Pebbles, Sushi, Jenatalia, Astor Earl, Desi Monster, and Brandywine, to name just a few. Each had their place and designated role. Some were paid to bring in their friends and additional customers to the club. Others dressed as the life of the party, creating a festive atmosphere for club-goers while encouraging them to dress up as well. "Dressing up" encompassed anything from wearing nothing but a G-string and a pink fright wig to donning twisted *Dangerous Liaisons* regalia, with drag being the twist. The more outlandish, the better.

Of course, I could have just shut my converted bishop's bedroom door, but I was too fascinated to do so. Instead, I found myself engaged in conversations with the cavalcade of lieges who arrived to both kiss the ring and conspire. As we spoke in the hallway or as they meandered into my office, I could actually hear my mother's glass-shattering voice: "Stevennn, why are you talking to these people? You have work to dooo."

There was Sebastian, an FIT design student by day who became a nightlife Pee Wee Herman after dark, accessorized with a sparkling designer lunchbox where he stashed guest invitations. And Maureen, a Rebel Wilson clone who worked as a realtor and transformed into Misty at night to show off her weekly updated dance routines in short shorts, a colorful matching vest, Day-Glo sunglasses, custom-designed platform sneakers, and a Yankees cap. At over forty years old, she was walking proof that being a Club Kid had nothing to do with age. Others, such as Amanda Lepore and Sophia Lamar, were Club Kid full-timers.

I soon realized that being a Club Kid involved much more than what appeared on the surface. It was more of a movement than a circus, based on freedom of choice and expression. Much of the group hailed from small towns, and the nightlife scene was a place where they were accepted as transgender or gay; for others, it was a creative outlet through fashion statements and party promotion; and for many, it was a safe place to simply be who they wanted to be.

With Limelight now a significant nightlife employer, I quickly became a lightning rod for job requests. There were no resumes, just nonstop in-person pitches that could take place at any hour. One day it could be a drag queen looking to debut her ukulele act. Another day, I could be eating lunch at my desk when a "little person" DJ would appear in my office doorway, looking for an opening time slot.

There were all sorts of positions that needed to be filled—traditional ones like bartenders, security guards, and cashiers. And then there were the not-so-traditional ones. Like candy girls, modern-day incarnations of 1920s cigarette girls who walked around with large trays and sold everything from Oreos to condoms. And performers to participate in live installations, such as a modern-day Rapunzel in a fiberglass box, outfitted with a seven-foot platinum wig and pretending to get ready to go out for the night.

The majority of those who approached me were interested in one position: go-go dancer. These performers were paid to dance on one of the six platforms dotting the dance floor. They eventually graduated to the two metal cages suspended twenty feet above the crowd. Supported by a chain hoist system, the cages were lowered and raised by an electric motor and, when airborne, were highly unstable, swaying back and forth if the occupant was unable to maintain a center of gravity.

Over time, dancers would not only learn to maintain the cage's stability, but also develop elaborate Cirque du Soleil-type routines incorporating the cage itself. These ranged from hooking their legs around the bars and raising themselves off the cage floor, to dangling their legs outside its bars while leaning back to steady the cage.

"Ize can do that," a woman told me confidently one night, pointing up at one of the cages. She had suddenly materialized next to me, dressed in a pink latex miniskirt, a matching crop top, knee-high boots, and some sort of riding stick.

"It's harder than it looks," I replied, caught off guard.

"I don't think so," she said. "I can dance anywhere. Let me show you, and then you can hire me."

"We're not really hiring now, but I'm sure you'd be great."

"That's a bunch of bullshit. I know you guys always hiring. Especially someone as good as me."

She does have confidence.

For obvious reasons, putting someone in an unstable cage without any practice, while hovering over a thousand people, was out of the question. Frankly, even with those dancers who were well-versed, it was a liability nightmare. The other issue was that this woman would barely fit into the cage. Over six feet tall and built like a brick house, she certainly was physically imposing, to a point of being intimidating.

"What did you say your name was?" I asked.

"I didn't," she replied. "My friends call me Mo—as in mo' than most men can handle."

"Okay, Mo. How about trying out one of the podiums when they become clear?"

"Trying out . . . you asking Mo to do what? Mo don't do no tryouts, honey." With that, she walked away.

Entering the bathroom two hours later, there was Mo in the mirror, redoing her makeup. Without her perfectly coiffed wig on, it was clear that Mo was not short for Maureen.

"You don't know what you're missing, honey," she said, spotting me as I walked by. "Maybe someday you'll find out."

One late Friday night, I spied an older Asian man on one of the podiums. Outfitted in a frilly white tank top, sequined ballerina tutu, and three-inch stilettos, he was both conspicuously out of place and right at home. The following night, he was back at it again, this time incorporating two ornate hand-fans into his elegant routine. This went on for weeks, prompting me to approach King Michael about the dancer's status in his realm.

"Oh, that's just Mr. J," Michael replied, waving me off in his typical preoccupied manner. "We don't even need to pay him. He just loves dancing."

Mr. J's night was like clockwork. He appeared at midnight and left at 4:00 AM. Each week, he brought in new props to assist his performance. One Friday it was a Fred Astaire cane and top hat; on another it was a hand bubble-blower or a flashlight, which he would direct on the dance floor crowd. The tutu and stilettos always stayed.

After one of his most memorable nights involving multiple feathered boas, I watched Mr. J exit Limelight and stop to talk with a woman in her mid-forties who was entering the club. She handed him a paper bag, setting off alarm bells to my detective-self. Something was definitely off here. Some sort of drug deal, no doubt.

I alerted security and we waited until the next week's exchange. After Mr. J refused to open the bag, we confronted his co-conspirator as she waited to check her coat.

"Can you please let me know what's in the bag you keep giving to one of the customers?" I inquired.

"In what bag?" she asked. "You mean the paper bag with raisins? It's for my husband. He has a long subway ride home and gets hungry before he can eat dinner."

"Raisins. That's it?"

"Well, not exactly."

Here it comes.

"There are instructions for heating up his food," she continued. "And what to give our daughter for breakfast in the morning."

"Am I supposed to believe that man is your husband?"

"Of course. Who did you think it was? He just hates the kitchen. But he *does* love to dance, and so do I, so we decided to take shifts. He thinks he is a better dancer than me, but of course that's not true."

Back outside, I spotted Mr. J and his detainer now sharing the bag of raisins together on the sidewalk. Still not fully believing the alibi, I headed to the dance floor, where Mrs. J was indeed up on her husband's platform in a full S-and-M cat suit, to the delight of the early morning party animals. Transfixed as she executed a flawless combination of salsa and whip-wielding, I came to the conclusion that she wasn't actually a better dancer than her husband, as she had claimed—just, well . . . different.

Getting jaded New Yorkers to come to Limelight every week was not an easy task. The process of constantly reinventing oneself was both exhausting and stressful. Imagine if, every Monday morning when you arrived at work, you had to start over, finding all new clients or customers every week to pay your bills. Welcome to NYC nightlife.

With the perfect storm of ingenuity and audacity, no one at the time was better than the Club Kids in coming up with new ways to get people to attend club nights. Many had spent a good deal of their lives as outsiders, fending off bullying and ridicule. This helped many in the group develop a unique skill set of self-preservation and out-of-the-box thinking, which was perfectly tailored to make them natural promoters with a touch of deviousness.

This was never more evident than at an "outlaw party." Using photocopy invites, Club Kids would spread out across NYC summoning club-goers, and anyone else for that matter, to meet at a predetermined location at 9:00 PM. The most notorious of these meeting spots was Madison Square Park, where Fifth Avenue meets Twenty-Third Street in Manhattan. Attendees were met by stalwart Club Kid DJ Keoki, blaring the latest beats from a boom box connected to portable speakers. Bottles of vodka were provided by Limelight and poured into plastic cups, distributed for all to enjoy.

When the inevitable arrival of the police broke up the illegal gathering of over three hundred "bandits," the assemblage was more than happy to move along... now taking the party to the subway. Hundreds of nightcrawlers, the majority of whom were dressed in their flamboyant garb for a late night out, packed into one train as Keoki's music continued to keep pace. This spectacle felt like the Met Gala meets Mardi Gras, held in Lady Gaga's basement. As the one-step-slow NYPD again arrived to dampen the festivities, the outlaws were already moseying along to the next planned stop: McDonald's.

As they gawked at the traveling circus, the unsuspecting McDonald's workers, consisting mainly of high schoolers, were quickly overwhelmed by dozens of drunken orders for burgers and fries. Lines formed around the block, a scenario that Michael had planned out to the last detail. Unbeknownst to the staff, that day Michael had prepaid the manager for a hundred burgers, which now sat boxed and read to go in the storage area.

Jumping up onto the counter, Michael was able to command the drunk-hungry by tossing morsels into the sea of outstretched hands, ironically becoming the first-ever Burger King of a McDonald's. A Big Mac sighting caused hair-pulling and catfighting, wigs flying over the crowd like caps at a graduation. An overthrown Quarter Pounder bounced off a back wall, causing a mad scramble to the floor as if rushing to claim a coveted Mickey Mantle homerun ball.

From McDonald's, it was only a few blocks away to Limelight. There, the throng discussed their adventure deep into the morning while paying for drinks and speculating about what Michael would come up with next. Disguised as complete chaos, this was the perfectly executed loss-leader. Of course, the entire event was covered by news cameras and appeared in the papers the next day with the headline: "Club Kids take over NYC." Apparently, I wasn't the only person who had been talking to Maurice Brahms.

My arrival at Limelight coincided with that of a promoter Michael had also recruited, named Michael Caruso. It began with Michael Alig attending Caruso's parties in Staten Island, where New Yorkers rarely visited. He had one sole purpose: to find young, outer-borough types who had yet to come out of the closet, an apparent wet dream he had been harboring for years.

Caruso saw Michael's appearance as a way to get into the NYC club scene, which had long rejected those like himself. In the early 1990s, this included only Manhattan and, a decade later, some enclaves in Brooklyn—never Staten Island. Infamously named the "Bridge and Tunnel" crowd, Caruso and his friends were blacklisted, standing outside NYC clubs and being refused entrance. They possessed neither the fashion sense nor the daytime positions in society to deem them worthy. So, with nowhere else to turn, they created their own nightlife scene at home.

For all intents and purposes, it was the *Sopranos* version of the Club Kid movement, characterized by its crowd of high-testosterone sons and cousins of tough-guy-types. They jump-danced to a unique dance music genre deemed "hard techno," played by local hero DJ Repeat. Standard nightclub dance music involves a tempo of around 120 beats per minute (BPMs). Hard techno had adopted a style of over 150 BPMs, with minimal vocals. The harsh, hard-hitting electronic beat was a natural fit for the lives of its growing young followers.

Always the entrepreneur, Michael Alig saw the financial (and personal) potential of what was happening across the Upper Bay. Before long, the two groups had joined forces at Limelight, with Caruso adopting the fitting stage name of Lord Michael. The unprecedented mix of lifestyles, ethnicities, race, and sexual orientation on the Limelight dance floor on any given night left the impression that no matter what prejudices and judgment one faced outside of its walls, within its hallowed halls there was a place for everyone to feel at home. With the exception, perhaps, of one person.

My presence at Limelight had not gone over well with Steven Lewis, who saw it as a slight and a challenge to his vainglorious authority. On a daily basis, he came up with ways to undermine my situation. This consisted mainly of complaining to Peter about everything I was doing. In his characteristic reserved style, Peter just let Lewis vent, saying nothing, which infuriated Lewis even more. In a fuck-you moment, he quit, moving to the famed Palladium that had been off the relevant map for years. With this move, Lewis laid down the gauntlet as a competitor.

But after six months of being open and unsuccessfully trying to steal Limelight promoters and staff, the Palladium ran out of money, putting its future in dire straits. For a relatively minimal cost, Peter was able to take over the lease, putting Lewis right back in his old office.

"After all that, you're bringing Lewis back?" I asked Peter, disheartened and confused by his logic.

"We have no choice," he said in one of his rare direct responses. "His leaving for the Palladium cost us a lot of money. Letting everyone in over there for free and spending money like water bankrupted them, but it's also hurt us for the last few months. I can't have him doing that again. It's cheaper just to pay him here, even if he does nothing."

In a move of either pure genius or luck, Lewis had now become a loss-leader himself, ensuring himself a place at the table without having to pay for dinner.

LAXIOM #4
Have a capacity for success.
One point Peter made to me whenever the mood struck him was, "What's the point of opening a small club or local bar? You bust your ass to be successful, but then are limited by your size. Instead, you can put the same amount of work into a club that holds two thousand people and make five times the money."

When the long-dormant nightclub Tunnel, which had the capacity to hold over three thousand people, became available, Peter hired Eric Goode and Serge Becker of Area nightclub fame to renovate it, reopening six months later. Later that year, the *Blade Runner*-themed Club USA was built in Times Square, again with Goode and Becker at the design helm, equipped with a three-story slide. This now put the four largest nightclubs in NYC under our direction, which meant that I needed to travel between multiple clubs per night.

On one particular Saturday, my last stop put me at Club USA, where one of Club Kids grabbed me with excitement and pulled me near the dance floor.

"Your fabulous grandma is back," he exclaimed, pointing to a group of security leading someone of apparent diminutive stature through the crowd with a trail of onlookers.

"What? That's not possible."

"It has to be. Who else so small draws a crowd of so many in a place so big?" He sounded like he was trying to paraphrase Churchill.

I stared out at the dance floor. *Could it be? Without calling?*

Quickly making my way towards the group, I peered between its protectors until I could get a good look at their prize.

"Who do I have to screw to get a drink around here?" said Danny DeVito in his distinctive voice. "Let me rephrase that. Who can I screw around here, and a drink would be nice."

As those around Danny laughed, I had to join in. One thing was for certain—standing barely four-foot-ten, he *was* small, but certainly not on the scale I would soon come to consider little.

The Club Kid influence had now gone from fringe to mainstream, appearing on national talk shows and in Calvin Klein ad campaigns, while influencing the fashion sense of a generation nationwide. On any given weekend night, a combined ten thousand people made their way through our clubs. From Jennifer Lopez and Club Kid devotee Chloë Sevigny to Mary J. Blige and Malcolm Forbes, practically anyone of note from all walks of life passed through the doors of our four clubs and rubbed elbows. Encompassing a staff of over sixty bartenders, twenty DJs, and a virtual army of promoters per night, the heyday of the newly coined "mega-club" was here.

Just before midnight on New Year's Eve 1995, I escaped out of my Club USA office window and onto the fifth-floor fire escape for some fresh air. Behind me, an enormous foot belonging to Kate Moss, one of the Calvin Klein models in the four-story billboard covering the building, met me at eye level. Below, over a million revelers were jammed into Times Square, braving the near-zero temperature.

Inside, a sold-out crowd waited for the countdown, led by the legendary Cab Calloway and his orchestra, getting everyone out of their last "hidey-ho" before the year's end. Master of ceremonies Sandra Bernhardt revved up the crowd with lewd jokes, with an occasional "fuck" or "dick" making its way through the crowd noise. Only in New York!

As the ball dropped and pandemonium hit the world's epicenter of nightlife, from my private vantage point above I felt like a king, reaching heights I never thought possible.

Like a perfectly timed UFC kick to the head, I would find out soon enough that it would all be over quicker than it began.

Much has been written about the collapse of the New York club scene at this time, focusing on Limelight, Tunnel, Club USA, and the Palladium. Movies have been made glorifying the drug use, the murder of a promoter, the Club Kids, and Peter Gatien himself. Rudy Giuliani has been cast as the maniacal, ambitious mayor who deemed these mega-clubs a menace against his effort to "clean up" NYC, and made them into a scapegoat to further his own political career. This was indeed an accurate character study. However, I also attributed the downfall to an additional factor: Yertle Syndrome.

Yertle the Turtle and Other Stories, the much beloved and analyzed Dr. Seuss narrative, was one of my favorite stories as a child. By the age of four, I had memorized every page. It's a tale about King Yertle, who ruled over his pond, Sala-ma-Sond, where all the turtles were happy and had enough to eat, which, for turtles, put them all together in the upper middle class. Yertle, as is the case with most kings, was full of ambition, deciding that the pond he ruled over was too small. Yertle needed more.

He then made the arrogant proclamation that he was to be king of all he could see, in some sort of eminent domain power play which would never have held up in court had it been contested. He commanded his turtle subjects to stack themselves as high as possible to make a perch for his throne and give him the view he needed to make his claim. Now, with the ability to see a great distance, he felt like Jeff Bezos without having to go through the arduous bidding process associated with additional head-quarter locations.

But that still wasn't enough. King Yertle directed the turtle stack to go higher still, to the point where he could see forty miles. In the evening as the moon rose, Yertle was outraged by the moon's audacity to rise higher than himself. He called on additional turtles—5,607, to be exact—to join the pile. With a calculation that precise, it must have appeared to all that Yertle had really thought this through.

The problem ol' Yertle now had, which he could not see from on high, was that his throne was teetering on an unstable foundation. It only took a burp from one of the turtles below to cause the entire stack to come toppling down.

One mega-club is a world in and of itself. Add three more to the mix, and you've got a situation you just can't control. Just too many nightlife people doing too many things to keep track of. Someone was bound to burp. In this case, it was more like a large-scale belching contest.

The problem with Yertle Syndrome is that it can lay dormant for years before coming to the surface. By that time, it's too late to contain it. Unknowingly, I had already contracted it, the diagnosis of which I would receive a decade later.

One early morning, a young club-goer was found unconscious outside of Limelight, and later died from a lethal dose of MDMA. His father was a prominent politician in New Jersey. It was the first time an Ecstasy overdose had been widely reported. Ecstasy, at the time, was viewed as being a somewhat harmless club drug, like weed at a Grateful Dead concert. It was recalled that he was dragged out of the club at closing and left there to recover. His dad needed answers.

On almost any given Disco 2000, those in the know could partake in Ecstasy Punch, which was considered an adult version of a prom drink; no one thought twice about it. With the pressure to keep up attendance at the clubs, the kitschy and outrageous were increasingly joined by the shocking and borderline illegal. The "pee drinker" and simulated sex acts became as common onstage as Edith Fore, Don Knotts, and Gary Coleman. Anything and everything had now become fair game, with no apparent consequences.

When, in a drug-induced haze, Michael Alig unspeakably murdered fellow promoter Angel Melendez over drug money—followed by rumors of drug parties held by Peter Gatien at the Four Seasons Hotel—the DEA moved in and began shutting the whole thing down, with Peter becoming Giuliani's public enemy number one and facing federal charges.

The sad moral of the story? All could have been avoided with a one-word intervention: *enough*.

Michael Alig, the most unlikely personality to become a heavy heroin user, explained his thinking to Gregory, who was now the creative director for all four clubs. "After a while it just became harder and harder to shock people," he said. "I had to stay one step ahead, and I thought the sight of me as a heroin addict would do the trick."

The clubs in question had as haphazard an organizational structure as one could imagine. All the Business 101 characteristics that form the fundamentals of a thriving company culture—structure, accountability, and communication—never existed. The irony was that this same culture had made the clubs so iconic in the first place, fostering a creative atmosphere which broke both social and musical barriers. That was Peter's genius. The functionality of the business may have been a mess, but that's not a federal crime.

In the winter of 1997, everywhere I went, the trial was all around me. Newsstands displaying *New York Post* covers, constant television coverage, and prevalent on-the-street gossip made it impossible to avoid. It had all the essential elements of a Greek tragedy, which, together with gratuitous sensationalism, made it an engrossing spectacle. Media-proclaimed "Club King" Peter Gatien was charged with running drug supermarkets out of New York City's two largest nightclubs, Limelight and Tunnel, along with a cast of accomplices too outrageous for a Hollywood script.

The legal proceedings had been going on for three weeks, with the prosecution about to conclude their case, when I made a reconnaissance trip to the U.S. District Court in downtown Manhattan. As I entered the vast, overflowing courtroom, I felt intimidation that quickly gave way to dread. This legal drama wasn't like anything I'd seen in movies, though *A Few Good Men* did jump to mind. No, this was something altogether different. This was *real*.

I took the last seat in the back and spotted Michele Adelman behind the prosecution table. I recognized her from multiple on-air interviews. We shared the same last name and were in no way related, but that didn't stop the barrage of hate calls I'd been receiving on a daily basis: "Is your sister trying to ruin Peter's life? Fuck you, traitor asshole." This extended to elaborate conspiracy theories, including one in which I had been recruited by the DEA as a confidential informant years ago.

As I caught glances from others in attendance, I got the sense that many of them thought I was there to testify against Peter. Reality painted a much different picture. I'd been contacted two days prior with a request to appear as a material witness . . . for the defense. My scheduled testimony would take place in two weeks.

On the other side of the aisle sat Peter, stoic while in a whispered conversation with his attorney, Ben Branfman, known to the press for his defense of Michael Jackson, Sean Combs, and mafia boss Sammy "The Bull" Gravano. The day before, as I'd sat reviewing potential testimony in Branfman's office, I could only think that he was someone I'd want on my side in any type of brawl, courtroom, or barroom. I had no idea at the time that, twenty years later, I'd need my own defense lawyer and would use Branfman as my who-to-hire prototype.

Behind Peter, a large contingent of well-wishers and supporters had convened. Their mere presence fueled the scandalous narrative. Drag queens in casual attire, hulking security guards, flamboyant party promoters, and young club-going, Brooklyn tough-guy types formed an eclectic group that could be encountered on any night at Limelight. But by day, they looked like a casting call for *Mad Max: They Only Come Out at Night*.

To the side of the witness stand, a mafia-like organizational chart was on display that included headshots of each alleged "drug ring" member. The photos had clearly been chosen to make each person look as sinister as possible—particularly the one of Michael Alig, taken from a Halloween-party invitation for "Disco Bloodbath" that showed him with gore streaming down his face. With the eye-patched Peter at the top of the chart (legend has it, he lost an eye in a hockey accident in his twenties) and "lieutenants" with names like Lord Michael, Desi Monster, and Baby Joe, to the non-nightlife-world onlookers and tabloids, the group appeared almost too lurid to be true . . . and they were right. As a director of the clubs, my tailored mugshot was nowhere to be found, further fueling rumors of my cooperation with the Feds. My continued late-night sleuthing took me out of those same clubs during the hours the DEA had been conducting covert sting operations, which included detectives dressing up as Club Kids, with the intent of infiltrating the fictional Gatien cartel. I never appeared on their radar.

As inconspicuous as a thirty-year-old man in drag could be at a club like Tunnel, the undercover detectives managed to stick out based on their nonexistent fashion sense and excessive body hair. My alter ego had not only served me well learning the ropes, but had helped me avoid landing on them after being punched in the nuts by a gloveless, misinformed prosecutor.

The night before I was set to testify, I put a call in to my sister, an actual attorney, at 2:00 AM. Her advice was straightforward: "Don't testify under any circumstances. Get as far away from this as you can." This put me in a difficult dilemma, as Peter was anything but a drug kingpin; his hands-off management style, which at times left the inmates running the asylum, didn't allow for it. He was simply too unorganized. I was apprehensive about throwing myself into the middle of the high-stakes fray, and taking the stand was something I desperately wanted to avoid.

With Peter facing a potentially long prison sentence, I thought back to my arrival in NYC. Since that fortuitous first-day meeting with Gregory, I had gone from unknown to sought after, rookie to seasoned veteran, naïve to aware, sheltered to self-sufficient, Urban Outfitters to Helmut Lang—Steve from Boston to Steve Adelman. I'd attended one of the most intensive nightlife training programs ever devised. All the experience I had gained was now speaking to me, telling me that what was happening to Peter just wasn't *right*. With that, I made my choice. I would testify. Fuck you, Giuliani.

The morning of my testimony, I rose at dawn, with multiple scenarios unrelentingly repeating themselves in my head. *Will pissing off federal prosecutors land me in jail? Who will come bail me out? Will I have to wear an ankle monitor?* I jumped when the phone suddenly rang, but I was in no state of mind to talk with anyone. When it rang a third time, I finally picked up, sensing the urgency. It was Ben Branfman's office.

Ben told me that he felt the prosecution had not made its case and, as such, had decided *not* to call witnesses. I did not have to appear in court.

Branfman was spot on. Peter was exonerated of all charges—but was eventually sent to jail on tax evasion and deported back to Canada. Michael went to jail along with his accomplice, Robert "Freeze" Riggs, followed by Lewis, whose braggadocio exploits at the door had been captured on tape. It was the first I've ever heard of someone being convicted for being a narcissist.[6]

A short time later, the Roxy was closed to make way for Frank Gehry-designed condominiums. As the development plans stalled, and with his money running out, Gene DiNino was able to access his former club through a little-known back entrance, squatting undetected in his cluttered office with a few prized antiques and two cats for the next two years before returning to his hometown of Syracuse.

A golden era of NYC nightlife had all but come to an end. The music was turned off for good in the five largest clubs in the country, which I directed, all within a span of two years. Giuliani was not about to make it easier for those in nightlife anytime soon. He quickly raided other clubs, and his campaign to clean up NYC extended to going after jaywalkers, bike riders, and, famously, art exhibits that he didn't understand. Given what NYC had now become, it was time to pick my cards up off the table and move on.

I had come to the realization that, if I wasn't in control of what was

6 Officially defined by the State of New York as drug conspiracy.

happening around me, my fortunes were dependent on someone else. I made the decision then and there that the only way for me to move forward was to venture out on my own. Now, the only things I needed were the money and a location.

Boston seemed like a good place as any to start.

CHAPTER 5

SMALL*ISH*VILLE

"There's no place like home."
—DOROTHY GALE

After living in New York City, residing anywhere else can have its challenges, one being that almost every other city seems . . . well . . . *small.* This was certainly the case with Boston, which, in the traditional sense, is no small town by any means and boasts its own beauty and rich culture. Arriving back in Boston from NYC for the first time in over eight years, the first thing that hit me was the *less* of everything, from the restaurant choices, entertainment options, cost of living, and number and diversity of people on the street. I was experiencing Boston much differently this time around and, most vividly, the culture of the city itself.

In 1998, it felt as if the psychological effect of what had become infamously known as the "Curse of the Bambino" still manifested itself, permeating aspects of local life even outside of sports. For non-sports fans, the Red Sox selling Babe Ruth to the New York Yankees in 1920 for a mere $125,000 set off an eighty-six-year championship drought for Boston. It was finally broken in dramatic fashion in 2004, with the Sox coming from 0-3 to win the American League pennant from the Yankees, and then going on to win the World Series.

For sports-crazed Bostonians, this built up not only a generational distain for being swindled, but a deep sense of inferiority as the Yankees went on to win a record twenty-six World Series, making them the most successful sports franchise in U.S. history. No longer referred to as Steve from Boston, but Steve from New York, upon my return local attitudes toward me changed—something I experienced on a daily basis.

Oddly, I wasn't shunned by the locals or, in unique Boston fashion, called a "tool." Instead, I was the subject of an idiosyncratic reverence, especially along the lines of my reputation in nightlife. Like the soldier who goes off to war and finally returns home after winning hard-fought battles, my legend and exploits had grown over time. "How did it feel to tell Giuliani 'fuck you' to his face?" *Huh?* "What is Amber Valletta like, and did you really date her?" *No idea, and I've never spoken to her.* "I heard Mark Wahlberg is a tool, is that true?" *When I said hi, he seemed nice enough.*

With regards to nightlife itself, Boston had long been hindered by its Puritanical heritage, which translated to outdated practices like alcohol not being sold on Sundays, a 10:00 PM last call for restaurants, and night-clubs being mandated to close at 2:00 AM. With NYC only a few hours away by train or an hour's flight, Bostonians I knew had made it a habit to leave town for a "big-time" weekend in NYC, where clubs raged on into the early morning hours, Broadway staged performances that would take years to make their way to Boston, and 10:00 PM was prime time for dinner to begin. While NYC was nicknamed the "Big Apple," Boston was saddled with "Beantown." Enough said.

Long thought of as one of the most segregated and prejudiced cit-ies in the U.S., Boston at the same time played host to the world's larg-est per-capita student population, with over one hundred colleges and universities in its greater metropolitan area. It also had perhaps the best young, vibrant workforce in the country. If Beantown would never become a nightlife mecca, it certainly wasn't for lack of a captive audience seeking to be entertained. Known for its pubs and live music scene, Boston had a well-earned reputation as a "real man's" drinking town, similar to Chicago. It was also home to long-standing rock venues such as the Orpheum and Paradise, and served as the launching pad for the likes of Aerosmith, Godsmack, Pixies, Dropkick Murphys, and, of course, Boston the band.

Early one morning, as I lay on a friend's oversized faux leather couch after spending the night contemplating my self-imposed exile, I craved my morning espresso with just the right amount of cream and a coffee cake muffin from Dean & Deluca. Dinners at Raoul's in SoHo, conversations with the Club Kids, crazed interactions with Lewis, and late nights in the shadows were already disappearing memories.

It had only been three months since I'd been introduced to Patrick Lyons, one of the principal owners of That's Entertainment, a Boston group that owned numerous bars and nightclubs on Lansdowne Street, adjacent to the famed Fenway Park (birthplace of Bambino lore). Patrick had quickly introduced me to his brother, John, explaining that he was the one who oversaw the day-to-day operations.

John Lyons' office was located in a nondescript building on an abandoned-by-day street. Ringing the entry bell with no answer, I waited outside for twenty minutes before John's car pulled up. "Get in," he said.

I climbed into the car. As we sped off, I organized my pages of ideas for what I believed would be a formal get-to-know-each-other, and hopefully a strategic planning session.

"Got some errands to do," John explained abruptly, holding a phone up to his ear.

First stop was the car wash, followed by the traditional Boston Dunkin' Donuts run, and, finally, a trip to Star Market for groceries.

"If you need something, this is the best place to get it," John advised as he loaded up his cart with enough pasta sauce and rigatoni to feed the Bambino himself for a month.

"I'm good," I replied, checking my watch. It had now been almost two hours since I had been lured into John's car. After driving around for another thirty minutes, we finally arrived back at his office.

"There's an office upstairs," he said, handing me a key. "Gotta go." And with that, I became a managing partner.

By this time, I had come to accept that no matter how well strategies are formulated, plans analyzed, and ideas scrutinized, timing and good fortune are always factors in success. It's true for all businesses and life in general, but it's especially true in the nightlife world. This derives from the fickle nature of potential customers searching for an experience that facilitates sexual encounters and an escape from reality. Not an easy product to deliver, but if it's executed correctly and the stars are aligned, you'll have a proverbial "hotspot"—a term often thrown around a lot in nightlife defined by current popularity and, more than likely, the line waiting to get in. But below the surface, there is more than meets the eye, a third box to be checked: a feeling of superiority.

Rubbing elbows with those who define *themselves* as an integral part of a hotspot has always given club-goers the feeling that they're part of an exceptional group. In reality, it constitutes nothing more than jumping on the bandwagon. However, the psychology here is key. No matter what happened at work that day with your berating boss or condescending co-worker, you can always depend on the hotspot to make you feel important.

In mega-clubs, this was taken a step further with the creation of the VIP room, denoting a select few "superior" even to their superior comrades. Here's a little secret: that long line you see outside is just the hotspot keeping people out for no reason other than to heighten the illusion of exclusivity.

Even when building clubs, the location's blueprints versus what actually happens in each space is a bit of a crap shoot. For example, a large unisex bathroom was built at Tunnel and decorated with edgy, baby-blue custom furniture, with the intention that it would serve as an escape from the crowded dance floor. However, this area quickly became used as *another* dance floor, to the point that an additional DJ booth was installed to replace the piped-in music. Apparently, getting away from the action lent itself to feelings of being *left out* of the action. At Limelight, a back VIP entrance intended for important guests was never used for its designated purpose; instead, it was converted into an additional bar location. Turns out, it wasn't the waiting that VIPs didn't like, but not having the chance to complain about it—which is what made them feel like the bona-fide elite they believed themselves to be.

> ## LAXIOM #5
> ### Prepare, but don't over-prepare.
> On a trip to the vet with my dog, I witnessed a woman, who was there for the first time, hand the receptionist her dog's medical history (prepared), followed by a stool sample she had been carrying around all day, knowing they would be needing one (over-prepared).

As plans for Lansdowne Street pressed forward with a degree of nightlife-inherited uncertainty, I caught my first critical break from the most unlikely of sources: Giuliani. Ironically, by that time, the mayor had recreated the same ridiculous look seemingly originated by DEA undercover agents by appearing publicly in drag multiple times (including on *Saturday Night Live*), in some sort of nightlife-pilfered, hypocritical effort to make over his personality and attract gay voters for his mayoral run. If Rudy had just taken a second to talk with any of the dozens of drag queens he had put out of work, I'm sure they would have had a few things to say about his newly adopted persona: "Rudy, you must have a talented makeup artist. I have never met anybody who's able to shove their head so far up their own ass without smudging their eyeliner."

Giuliani's continued efforts against nightclubs were directed at Twilo in West Chelsea, just a few blocks from Tunnel. This would have an inadvertent and significant impact on Boston nightlife for the next decade.[7] In 1996, Twilo had become the first major U.S. nightclub to significantly embrace European DJ culture, beginning with a monthly party featuring British DJs Sasha and John Digweed. From day one, it drew sold-out crowds, with lines around the block waiting for the chance to pay the forty-dollar entrance fee. Within a year, British DJ Carl Cox was hosting his own monthly event at Twilo, with the same overwhelmingly positive response.

Limelight had tried to export this same culture two years earlier, but with disastrous results. On a night themed "Hacienda" after the groundbreaking Manchester UK nightclub, DJs such as Paul Oakenfold, Sasha, and Judge Jules took to the turntables for their NYC debuts. Their European musical style, deemed "trance" music, was an unexpected and unwelcome addition for the confused party-goers on the dance floor. Up against the hard techno of DJ Repeat, trance—named for the emotional feeling its listeners claimed to experience—had the effect of dirt being dumped on a campfire.

As the dance floor stopped cold for over thirty minutes, Arthur Weinstein (the same ex-owner of the World who, since its closing, had been working as the Limelight lighting technician) made the decision to have the whole lot of them removed from the DJ booth. This prompted pushing and shoving and ended with Weinstein, in his distinctive sarcastic manner, announcing to the dance floor crowd over a microphone, "The British are leaving . . . the British are leaving." The British DJ Invasion, as it had been promoted, was off to a conspicuous start.

By 1998, trance had become the main dance music of choice, and it soon became evident that the influence of foreign DJs on the U.S. music scene was here to stay. With Twilo facing an uncertain future, the rapidly growing scene was desperately seeking both a city and venue to call home. Avalon was now poised to pick up the baton and run with it.

---

7 Qualifying him for tool status. Giuliani would later try and succeed in taking his tool status to new lows during the now infamous bedroom scene in *Borat Subsequent Moviefilm*, and dying while peddling presidential election conspiracy theories.

Originally built in the early 1900s by *Boston Globe* owner Eben Jordan to house his delivery horses and carriages, 15 Lansdowne Street had existed as a music venue in one form or another since 1968. That year, newcomer Charlie Thibeaux opened the psychedelic rock club The Ark at the location. Though it lasted only one year, it established Lansdowne Street as an entertainment district.

Next came the live music club the Boston Tea Party, run by local promoter Don Law. The venue hosted some of rock's most celebrated acts, including the Who, Elton John, Fleetwood Mac, and Led Zeppelin. The Tea Party gave way to the rise of disco in the '70s, passing to new owners Ian Schrager, Steve Rubell, and John Addison, who converted the space into a glitzy dance club aptly named 15 Lansdowne.

By 1977, Schrager and Rubell had abandoned Boston for NYC to open the famed Studio 54. Addison, now the sole owner, renamed the space Boston-Boston, which was run by manager Patrick Lyons. In 1980, Lyons, along with a group of investors including Don Law, bought the property from Addison and eventually the other available buildings on Lansdowne Street as well, converting them into multiple clubs and bars.

In 1988, a large domed roof was installed at the venue for better concert viewing as Law and Lyons worked to host both live music and dance nights under one roof, renaming their brainchild Citi. In 1992, the space was again reconceived and renamed Avalon, featuring an updated layout and interior design. By 1998, Patrick had shifted his focus to restaurants and Don Law had become one of the country's premiere concert promoters, expanding his reach to multiple venues not only in Boston but in neighboring states as well.

Tasked with operating the now six Lansdowne locations—including local music showcase Mama Kin, co-owned by Steven Tyler and the other members of Aerosmith—John Lyons had other ideas in mind. His true passion for the technical aspects of nightclubs had led him to Los Angeles, where he spent the majority of his time working on the sound and light installations for the soon-to-be-opened House of Blues in West

Hollywood, founded by John's longtime friend, Dan Aykroyd.

While the concert business was on the rise, to the point of requiring additional capacity, the nightclub portion of Avalon had remained stagnant for years. Managers with limited experience, especially in the areas of marketing and promotion, were left to their own devices to generate business, with not unexpected results. As Law pushed for the expansion of the club, which included capturing additional space from the adjacent building, something profitable late at night would be required to help foot the bill. Out of this need, the club concept Avaland was born.

Billed as a "world at night," Avaland combined the theatrics and themes from Locomotion with the growing demand for European DJs in the U.S. When Avalon finally went under construction, the launch of Avaland would mark its reopening, opening its doors every Friday night thereafter. John became reengaged as the upgraded lights and sound system took shape. A new foosball table was installed in a back corner, where John could take on unsuspecting workers for money who had no inkling that they were about to face a world-class-caliber foe.

As the opening night of the "new" Avalon approached, delays in one inspection, another looming wildcard factor, had the potential to derail what had now been months in planning. Unlike Big Mac's place, where the only inspection was likely done by Mac himself to check that the back alley was clear as an emergency exit in case of a police raid, for Avalon to legally reopen, multiple city sign-offs were needed. That included electrical, plumbing, sprinkler, fire safety, and health code inspections leading to the issue of a Certificate of Occupancy, stating the new legal capacity for patrons. Each one of these inspections was performed by a different department and inspector.

After scheduling an inspection with over a month's waiting time, if you didn't pass, it could be another two months before the inspector was able to return, all the while facing a ticking clock. This, as you can imagine, left the door open for bribes to look the other way, or creative solutions to give the inspector what he most wanted: the ability to check the

YES box and move on to the next of his ten appointments that day. Within this entire process, only one thing was certain: you could always count on an Inspector Asshole to make life difficult for those awaiting his sign-off. Why? Like *America's Got Talent*'s Simon Cowell holding off praise for an act that had worked so hard to make it to that point—because he could.

We had now been waiting for the Buildings Department to sign off on our handicapped access for six weeks. This involved compliance with the handicapped bathroom stalls, ramps leading to all the exits and the dance floor, and an elevator allowing access to the balcony overlooking the dance floor.

When Inspector O'Rourke finally arrived, the first thing that struck me was his uncanny likeness to actor Chris Farley. "Let's get this a-goin," he said in a deep Irish accent, already eyeing his clipboard intently.

Breathing a sigh of relief as he finally appeared to tick off all his boxes, I ushered him toward the door; I was unprepared for his request to stop at the bar, thinking with unconscious bias that it must be an Irish thing.

"Can I get you something to drink?" I asked, hoping to quickly grab something from the cooler and push him on his way.

"No, I need to get *behind* the bar," he said. From there, he took out a tape measure and began measuring what seemed like every inch of the space. "This is not handicapped-compliant."

"The bar?" I asked, thinking I had misheard.

"By law, the area behind the bar needs to be able to accommodate a bartender in a wheelchair. You need a ramp here—" he pointed to the back-bar entry point "—and the ability for someone to turn three hundred and sixty degrees." He pivoted in a circle to demonstrate.

"I never knew this was needed," I said, handing him the checklist we had been given weeks earlier.

"The other inspector must have missed it," he replied without looking at the list.

This sounded, well, a little off. I could appreciate the need for the area behind the bar being accessible, but it was a little late to be bringing it up. *Is this guy looking for some cash to let it slide? A maître d' handshake, maybe?*

As "A-hole" further explained, the fix would involve building a four-foot-long ramp leading to the back bar area due to its two-step elevation, and then ripping out the entire row of six cabinets behind the bar—which were essential for liquor storage—to create the necessary space. Even if the work started today, to rip out carpet and then pour a sloped surface out of concrete would take days . . . days that we didn't have.

"Call me when the work is done, and I'll schedule a time to come back," said Inspector O'Rourke.

I was not about to let him out of my sight until I was assured that we could open tomorrow.

"Wait," I blurted out. "What if we built a wooden ramp over the carpet that served the same purpose." I knew I couldn't take no for an answer.

"Wood isn't fire-retardant, so I couldn't accept that," he replied.

"We'd cover the wood with a fireproof paint."

"You also need to have handrails."

"Can do."

"And the cabinets?"

"Consider them moved," I replied, talking out of my ass. "Can you *please* come back tomorrow morning? Everything will be done by then."

"I could make time tomorrow before my first inspection, at eight-thirty."

"Great, see you then."

My "what if" was purely speculation. We only had hours to turn it into reality.

With John's help, we were able to locate wood and have a ramp—with railings—built and painted by 3:00 AM. At 4:00 AM, we made the decision to rip out the cabinets and relocate them *near* the bar. When stacked vertically and covered with a piece of plywood and a long, black tablecloth, they made great standing bar tables.

Beyond having a barback crawl under your table from time to time and emerge with three full bottles, this proved to work quite well. It worked out even better for the barback, who was mistaken for some sort of nightclub magician and tipped to show how the trick was done.

At exactly 8:30 AM, the inspector arrived. Fifteen minutes later, as I handed him $200, he gave his approval.

"Please come tonight if you get the chance," I said. "Consider this a prepaid bar tab for all your efforts.

Avaland launched in grand fashion with a "Wizard of Odds" theme featuring Dutch DJ Paul Van Dyk, deemed the number-one DJ in the world at the time. Gregory Homs, who I'd worked closely with since the Roxy, had followed me to Boston as creative director for Avalon. He and his partner, Candi, marked the occasion by creating an elaborate hand-drawn, poster-sized invitation that took three months to complete.

The local design team, recruited by the now-artist-in-residence John Dellarocco, executed the night's installation. It consisted of twenty feet of chicken wire on which tree limbs, mismatched pieces of wood, a mini stuffed cow, ten stuffed chickens, and five small TVs playing disaster footage were fastened. When an image of a whirling tornado was then projected on the chaotic installation, it gave a vivid and largely comical illusion of the real thing, with industrial fans staged around the dance floor to heighten the effect.

In the center of it all was a large twenty-foot platform that supported a partially damaged house. Our eclectic group of performers was headed by Girlina, a plus-sized drag queen playing Dorothy who held a perfect Toto lookalike and threw fake poppies into the adoring crowd dancing around her. Around her were fourth and fifth graders (closely supervised by their cousins, two of the night's six Avaland dancers) playing munchkins, as well as a Tin Man, Lion, and Scarecrow prancing around a "horse of a different color" (a fiberglass "mare" covered in UV paint that appeared to change color when special overhead lights were activated).

John Lyons had installed a twenty-foot video wall that he'd some-how obtained from MTV, which would simultaneously run videos of live crowd shots, the performers, and a prerecorded drag wizard who would utter the famous phrase from the movie: "Pay no attention to that man behind the curtain." To top it off, an old-school bicycle was welded to one of the giant moving light trusses. As the truss lowered to the ground an Avaland dancer, wearing next to nothing other than a large hat and painted head to toe in green, mounted the bike and was raised to the rafters—a wicked witch to behold.

A universal truth at nightclubs is that, around one hour before clos-ing, in a joyful ritual that has most likely played out in some form since the invention of alcohol itself, almost *everyone* transforms into a self-pro-claimed magnificent exhibitionist dancer. During this period, if a live camera is directed on the crowd, the ceremony evolves into an elaborate audition for *Dancing with the Stars*. In cities such as NYC, Madrid, and Singapore, where there is no mandated closing time, this highly un-cho-reographed "Ceremony of the Smashed" can last for hours. It frequently ends in a loss of either consciousness or clothing and accessories, but nev-er the will to continue on, like some Paula Abdul-inspired, spring-break Tasmanian Devil.

This was perfectly demonstrated by the blotto bachelorette parties that pranced around endlessly, until one of the mascara-smeared ladies either face-planted on the floor (which, in many instances, didn't halt the runaway party train) or, in the definitive case, misplaced her purse, at which time a manhunt was formed with anyone in the vicinity viewed as a prime suspect.

With 1:00 AM quickly approaching, the Avaland version of a pickled *American Bandstand* was already getting underway, with dance floor rev-elers climbing onto the performer's platform and grinding away against their paid counterparts. Fashion-forward Emerson College students grabbed leftover poppies and created impromptu headbands for both the

Cowardly Lion and two members of the Red Sox, who, by the smiles on their faces, appeared to have anything but curses on their minds. "Mass-holes" (the Boston version of the Bridge and Tunnel crowd) sashayed with Financial District yuppies. Two twinks, both dressed for the occasion as twin Glindas, mounted the horse and played bucking bronco, their lipstick illuminated under the black light as Dan Aykroyd, his wife Donna Dixon, and a trio of Baldwin brothers looked on.

In the center of all this chaos, one man emerged as a true sensation.

Inspector O'Rourke had taken to playing out the famous Farley *SNL* Chippendales skit, adding in his own special touch. Shirtless, he alternated between a stripper performance and what I interpreted (once again with unconscious prejudice) as an Irish folk dance. His expression of pure joy mixed with unwavering concentration made it clear that he might be an inspector by day, but a perfect fit for the Club Kids at night, perhaps adopting the name "Jiggy."

This quickly reminded me of my time in New York, where, living in the Rutherford Building on Seventeenth and Second, I would frequently see Farley in the lobby at 5:00 AM with his trusted bulldog, which never failed to greet me with a bowling ball-like beeline. As we discussed matters at *SNL* or Limelight, it was common to be interrupted by David Lee Roth, on his way to Washington Square Park to meet his pot dealer. Always the gentleman, "Diamond Dave" never failed to inquire if we needed some weed ourselves. Chris always answered with, "A bit early in the day for me." He died tragically the very day I moved back to Boston.

When I was finally able to pull my gaze away from the riveting Jiggy, I realized that a mounting problem needed immediate attention. The platform built to accommodate fifteen people was now overrun with over thirty, and about to buckle. Technically, the platform was not licensed to hold anyone, not performers and certainly not drunk patrons. Even worse, it had been erected that morning, *after* the inspector had left.

Expecting to see any number of people thrown off the side due to lack of proper railings, I could see the *Boston Globe* headline now:

INTOXICATED INSPECTOR BREAKS BACK AFTER FALLING FROM PLATFORM HE WAS SUPPOSED TO HAVE INSPECTED

Witness Stephen Baldwin claims the South Boston resident plunged into the crowd while doing an odd striptease-jig

Frantically radioing to clear the platform, security was running up against a barrier due to the crowd size. In a moment of unparalleled nightlife poetic justice, Will Smith's recently released dance hit "Gettin' Jiggy Wit It" blared as the platform now began to give way. Looking on from the balcony in horror, I caught my second big break as the music and dance lights stopped, leaving the crowd chanting for more. It was 2:00 AM, the Boston witching hour (literally, in this case, as the Glindas stopped dancing).

The one thing that had always set Boston nightlife back had saved the day.

Back on my friend's faux leather couch, I replayed what had occurred that night. I was beginning to feel more at home. The reopening of Avalon had left me feeling like I was back at Limelight, as a group of people from all walks of society, rarely seen collectively in Boston, had come together for one memorable night.

Only in the world of nightlife.

So what if there were less of them and they had to go to bed earlier. My self-imposed exile now seemed to be turning into opportunity, with a light at the end of the tunnel coming into view as my future.

CHAPTER 6

AN EVENT FULL YEAR

"Why party like it's 1999,
when you can party like it's your birthday."
—PRINCE

One clear summer's night, I stood outside Avalon as the lengthy entrance line snaked around the block and moved slowly past me. Taking a step back into Lansdowne Street, I was too preoccupied to notice a large black SUV whizzing by.

"Dude, that Tahoe almost took you out," a voice said from somewhere in the slowly moving rank and file. "You all right, bro?"

"Yeah fine, thanks," I replied to no one in particular. My gaze was still fixed down the block, taking in the scene of two police officers stuffing one of my now ex-employees into the back of their car.

"I would still really like to use you as a reference, if possible," Nick, my former manager, called out to me, looking back over his left shoulder. The thing was, he was being serious.

As the police drove him way, I all but expected a friendly wave, or perhaps a thumbs up, to appear in the back window, if Nick's handcuffs hadn't preventing him from doing so. I have to say, up until three days earlier, I'd considered him to be one of the best managers I had ever worked with.

My thoughts were interrupted by my phone ringing. I searched for it in my pocket amongst the complimentary drink tickets.

"Traffic was horrible . . . it took us two hours to get here from Providence . . . we are outside . . . how do we get in?" the snappy voice asked, with an easily recognizable Brooklyn accent.

"Who is this, and how did you get this number?"

"This is Perry's Aunt Myra . . . I'm here with Perry now."

A few minutes later, Perry Farrell, the frontman for the hipster Los Angeles rock band Jane's Addiction, his Aunt Myra, and her friend, Marla, were all upstairs together in my office.

"Look at this boy. Have you ever seen anything so handsome? And talented?" Aunt Myra grabbed her object of affection with both arms.

I was expecting Perry to show up with guitarist Dave Navarro or perhaps his manager—not Aunt Myra, who, after completing her bonus cut scene from *Annie Hall* had a list of questions. "Are there any more chairs? Who has an office with no furniture? Do you serve food? I didn't get a chance to eat dinner. Where do I go to watch the show?"

Perry had been booked to DJ for Avaland's first anniversary. Club-goers were anxious to see a DJ rock persona, more as a novelty than anything else. *Would he be DJ'ing with the band? Can he actually DJ? What type of music?* Truth be told, I didn't really know myself. Dave, our booker, who doubled as our in-house DJ, assured me that Perry could play anything.

The past year had been one of nonstop construction and promotion as Lansdowne went through a complete overhaul. After the completion of Avalon in 1998, five other clubs had followed suit within the year. Mama Kin and the adjacent Music Hall were converted into the Carlos Zapata-designed, minimalistic lounge Modern, and Embassy, a nightclub catering to the now overflow of international students in Boston, who had adopted it as their prime party destination.

Just blocks away in Kenmore Square, Boston University had found creative ways to lure the sons of affluent Middle Eastern families to campus, who brought a new element to Boston nightlife: their fathers' Amex Black cards. Their own variation of the last-hour dance ritual involved credit cards being bandied about for champagne, in a free-for-all spendathon to determine who would emerge with the largest tab and the coveted reality show title of "Top Spender."

Over the last year, European DJs had found a home at Avaland every Friday night. This marked the beginning of "superstar" DJ culture in the U.S., which would continue to flourish for the next twenty years. In a nightlife version of the classic Aykroyd comedy *Trading Places*, New Yorkers were now starting to travel to Boston to experience the likes of DJs Paul Oakenfold, Fatboy Slim, the Chemical Brothers, and Daft Punk. These acts were set against the backdrop of weekly elaborate themes—such as "Heaven and Hell," starring a dozen scantily clad angels and devils on trapeze swings hovering over the crowd, and "Hoedown," which featured two dozen hay bales and the "horse of a different color" now painted to look realistic and saddled up with a drag Wyatt Earp in an oversized cowboy hat, twirling a lasso. As far as cities went, Boston had ostensibly answered the movie's one-dollar bet of nature versus nurture.

Avaland's Friday nights had their own mascot: Gnomar, a three-foot nightlife version of the Travelocity gnome, complete with a custom fabricated Avaland wizard hat. Named after Red Sox star shortstop Nomar Garciaparra, the prized statue was hidden somewhere in the club every Friday night, and the person who discovered his location received $50 in free drinks. On any given Friday, the frenzied question was asked dozens of times: "Have you seen Gnomar?"

When the actual Nomar showed up with Red Sox teammate David "Big Papi" Ortiz, he was inundated with fans who couldn't help but see the humor.

"It's the real Nomar," they commented in passing, many following up with, "Have you seen Gnomar?" This must have made Nomar feel like he was trapped in an Abbot and Costello bit. Big Papi, being a man of the people, high-fived everyone in his vicinity, giving the impression of being an inside-joke collaborator.

When Boy George came to town to DJ for our "A Night in Gay Paris" theme, he became furious at his manager; he'd been under the impression that he was booked to play an exclusively gay night. But after entering the club that evening and witnessing a combination of male and female body-painted mimes and chatting with host Carmen Electra, he was quickly sold. Later that same night, the Backstreet Boys, in town for an arena show at the Boston Garden, arrived to pay homage to the pop icon. Not recognizing them, Boy raved, "Oh, this is just so much funner than the boring go-go boy dancers I always see. Are you sure we're in Boston?" As he looked around at the mingling of humanity, Boy borrowed the one sentiment that seemed to fit the moment, saying enthusiastically, "I don't believe it." The other "Boys" stood in confused silence.

In a page right out of the early Disco 2000 playbook, Verne Troyer (aka Mini Me from the *Austin Powers* movies) was brought in to host the '70s psychedelic-themed "The Spy Who Shagged Me" event. Even for a little person, Verne was undersized, having to improvise a version of rock-climbing to get into a car. After issues on his flight, where he refused to fly in anything other than the first row in first class, he spent the day pulling up to pedestrians in his negotiated limo on swanky Newbury Street, rolling down the window, and shouting, "I'm Mini Me!" to stunned shoppers. A true prankster at heart.

Verne's diminutive stature was put in even starker contrast when he spent his night at Avaland smoking cigars with Michael Jordan while sitting *on* Michael's table, where, from afar, he might be mistaken as an ornate centerpiece if not for Gnomar positioned next to him.

Soon after, we hosted a night with two of Howard Stern's Wack Pack: Beetlejuice and Hank the Angry Drunken Dwarf. However, at Disco 2000 we'd already seen how quickly hiring hosts for their kitsch value could quickly turn from clever and humorous to ugly, a moratorium was put on little people after that.

As hard as I tried, I couldn't get Dellarocco to buy into the return of my "Attack of the Killer Tomatoes" theme. "Sequels are never as good as the original," he said, "and that's especially true if no one ever *saw* the original." He had a point.

Now, at Avaland's first anniversary, Perry had not said a word in over fifteen minutes. Not that it was easy getting a word in with Aunt Myra in the room. Finally he broke his silence.

"So, is that the dance floor we passed on the way up here?" he quietly asked.

"That's one of them. Tonight we've opened all six clubs together, so there are actually six dance floors. You're playing in the biggest one."

"How big's that?" Perry asked, looking somewhat concerned.

"Two thousand people," I replied matter-of-factly.

"Oh my," Aunt Myra chimed in. "That's a big club just for dancing. Does it serve food?" She was still trying to come up with a dining option.

"I'm afraid not, but if you take a left outside and go about five blocks, there's a great pizza place called Nemo's. I eat there all the time." And away the *SNL* "Let's Talk" girls went.

Perry stood up nervously from his coveted chair. "Can we talk?" he asked. "I've only really DJ'd at small lounges, for about one hundred people, using my personal play list. I took this gig thinking it was like that. I'm in way over my head here, man."

"How much music do you have . . . and what kind?" I asked quietly, trying to calm down both myself and Mr. Lollapalooza.

"About forty minutes' worth. Almost all rock and old-school hip-hop tracks. Stuff like Run-DMC and De La Soul." Perry was now pacing in front of me.

Thus far, I'd never been in a situation where a DJ didn't have enough music—and was going to feature tracks in a completely different format. I mean, what major nightclub runs out of music?

"And," Perry went on, "I don't really mix my songs. I just kind of play them back to back." *Great.*

As a DJ, getting a few hundred party people to dance is one thing; a few thousand is, well, a horse of a different color. But practically speaking, it's easier to get a small number of people to act in unison than a large group. Usually the DJ has the expertise to overlap songs, or "mix them," at around the same BPM with a seamless transition, creating the experience of dancing to one extended song. Every DJ will tell you it takes time to warm up a large dance floor, literally because of all the moving parts. Wisdom would have it that combining the 80 BPMs of classic hip-hop with the 120 BPMs of dance music would result in a schizophrenic dance experience.

With midnight fast approaching and our star attraction due in the DJ booth, two potential scenarios crossed my mind. In the first, Perry would play music from our resident DJ, Dave, who had been working the stage since 10:00 PM. But I quickly abandoned this idea—Perry wouldn't know the tracks, and the same music would be playing at another Lansdowne club that night. My second idea was to have Perry pretend to play Dave's tracks, which, after thoughts of Milli Vanilli, was also ruled out as simply a bad idea.

There was one other risky option . . . maybe. We could have Perry and DJ Dave play together, combining their sets. What was the worst that could happen, other than a dance floor train wreck?

Perry winced at my idea. "I really don't want to look like a fool in front of all these people. This is a big mistake." He hadn't even noticed Myra's return to my office.

"Perry, honey, we brought you back a calzone," Myra said, holding the wrapped pizza inches from his mouth. "You need to eat something."

"Not really hungry," he said despondently, seemingly resigning himself to an almost certain fate. But he agreed to go on with DJ Dave.

Perry appeared in the DJ booth overlooking the at-capacity crowd, and just the glimpse of him brought cheers from below, much to his apparent chagrin. My only thought was of the Limelight "British DJ Invasion" debacle. I looked over my shoulder, expecting Arthur Weinstein to appear and announce to the eager crowd, "Jane says . . . we're done with Pare-e-o."

Dave stepped aside, and Perry waved to the crowd as his name and photo flashed across the video wall. Dave then led off with some sure-fire dance tracks, including Daft Punk's "Harder, Better, Faster." Then it was Perry's turn. As "Rapper's Delight" came on, drastically dropping the BPMs, the crowd collectively stopped and looked around in bewilder-ment, as if lost in the forest and left to decipher strange sounds emanating from the threatening darkness. But then something strange happened. Like the famous scene from *The Grinch*, a sound began to emanate from below like the Whos down in Whoville . . . starting off slow, it continued to grow.

All two thousand people were collectively chanting every "bang bang," and "boogie," including Jiggy, who now made weekly Avaland appearances and, with his new accessories of multi-color glow sticks and matching necklaces, had become the blue-collar version of Mr. J, al-though I had yet to meet his wife. As Perry realized what was happening, his innate rock star persona took over. He began to work the crowd, fol-lowing up with Kurtis Blow's "The Breaks" and the Run-DMC remix of Aerosmith's "Walk This Way." When Dave finally came back on thirty minutes later with "Dare" from the Gorillaz and a remix of Madonna's "Get Together," the crowd was in a frenzy. In true unpredictable nightlife fashion, we had accidentally launched what would soon become the most popular DJ format in the country: the "mash-up," as it's now known.

One week before the Avaland anniversary, I had been given the monthly financial reports for all of the Lansdowne Street clubs, and the door ad-mission totals for Avalon immediately jumped off the page. On two sep-arate nights, total bar sales were over $35,000, but admissions were below $20,000. On average, patrons were spending $20 per person for drinks, which meant that approximately 1,750 people had entered the club that night. Given our cover charge of $20, the door revenue should have been almost equivalent to the total bar sales.

Even if the crowd on these nights drank more than average, say $25 per person, that would mean we'd had 1,400 in attendance. Let's say 100 of them got in for free as guests—that would still leave the door around $5,000 short on each night. No, this wasn't adding up. Obscure-Locks Roams once again made an appearance in my mind, and I was sure of one thing—I needed to investigate.

Going back over the numbers for the last three months, it became apparent that there were similar inconsistencies, the majority of which took place on our busiest nights. If money *was* missing, it was most likely that the door cashier was pocketing cash sales, to the tune of thousands of dollars on some nights.

I had seen this happen in New York—the customer was not given a door receipt and the ticket taker allowed the customer to pass, putting the ticket taker and cashier in cahoots. It took place right under the nose of the manager, whose job it was to prevent this exact scenario. It was time to have a chat with our cashier and ticket taker, who, it became apparent after checking the nightly staff schedule, were the same person for the nights in question: Gina.

When Gina entered my office the next day, she was quick to notice James, our ex-police detective turned head of security, standing in the back of the room. She looked back at him with a pained smile as she sat down.

"Thanks for coming on such short notice," I said, reaching into the folder on my desk. "I have a few questions about the door numbers."

Before I could pull out my evidence, the color drained from Gina's face.

"I'm so sorry . . . it was all Nick's idea," she blurted out, now in tears.

Nick had approached Gina months earlier with a plan, a way for her to make some "extra money," as she put it. He had conceived a more elaborate scheme than I'd suspected, which involved printing counterfeit door receipts that he gave Gina at the beginning of the night. All Gina needed to do was take the cash and hand the customer the fake door receipt, leaving no money trail. To ensure that this was working, the ticket taker was recruited to accept the fake receipt, later removing them from the night's total collected tickets.

At first, this happened around fifty times a night. As the trio became more emboldened, the number rose to well over a hundred. In a few short months, an estimated $30,000 was taken right out from under my nose, by a crime syndicate that consisted of two Boston University students and a barback-turned-manager. I never saw it coming; my slowly inflating ego hadn't even considered that stealing under my watch was a possibility. I felt like I'd actually been hit by that Chevy Tahoe that had barely missed me on the street.

When I asked Gina why she'd decided to get involved in something like this, her answer surprised me.

"Because I could, I guess," she said without hesitation. Her part of the take started at $150 a night, later increasing to $250.

On anniversary night, our sting operation was in place. Gina had agreed to cooperate as a now-undercover operative. As we had planned, James went into the box office and took the unaccounted-for cash, which Gina had been keeping under the counter. Then he asked very calmly for Gina and Nick to meet him in the office.

Knowing the jig was up, within minutes they had all confessed on the spot. Five minutes later, Nick was led out of the building. Meticulous as always, he actually had a handwritten record of exactly what had been taken: $28,800. Later he was asked why he did it—was he underpaid, or did he feel undervalued or disgruntled? His answer was, "No, actually this was the best job I ever had, my dream job. I guess I just saw an opportunity."

John's idea of having Nick removed publicly in handcuffs did pay dividends. The scare tactic made it easy to convince him to pay back the stolen money. Over the next two years, Nick had been unable to find steady work and had only repaid $3,000. When I received a voicemail from him asking for a reference, I was more than happy to accommodate. He was applying to be the general manager for our biggest competitor.

LAXIOM #6
Hire slow, fire quick.
The walking dead never come back to life. As such, I've never once thought I fired someone too soon. Hiring them too quickly . . . that's another story.

As the millennium was coming to an end, my reinvented life was now taking shape. The remake of Lansdowne was complete, and the ever-growing international student population continued to flash their no-limit Amexes with no end in sight. Even Hollywood was having its best year ever, releasing *The Matrix*, *The Green Mile*, *American Pie*, and *The Sixth Sense*, to name just a few.

To top matters off, New Year's 2000 was being considered the largest nightclub financial opportunity ever, with millions of revelers taking to the streets. Plans were already underway, including live performances from iconic Boston bands booked by Don Law. Things felt good as I finally made my way from my friend's couch to my own house, a converted flower shop in the up-and-coming South End District. The next year promised to be the best I had experienced in nightlife. I mean, what could go wrong?

Weeks later, the answer would come: *everything*, including a day that would change life and everything we thought we knew about it.

PART II
2000–2007

Avalon Boston, Avalon Hollywood,
Spider Club, Avalon NYC

CHAPTER 7

FEAR FACTOR

"Drink and dance and laugh and lie /
Love, the reeling midnight through, /
For tomorrow we shall die! (But, alas, we never do.)"
—DOROTHY PARKER

Think of the feeling of winning the lottery. More specifically, the feeling of knowing you're *going* to win the lottery—all you have to do is wait two months, and then the money will be yours.

This was the elevated mood in nightlife around the world as the new century approached. New Year's Eve was always the biggest night of the year, traditionally making two months' profit in one shot. But this was a once-in-a-lifetime historic event and a chance to cash in on the biggest celebration the world had ever seen.

With the Lansdowne clubs able to hold a maximum of five thousand people, I'd been working on alternative locations to house the expected twenty thousand revelers. This included renting and tenting the nearby Fenway Park, which would feature live, pre-midnight countdown performances by Aerosmith and New Kids on the Block. Negotiations for Fenway had been dragging for some time, due mainly to the intricate logistics needed to pull off such an event. Not helping matters was band management, who, also seeing the opportunity to make hay, were asking double their acts' going rates. After months of meetings, proposals, and counterproposals, the Fenway plan fell through, due mainly to a growing sense that a major crises was looming of apocalyptic proportions.

The "Y2K Problem" evolved from the computer-programming practice of representing years with only two digits: 97, 98, 99. Many believed that when the year 2000 arrived, denoted as 00, computer systems would break down as their numbering systems became invalid. This could disrupt anything from FAA flight-tracking systems to municipal traffic lights or any number of electrical grids, leaving society in chaos.

"The Y2K Problem is the electronic equivalent of El Niño, and there will be nasty surprises around the globe," U.S. Deputy Secretary of Defense John Hamre said.

Quickly pivoting, we drew up plans to use Lansdowne Street as an outdoor party location, creating a mini Times Square. However, without time to get the necessary permits, we quickly found ourselves back at square one.

LAXIOM #7
The deal you don't do won't hurt you.
Financial deals are like dating. They have a rhythm to them, and if the other side isn't responding positively, you should move on, no matter how great the disappointment. Better to have made no deal than a bad one—words that could also be applied to lessen the divorce rate.

To complicate matters, a new promoter had come to town to exploit the same fiscal opportunity with all but unlimited funds for promotion and a group of devoted regulars numbering in the millions: the Moral Majority.

A growing number of Christian leaders had taken up Y2K as a pronounced prophecy, led by Reverend Jerry Falwell, who proclaimed it "God's instrument to shake and humble this nation." His belief—and I use that word dubiously—was that the impending Y2K crisis would incite a worldwide revival of the church.

Jerry had taken up the cause after his latest call to arms, an attack on the purple Teletubby Tinky Winky, had fallen flat. After he claimed that Tinky Winky was intended as a gay role model that was damaging the moral lives of children, a spokesman for Itsy Bitsy Entertainment, who aired the show in the United States, gave a one-line response: "We find this absurd and offensive, as the show is aimed at preschool children."

Unrepentant, Falwell continued to beleaguer his non-point by insisting that "he's purple, the gay pride color, and his antenna is shaped like a triangle, the gay-pride symbol."

Not surprisingly, Falwell's scare-mongering tactics were followed with ministry sales of Y2K preparation kits, ordained generators, and memorabilia items marking the end of days. Many of these were emblazoned with catchy pop-culture references like "Apocalypse Now" (a theme, by the way, we'd used a month earlier at Avaland, with recreated helicopter wind blowing off our dancers' tops and drinks from the tables).

In a moment of "crossing the aisle" in respect, I broke down and ordered what can only be described as a flair-inspired Club Kid t-shirt with a world map surrounded by bowling balls and the message "You Don't Fuck with the Jesus" (in reference to the John Turturro character in *The Big Lebowski*). I mean, good is good. The group selling the item was actually Dudes for Disarray, whose retail outlet consisted of a table outside a 7-Eleven and who, unlike Falwell's PTL Club, accepted cash only.

Falwell's group, which I aptly dubbed the "False Profits," were the Yankees of manipulation and hyperbole, the true masters of their own national "outlaw party." Compared to them, the Avalon promoters were nothing but a version of the Bambino-less Red Sox. Fearmongering writers sold over forty-five million books citing Y2K-disaster scenarios, from civil war and planes dropping out of the sky to the total collapse of the banking system, advocating food hoarding and a bunker mentality.

I'd faced nefarious tactics from competitors before—such as calling the fire department to falsely claim overcrowding, resulting in a visit from two screaming fire trucks and the fire chief, who proceeded to stop the music and actually count the number of guests. On numerous occasions, underage girls were paid by rivals to enter Limelight or the Palladium with well-doctored fake IDs. After they were served, a call would be made to the police impersonating the mother of the minor, complaining that her daughter had been given alcohol. Squad cars pulled up and cops checked guest IDs, which had the intended negative impact on our customers.

These cutthroat opponents of ours lacked moral clarity and were willing to do anything to survive, but none had the False Profits' ability to inflict financial damage. They lacked the one great equalizer to turn the tide: God and his only perceived son.

I'm sure Evangelists would have said my uneasiness and potential loss of revenue from their scheme was my just reward for spending all that time at Limelight, desecrating a church for profit. To them, I'd point out that at least I never had to resort to prophesizing the "end of days," or use fearmongering to drum up business.

The original New Year's revenue was projected to be over $3.5 million, but now that the False Profits were gaining momentum and we were confined to the capacity of the Lansdowne clubs, this number had dropped to under $1.5 million. With December approaching, cable news couldn't resist the drama, broadcasting segments that gave credence to outlandish theories. One revealed a political agenda in which the downfall of the government was needed to usher in the reign of Jesus. Ironically mirroring nightlife's relationship with pop culture, the False Profits had brought Y2K from the fringe to mainstream.

Nightclub admission ticketing had yet to move to the live-concert model of advance online purchasing, leaving tickets to be purchased solely at the box office. With presales falling far below expectations, two days before New Year's Eve we were forced to cut our pricing to help generate sales.

On that same day, Patrick Lyons called me asking if I might help him get a group from one of his restaurants, Sonsie, to Avalon (eight blocks away) and ensure that they got in without waiting. Ben Affleck and Matt Damon had rented out the entire restaurant for their private family New Year's celebration, Moral Majority be damned.

At around 8:00 PM, an hour before doors opened, I made my way to Lansdowne Street. The design crew had outdone themselves with more glitter and mylar than one thought possible. A giant countdown clock hung above the Avalon dance floor with a camera system linking all six clubs, including a live feed of Times Square. Thousands of party hats, poppers, and noisemakers lay on large tables in the entryway, anticipating guest arrivals in the thousands.

Most never came.

The Moral Majority's message had landed with its desired impact (though it was eventually pushed back on by government officials who portrayed comments from the likes of the secretary of defense as being a "proactive precaution," along with scholars and computer-industry experts worldwide). Fear had claimed a temporary victory over facts.

No planes fell from the sky. No banks failed. No civil wars materialized.

In the United States, the most severe incident pertaining to Y2K took place in Delaware, where 150 lottery machines stopped working.

As 11:00 PM came and went, the Lansdowne clubs were at less than fifty percent capacity. I stepped outside onto the street, which was as desolate as the day I'd arrived at John's office. With no taxi in sight and a dark, ominous, empty Fenway Park looming over me, I made my way to Sonsie as promised, on foot as snow fell heavier by the minute. Fortunately, now that I was Steve from New York in Boston, I knew exactly where I was going.

I arrived to a half-empty celebration at Sonsie and searched for the hosts, who had yet to arrive, unable to find transportation. The majority of taxis and car services had taken the night off to avoid anarchy in the streets.

Ma Damon-Affleck (I can't recall whose mother it was, but a composite seems appropriate given that Matt and Ben seemed inseparable at that time) watched the action on the restaurant's makeshift dance floor. I was surprised as she rose and motioned to me to join her. Though I'd been surrounded for the past decade by thousands of people dancing on a weekly basis, this was the first time I'd actually danced myself, too busy to partake while working and purposely avoiding clubs in my free time. As I dusted off moves dating back to junior high, I envisioned all the righteous followers at home in their shelters, each with enough stored canned meat to feed a congregation. Breaking out the robot under the illuminated disco ball for what would be the last time in public, I couldn't help but think that, even though tonight might end up being the biggest financial letdown I'd experienced, no one could take this away from me. Contrary to the teachings of the False Profits, there's always tomorrow.

On September 11 the next year, it felt like the False Profits had been right after all. Like everyone across the world, I stared at the television in disbelief and horror as two planes kamikazed into the World Trade Center. Both flights had taken off earlier that morning from Boston's Logan Airport, just a few miles from my apartment.

After three days of total numbness, I made my way into the office to meet with John and the now eight managers on Lansdowne. Being the largest self-contained nightclub on the East Coast put us in a "code-red" category with respect to potential future attacks, according to a private police briefing earlier that day. I had only one plan in mind: close everything until we get a clearer understanding of the situation. Not by choice, mind you, but at the urging of others looking out for my best interest. I would, however, break with that well-meaning advice one more time at a private event.

No one knew quite how to begin the meeting in such an unprecedented situation. I spoke first.

"I know you're all still in shock, as am I," I began, "but I thought it best to meet to discuss how to move forward. There are a lot of people involved on the street, and I'm sure they'll be looking for answers regarding work soon enough. With that being said, I think we can all agree that we need to close for the foreseeable future."

Silence.

"I don't see it that way," said John, breaking the awkward quiet. "If we close, the terrorists win." He had an air of defiance. "Rolling up in a ball with fear is exactly what they want."

This was met by nods all around. It was something I hadn't considered.

"How would we keep people safe? I'm not even sure people feel secure leaving the house, let alone being in any sort of mood to go to a club."

"It doesn't matter," said Scott, Nick's able replacement. "It's the idea that counts. We need to show that we won't be intimidated. I'll work for free until you can pay me."

This elicited more nods.

"I've got this," added James. "We'll have the buildings secured during the day—no ins or outs unless preauthorized. At night, we'll search everyone. It shouldn't be a problem."

"It looks like the room says yay, so let's open tonight," instructed John.

I feared the worst.

That night, guests did indeed trickle in, and the mood, though somber, was composed. The DJs kept the music sedate as Avalon turned into a large support group. The look of fear on hundreds of faces was unmistakable, but so was the look of comfort and feeling of support from sharing the experience with others. One thing was for sure: it might have taken another form, but nightlife continued on.

As the country began to grasp what had occurred, backlash was swift against those from the Middle East residing in America. Out of safety concerns, by November the majority of parents from countries such as Kuwait, Saudi Arabia, and Turkey had summoned their sons back home.

In one last hurrah, Embassy regulars gathered together in the club one more time to watch the "Top Spender All-Stars" battle to determine who would end up as the GOAT.

With the night coming to an end (designated by the Gipsy Kings' anthem "Bamboleo"), Hussain, son of an Egyptian cabinet minister, was hoisted onto the shoulders of his competitors and proclaimed victorious. He had spent four months of his tuition in one night—over $15,000—and would later say that the money was already earmarked to be spent, so he might as well do it in the most enjoyable way possible.

In the months after 9/11, nightlife took on a new importance in people's lives. With a tornado of uncertainty and fear swirling, no matter what happened, gathering and meeting friends for drinks and dancing was always something they could count on, now more than ever. No matter what, nightlife would always be there.

This would hold true for the next eighteen years, until, for the first time in over a century, nightlife would be stopped dead in its tracks.

Chapter 8

PORN IDOL

"Each player must accept the cards life deals him or her;
but once they are in hand, he or she alone must decide
how to play the cards in order to win the game."
—Voltaire

One thing that separated Avalon Boston from the NYC mega-clubs was the concept of combining both weekly live concerts and club nights under one roof. The idea originated from the Patrick Lyons/Don Law partnership of the late '80s and was born out of practicality: the more you are open, the more money you make. A successful concert venue in Boston was open for business a mere thirty hours per week, and a nightclub, sixteen at best. When you're up to forty-six hours, plus additional private events such as fundraisers and Christmas parties, you have the makings of a highly successful nightlife business.

As this operating model ramped up, by 2002 it was not uncommon to have a Green Day, Stone Temple Pilots, or Strokes show followed by Avaland later that night. The coordination needed to make this happen had become a management art form within itself. It was something John had come to master after years of working with his brother, earning him the distinguished nickname of "Mr. Turnover" for his ability to manage a turnover any room, even under the most trying of circumstances.

Although he was six foot four and over 250 pounds, John was nimble thanks to his bowling ball-sized calves. Incidentally, he'd earned the same moniker playing the sport he loved, basketball. He had a unique playing style, in the mode of a Charles Barkley with a little John Stockton thrown in. But a Magic Johnson, he would never be.

Doors for a typical concert would open at 6:00 PM, with the headline act set to play at 7:30. On the days when there was a "double," as we came to call it, the design crew would use Avalon as their work space, and then were forced to move their props either behind the building into temporary storage or hide them in inconspicuous places within Avalon itself. This proved a challenging endeavor at times—and never more so than the Friday night that Iggy Pop and a porn star came to town.

The day began at 9:00 AM, with Iggy's roadies unloading the band's sound equipment off their two semi-trucks into Avalon. They were surprised to be met by Dellarocco and his design team, already scurrying about to ready the club for that night's Avaland theme: "Erotic Island," featuring Carl Cox and hosted by porn actress Jenna Jameson, with Gregory's custom-engraved massage oil bottles serving as invitations.

In the nightlife version of *Survivor*, two distinct tribes were responsible for completing the designated challenges to ensure that the entire night went as planned. The first, Iggy's Irritables, consisted of band members, tech crew, and roadies, led by their tour manager. The second, the Avalon Avengers, was comprised of Avalon managers, security, bar staff, and the design team, led by John Lyons and myself.

"Why in bloody fucking hell is there a fucking lifeguard chair here . . . and what the fuck are *those*? Fucking beach balls?" The Irritables' de facto leader / tour manager was yelling at no one in particular. This complaint, along with a host of others, made its way to the Avalon "advance manager," Todd, whose job, ultimately, was to babysit the band. He handled any issues that came up in advance of the show, and settled what they were owed at the end of the night. His unenviable position put him squarely in-between both tribes. Of all the times to get a "Seen Better Days" tour manager when a "Let's Get It Done" one was needed.

I'd found that all touring or road managers, called "TMs" in the industry, fit into four categories:

1. Seen Better Days
2. King for a Day
3. Let's Get It Done
4. Absentee

The job of the TM is to travel with the act to make sure things go as planned. This can involve traveling with the act, significant others, and a sound and/or lighting crew by tour bus, or flying into a city for a one-off performance date. Their responsibilities entail, firstly, making sure the act's "rider" is correctly provided. The rider includes all of the artists' special requests, consisting mainly of food and alcohol and ranging from sandwiches to vegan whole wheat tempura. As a rule, the bigger the act, the more eccentric the requests. This is all arranged in advance and delivered throughout the day by the "show runner," whose job is exactly as it sounds.

Next on the list is making sure all the equipment is unloaded from the trailers that accompany the tour bus. The venue provides stage hands to load in and begin setting up the stage plot, attaching dozens of cables that create a zoo of giant black thermoplastic snakes leading to and from the equipment on stage.

Sound checks need to happen on time. There are complimentary ticket requests to see to, from friends, family, friends of family, press, and others. Most importantly for the act, the TM's function beyond all this is to make sure they get paid at the end of the night. How this whole process plays out has everything to do with the category the TM falls under. Most TMs happen to be men, so I'll use male pronouns for simplicity.

Seen Better Days

The SBD ranges in age from fifty to sixty-five, themselves falling into two subcategories: "Mr. Big Time" and the "Angry Lifer." Both groups have been TMs for at least twenty years, but Mr. Big Time has ascended at some point to manage an act playing arenas and stadiums.

Following the rule of thumb "what goes up must come down," like Mr. Big Time himself, this band's glory days have passed, leaving them to play out the clock while getting older and less relevant. As the years go by, they start to play smaller venues. Unfortunately, like the star high school quarterback stuck in time decades ago, Mr. Big Time has yet to move on.

"When we played the Forum, our dressing room was five times this size," he remarks coldly while being politely shown around backstage.

"When we headlined with the Doobie Brothers at the Spectrum, we never had to ask for extra champagne—it was just given to us," he snarls at a show runner, ignoring the rider.

"We would have walked off the stage at Yankee Stadium if your shitty, so-called sound man had been doing the mic checks," he yells to anyone in earshot.

When it comes time to settle up the band's payment at the end of the night, there is *always* a problem. "You were given twenty people on the guest list and I was told twenty-two came in," he bitches to the advance manager, who has now been at the venue for seventeen hours and just wants to go home. "That's taking money out of the fuckin' band's pocket. You owe us the price of two extra tickets. And it says in the contract you were to have twelve loaders . . . I only counted ten. That expense was taken out of the gross (sales), so you need to reimburse us."[8]

This could go on for as long as two hours, with Mr. Big Time and the advance manager hashing it out until they come up with a number Big is inevitably pissed about. His parting words: "I'm sick of this shit, so I'll agree to it, but the band is going to be pissed. This kind of shit never happened at the Rosemont. I can't believe I have to put up with this fucking unprofessionalism."

---

8 Almost all national touring bands are paid on total door sales minus pre-agreed expenses, which include line items such as the cost of the venue loaders, venue marketing, and any additional necessary rented equipment for the night.

In contrast, the Angry Lifer has one major issue: he has just been doing the same job, with grueling hours, for far too long. Making matters worse, you could bet he was once an aspiring musician himself, getting into tour managing because he needed the cash. He tells his friends, "I'm just doing this one tour," but that was forty tours ago. After too many years and too many drunken nights to count, he finds himself waking up one day realizing he should have started a 401(k) years ago. Mad at the world, he rains down irrelevant commands on the staff, accompanied by insults, that go ignored.

"Can someone please move this merch setup so people can actually see what we are selling?" he pontificates as if facing a life-or-death situation, while pointing two feet to his right. "Is everyone here a fucking idiot?" His heartfelt parting words as the act departs: "We need someone to direct us out of the parking lot . . . if the imbeciles here can manage that." To which the fed-up venue manager replies, "Just leave the same goddamn way you came in."

King For a Day

In every respect, this category of TM becomes annoying as hell within hours (sometimes minutes) of arriving on site. First, he makes it clear that he is the person in complete charge. This almost always involves an immediate sidebar with the advance manager. "I need to have everyone report to me," is his mantra. This involves having the venue production manager give him status updates for no other reason than making him feel he is ruling his subjects.

The KFAD is notorious for inserting himself into situations where he doesn't belong. "I just saw one of the loaders take off into the back for about twenty minutes," he'll tell the production manager. "Just thought I'd let you know, since I'm paying for the guy."

"Yeah, he had to take a shit. Do you want me to find out how it came out?"

Acting like a would-be king, the KFAD demands to be treated as one.

"Can someone get me some water," he yells out to no one in particular, leaning on the bar as the staff around him works to get the venue open. "Is there a menu I can order dinner from? Are there any good sushi places nearby that serve vegan whole wheat tempura?" *I don't think so, buddy.*

Let's Get It Done

This version of the TM is usually on the younger side (twenty-five to thirty-five) and is the type an advance manager hopes for. Though focused on his task at hand, he's already mastered the art of catching more flies with honey. Usually, he has been with the band from the beginning, and sees a bright future for himself if he can pull off the current tour without a major hitch, impressing the higher ups at the act's record label and their agent. Unlike both types of SBD, he is quick to throw out compliments.

"This is the best venue we've played this whole tour, and your staff is just great," he'll say, looking around in awe at his surroundings (never mind that he's been there all of thirty minutes and this is only their second show).

While the staff of bartenders, loaders, box office personnel, and managers scurry around, he's quick to jump in and help in any way he can.

"Let me help you with that," he tells a barback struggling to carry a case of vodka. "Can I lend a hand?" he asks two security guards, stepping in to help them move furniture.

This, in turn, leads the staff to bend over backwards to help him, without him even asking. "Do you like vegan whole wheat tempura?" asks an admiring bartender. "There's a great place right around the corner. I can order it for you."

It's amazing what a few well-placed compliments can buy you.

Absentee

My favorite TM by far. He realizes exactly what is actually needed of him before the show, which, if the venue has a good production manager and staff, is often very little. Upon his arrival, he introduces himself to the venue staff, giving out his number if they need to reach him, and then takes off for his pre-planned tour of the city or to catch up with friends. He returns before sound check with tales of his adventure.

"I stopped by the Berklee College of Music," he tells the sound engineer, who by chance had gone to school there. "Cool place . . . always wanted to check it out." A conversation ensues expounding philosophies on the best way to achieve primo concert sound.

The Absentee then makes his way around the venue, sharing stories about his exciting life on the road with an enthralled staff, who are happy to make time to listen. When it comes time to pay the band, he takes a quick look at the settlement sheet and declares, "Looks good to me" while on the phone laying out his excursion plans for the next stop on the tour.

One year later, when the band's tour again brings them to town, this time to play a larger venue, he will show up to see his old friends receiving a hero's welcome while surrounded by his admirers—a Michael Jordan appearing unannounced at his old high school just before tip-off.

"We're doing two nights across town," he tells his fan club, "so if anyone is free tomorrow night, I can get them tickets."

Todd assured the now irate SBD Ian that everything currently occupying the space other than furniture—including five barrels of sand we were using for a faux beach, six five-by-five foam core "sun" cut-outs, and a one-dimensional, false-front hot dog truck—would be removed by the Avalon Avengers long before Iggy took the stage.

This was indeed true . . . well, true-*ish*. Once constructed, the eight-foot-high lifeguard chairs were simply too large to move out of the building, the sand barrels too heavy, and the false-front hot dog truck too delicate. Instead of moving these props, they would have to be disguised or hidden—a fact that I had disguised and hidden from Todd.

As Iggy fans began to roll in, it appeared once again that the Avengers had completed their challenge, leaving no trace of what minutes earlier had been the site of a nightlife workshop. A closer look would have revealed the sun cut-outs hidden in the lighting trusses where they could drop down at a moment's notice, the lifeguard chairs on dollies hidden under a black tarp against a far wall, and the sand barrels, stage right, hidden by another tarp.

As Iggy took the stage to booming applause, the newly lubricated old-school rocker audience (with many of the men looking like a version of Iggy himself) pushed forward toward the stage to get a closer look at their hero. At the same time, some Pop-ites had discovered the concealed lifeguard chairs far across the room from the stage and climbed up on the them, three at a time, to improve their view. Sound reverberation jarred the foam core suns loose from their hiding place in the rafters. They dropped down and hung by their support wires, leaving the crowd below looking surprised and awed.

With now over twenty climbing enthusiasts draped over the elevated lifeguard chairs, the wheeled platforms supporting them began to slowly surge forward in unison, forcing those in its path into a wave of movement to avoid the encroaching barges. Security rushed to contain the rolling hazards. They elicited the help of four friends-of-Avalon police officers, who had stopped in to enjoy the show but were mistakenly interpreted as an ominous presence, heightening the crowd's trepidations.[9] At the same time, the sand barrels had been unearthed by some blitzed fan-atics who dumped them, turned them over, and sat on them, using the containers as viewing platforms.

Iggy played on—either impervious to what was transpiring or just not giving a bloody fucking hell—but his tour manager was beyond livid. Doing his best Ian Faith imitation in a scene right out of *Spinal*

---

9 At times, just off-duty police officers (whom the managers were friendly with) stopped into Avalon. On many of these occasions they were seen dancing, surrounded by young ladies with their hats on (the ladies wearing the police hats, that is). Everyone loves a man in a uniform.

Tap, with an *actual* cricket bat in hand (or what was deemed as one), he stormed Todd's office and threatened to pull Mr. Pop-star off-stage. Todd informed Real Ian that he'd been told all of the props would be moved.

By whom?

By *me* (which was true).

Enraged, Real Ian hunted me down. I was standing alone, watching security doorstop the rolling platforms with wedges crafted out of plastic serving cups and stacks of cocktail napkins. As Real Ian charged at me like a bat out of hell, I didn't know whether to run for cover or reach out for the police protection standing a few feet away.

With Iggy still going at it full volume, Real Ian's tirade could only be interpreted from the sweat now coming out of his beet-red eyeballs and exaggerated hand gestures. The rest was up to me to lip-read, and although it was difficult to catch any word other than "fucking," I quickly got the gist.

Real Ian was right—he had been screwed over, and if Iggy was pissed, as his TM it could mean his job. There was nothing I could do except perhaps make it up to him. Asking him to step outside, I had an idea.

LAXIOM #8
The law of always.
There is always a solution, and it's always easier than you think. When starting with this premise, you'll be surprised how fast ideas will come to you.

At the end of an Iggy Pop show, it was traditional for him to invite women from the audience onstage during his encore, until the band itself, the reunited Stooges, were almost squeezed out of the picture. In this case, the path for the ladies rushing to get onstage snaked through mounds of sand. Like a walk on the beach, they saw this as a sign to remove their shoes. Taking the beach theme one step further, with inspiration from the now hanging suns, they began to strip down to their underwear. The Stooges had no way of knowing what was happening and simply embraced the situation with smiles as wide as Cheshire cats.

This went on for thirty minutes longer than planned as Iggy, in an impromptu move no doubt motivated by the unexpected panty parade, added two songs to his set. This was a problem, however. It was 9:52 PM, which gave the Avengers and Irritables less than forty minutes to clear and clean the room in time for the 10:30 opening of Avaland. In all his years as a manager and club owner, Mr. Turnover had yet to be late for doors—a streak now seriously in jeopardy.

When the house lights finally came up to signify the end of the show, the result of the chaos and hours of heavy drinking left Avalon looking like a nightlife reenactment of London during The Blitz. Thousands of cups littered the ground, surrounded by a dozen large, overflowing garbage cans. Objects left behind included purses, shoes, underwear, glasses, bags of pot, driver's licenses, deodorant, greeting cards, Twinkies, credit cards, and family photos, all destined for the lost and found.

As security pleaded with fans to move toward the exits, many stopped to grab a Jack and Coke (or three) for the road. It was an odd spectacle, a drunken audience of spectators stumbling and drinking as the tribes began darting around.

Mr. Turnover had pre-assigned a single challenge to each of the thirty Avenger tribe members, laying down the gauntlet to best their time. The new goal was thirty-eight minutes. The beauty of his battle instructions was that only *he* had an understanding of the overall plan, leaving each tribe member free to carry out their specific assignment. Three busboys were tasked with cleaning the bathrooms, two others with rounding up all lost items. Designated security guards formed an orderly line of large brooms, walking in brotherly unison across the dance floor area, while another group ushered the concert crowd out of the building and onto Lansdowne Street.

At the same time, Dellarocco's group moved the lifeguard chairs into their final positions and laid painter tarps over the stage. Once in place, the sand (which had been frantically swept up) would be spread over them. Then we'd add some plastic crabs, lobsters, umbrellas, and coolers (the drink special for the night being a hand cooler of beer for $25, which include the cooler itself).

"Twenty-three minutes," John announced from the center of the room.

Outside, two thousand concert-goers milled around, some still in only their underwear, while one thousand club-goers anxiously waited for the doors to reopen for part two of the night. Both groups stared each other down in confusion.

"Eighteen minutes."

Ten bartenders were almost finished cleaning and reorganizing their bar stations. Nearly out of alcohol, appointed barbacks had begun frantically restocking the shelves. Props had been restored to their positions and the hot dog truck in the corner was functional, ready to serve Boston's beloved Fenway Franks to anyone willing to shell out $5.

"Ten minutes."

With the deadline at hand, loud voices erupted from the back door, where Iggy's packed-up equipment was being loaded out. After a standard show, the Irritables would have had two hours to pack up, load their trucks, and be off to the next tour stop. Tonight, the challenge needed to be completed in just over a quarter of that time, and the Irritables were in no mood to be rushed out the door.

As a clash of tribes ensued, and I had no choice but go to Real Ian for an improvised council meeting. After a short discussion, the Irritables emerged, pushing their cases into the street in a stunning show of cooperation.

"One minute," John announced.

The slightest aroma of Fenway Franks was intoxicating to the now hundred or so leftover concert stragglers, who had already begun forming a line to be served.

"They can stay," bellowed John, who was not going to let anything, or anyone impede his quest for the record.[10] "Time!" he called out.

In one fell swoop, the house lights went off, the truss lighting powered up, and artificial fog was pumped into the room. The staff took their positions. Living up to its billing as a "World at Night," Avaland now looked like anything but a place where a concert had taken place thirty-eight minutes earlier.

As the Avaland club crowd began to file in, a dinner was already underway at Sonsie as a "Welcome to Boston" party for Jenna, with her planned arrival at Avalon set for midnight. After some heavy lobbying, John, a big fan of her work, had been officially recognized as the ceremonial host.

The proclaimed Queen of Porn's late-night appearance had drawn more anticipation than any event I had yet seen, with dozens of calls coming into the office daily. *Is she signing autographs? Will she pose for pictures? Can I give her a gift I made?* Surprisingly enough, the majority of these calls were from women.

With the same detailed precision that had set a turnover record earlier that night, a plan was set for Jenna's grand entrance at Avalon. John would personally escort her in, surrounded by security, and up to a private booth he had arranged for her and some of his closest friends who had flown in from around the country for the occasion. As the custom Bentley (which John had borrowed for the evening) pulled up, groupies awaiting Jenna's entrance formed two lines behind the velvet ropes.

Giving the impression of a modern-day Marilyn Monroe, Jenna stepped out of the Bentley wearing a clinging white dress and heels. Flash bulbs went off, creating the effect of a 1950s Hollywood red carpet premiere. She stopped to quickly wave at the fans, as outstretched arms tried handing her everything from DVDs to dildos for her to sign.

Seconds later a man emerged from the car in what appeared to be a loose interpretation of a tuxedo, quickly putting his arm around Jenna's

---

10 The record would have an asterisk behind it, given that not all concert-goers had left. Given the profit made on hot dogs within fifteen minutes of Avaland opening, it was well worth it.

waist and escorting her in. Shortly after, John stepped out of the car. Trailing five paces behind, he needed to fight his way to the front door as the throng crowded behind the guest of honor.

After she thanked John for his hospitality, Jenna was directed by security to the reserved VIP booth, where the waiting group was surprised by her uninvited, tuxedoed plus-one. Before Jenna could sit down, a large group of fans surrounded her requesting pictures, and her husband graciously stepped to the side. Real Ian, the Stooges, and the Irritables posed for photos, and the earlier issues of the day were instantly forgotten, replaced by a night that many would remember for some time.

"Best fuckin' show we've ever played," said Real Ian (who's actual name was Richie). He put his arm around me. "Can't wait to come back, matey."

"Richie, you're a fucking genius," said Iggy's lead guitarist. "Those fucking sun-looking things . . . and the sand . . . bloody hell, mate. How in fuck's sake did you come up with that?"

Looking over at Richie, I couldn't help but think that, in the most improbable of outcomes, he had earned the title of "nightlife Boston Rob."

CHAPTER 9

SHOW-STOPPER

"When I was a little boy I told my dad,
'When I grow up, I want to be a musician.'
My dad said, 'You can't do both, son.'"
—CHET ATKINS

I n Boston, for the first time I was directly exposed to the concert promotion business. Booking occasional smaller live acts at Limelight or
Tunnel had provided me with a glimpse into dealing with performers
and agents. But with major concerts now being booked by Don Law and
integrated into the weekly Avalon schedule, live music played an important role in the overall success of the business.

I've always had a love for music. I can remember, at five years old,
spending countless hours alone in my room listening to albums on a Ze-
nith Victrola, memorizing the words. Even early on I had eclectic taste,
soaking up everything from *The Age of Aquarius* by the Fifth Dimension
to the entire Broadway soundtrack of *Fiddler on the Roof.*

It's amazing what sticks with you musically, as I demonstrated fifty
years later when reciting every line of the musical *1776* while attending
a local theater production. My wife watched in both horror and disbelief
as I sang the catchy number "Sit Down, John." Hell, I knew those songs
even better than the cast.

My favorite song by far as a child was the classic "Puff the Magic Dragon" by Peter, Paul and Mary. What I didn't realize, of course, was that the entire song was one big metaphor for smoking pot, with "dragon" being a variation of "dragin'," "land of autumn mist" being pot smoke, and "land of Honah Lee" being the Hawaiian town of Hanalei, famous for its pot farms. One of the song's writers, Peter Yarrow, actually denied these references, saying the song was about the loss of childhood innocence. I guess that could be true . . . if that child was Keith Richards.

The song would later make a splashy return to pop culture, inspiring Elon Musk's "Dragon" SpaceX astronaut capsule atop the Falcon 9 rocket, in the historic joint mission with NASA to the International Space Station on September 3, 2020. There was no skirting the reference this time around, as Musk himself became engulfed in the land of autumn mist during an infamous Joe Rogan podcast interview in the fall of 2018.

At age eleven, I began attending concerts with my dad and cousin, the first being KISS at our local community college gym. Mel sat unfazed as always through the entire blast fest, his only comment being, "That was something."

By the time I entered high school, I had discovered two other things that would follow me throughout my life: writing and storytelling. I looked forward to writing reports on classics such as *Beowulf* and *Lord of the Flies*, while little else held my academic interest. As we sat around the lunchroom talking as high schoolers do, I constantly found myself critiquing my fellow classmates' story delivery. *Can you just get to the point? Why didn't you just lead with that? Thaaat's a great detail to leave out . . .*

In college, I got my first real chance for formal storytelling success when I entered a contest for the best year abroad report. Having just come back from Madrid, Spain, I stood in front of an audience of two hundred and delivered my narrative about the Spanish obsession with clean laundry that is hung out to dry in a city of clotheslines. The punch line of the story was the sight of a semi-deflated blow-up doll hung from a clothesline and blowing in the wind. I won first prize and a $50 credit to the bookstore, which I used to buy copies of the *Harvard Lampoon*.

When the first season of HBO's *Curb Your Enthusiasm* aired, virtually everyone I knew had bowed out of watching by episode three. But I thought it was the funniest thing I had ever seen. Let me rephrase—I could *relate* to it more than anything I had seen on TV. I had always seen the inherent humor in everyday situations, and now it was playing out in front me on a TV show. It was the same premise as *Seinfeld*, only set in Los Angeles with creator Larry David cast as a fish out of water from NYC.

I viewed the show as something of a doppelganger for my life and began carrying a small recorder with me, documenting all that I saw and experienced. I'd then use these notes to craft specific episodes that I thought would be good for the show. I had no real plan to do anything with them, and treated them like the byproduct of an unusual hobby.

While playing golf on vacation in Martha's Vineyard with John and Patrick Lyons' other brother, Mike, we started discussing the current season of *Curb*, and I let him in on my closet writing career. As luck would have it, Patrick was good friends with Larry David, and they frequently played golf together. The next day I gave Mike my latest script outline with what I felt was my best stuff, including bits about Larry going to see a high-maintenance Buddhist lama, trying to find a way to attend synagogue during the Jewish holidays, and becoming obsessed with "obvious" signs. ("Fresh Meat" . . . is there another option?) Mike liked my ideas and said he would have it forwarded on to Larry.

A week or so later, I got a call from Larry's office in L.A. saying thank you for the submission, but they couldn't accept it unless it came from an agent. This was done to avoid any legal issues with copyrights and maintain industry protocol, and so it appeared that was that.

I would soon find out it was anything *but* that.

My introduction to the live concert world wasn't without its bumps in the road, resulting in some unexpected lessons learned. One afternoon, as I made my way up the stairs to my office, I was surprised to see none other than Bob Dylan pass by. Under normal circumstances, the dressing room areas were near the back of the Avalon stage, but in Dylan's case, he had demanded that the entire second floor of Axis, the club adjacent to Avalon, be converted into his dressing room. With my office located through a set of second-floor doors off of Axis, the only access available was through a singular staircase.

As I did a double take, Dylan quickly looked over his shoulder and continued on his way. Fifteen minutes later, my trusty assistant—Lauren by birth, "Lorno" by affable nickname—appeared in my office.

"What just happened?" Lorno asked in a panic.

Happened?

"Bob Dylan is refusing to perform. Apparently he had a run-in with someone, who by description appears to be you."

"Run-in? I passed him on the way up here for all of ten seconds."

"It must have been the way you looked at him then."

"That's ridiculous," I said, thinking the matter would pass.

Soon Todd was standing in my office as well. "I don't know what happened between you and Dylan, but he doesn't want to perform. I talked to his tour manager, who was able to convince him to play. But under one condition—that you leave the building."

I remembered a quote I had taken to heart: "Talent is king," spoken by famed MCA Talent honcho Lew Wasserman. I packed up my damaged ego and headed out the door, careful not to intimidate anyone by my mere presence. I tried my hardest to justify the situation with an explanation that I must come off more menacingly than I believed. But I'd never been accused of that before.

Less than a month later, I was surprised to see Alanis Morissette coming down the same flight of steps, having demanded the same overblown dressing room setup as Dylan. In a déjà vu moment as we passed each other, I could only smile and give a slight nod.

Minutes later, Lorno once again delivered a message: "Alanis wants you out of the building," she said with a shrug.

Not even questioning why, I packed up my carrier bag and headed for the door. Evidently, even the slightest unexpected encounter was enough to throw even the most experienced of performers off their game. I could understand if I was a crazed fan who had broken into the building, but in my case, the whole thing smelled of utter ridiculousness.

What I wasn't aware of was that everyone in the building had already been told they weren't allowed to talk to, engage, or even look at either Dylan or Alanis, as part of their rider. As a performer ascended in their success, it became accepted for them to be increasingly difficult. In the case of both Dylan and Alanis, they had reached the peak of Mount Demanding.

Not a fan of the double, which only served to cause him headaches, it most likely was not an error of omission by Todd that I wasn't told about the situation, but a punch in the nuts for causing him constant misery. Months later, karma would make an appearance during the Iggy night.

With a recently added "unannounced" show during the same week as Alanis, I was not about to fall for Todd's passive aggressive tactics. I sent Lorno on a reconnaissance mission to ensure that the coast was clear. When I arrived at the top of the stairs, a dense fog had enveloped the second floor; just a quick inhale was enough to chill out Peter, Paul, Mary, and Elon Musk.

"Yo, my man, what's happening?" I heard a voice ask through the haze. "What are you doing up here?"

Not wanting to be lured into the same trap again, I kept my head down and continued walking.

"Yo," the voice continued, "can you get Todd for us. Need to talk to him . . . like now. Don't act like you can't hear me. Where is Todd, man? What's the dealio, yo?"

I now recognized the voice. I quickly turned and made eye contact to confirm my suspicions while fumbling with my door keys. Once inside my office, I finally gathered myself; despite the aroma seeping through the walls, I was now safe, ready to begin my day on the right foot.

It would be a year before I'd hear that same voice again, and this time around I'd have some explaining to do.

By the end of the year, Electronic Dance Music (EDM) culture had begun to explode in the U.S., taking hold not only in Boston, but in San Francisco, Los Angeles, Denver, Washington DC, and Miami.[11] DJ booths themselves, traditionally hidden in the shadows, had moved to center stage, backed by increasingly sophisticated productions featuring customized videos and lighting. Over the next three years, DJ fees increased over a thousand percent. As one club-goer said to me matter-of-factly while watching Paul Oakenfold at Avalon, "Looks like DJs are becoming the next rock stars." Staring at the lone person onstage, he commented, "Hell . . . *I* can do that."

It was Oakenfold who had led this phenomenon and solved its biggest challenge: as a DJ, how do you actually *perform* when you are just playing pre-recorded songs? No live instruments, no live vocals?

Oakenfold's live performance now consisted of various choreographed movements, the most effective being "the Messiah." One aspect of EDM was that its tracks incorporated "drops," slow melodic buildups within the song culminating in a bass drop for dramatic affect.[12] As the music slowly built up, Oakenfold commenced to slowly raise his arms in unison, as if expecting to part the Red Sea. When the song peaked, he

---

11 With all the varying styles of dance music at the time, the term EDM was coined as an umbrella for the genre. By 2010, the term had become mainstream, used to describe DJ-produced radio hits for the likes of, Selena Gomez, and Cardi B.

12 This phenomenon was brilliantly parodied on *Saturday Night Live* in 2014 by Andy Samberg and Lil Jon in *When Will the Bass Drop?* Samberg played the fictional DJ Davincii, the name deriving from a cross between the two most celebrated DJs at that time, David Guetta and Avicii.

stood with hands overhead, palms facing him, seeming to proclaim, "Let my people dance." With the turn of a switch, he would then add the bass line and begin jumping up and down to the beat. His disciples ate it up.

Other DJs soon followed suit, customizing their own performances. This included everything from scantily clad performers dancing on either side of the stage, to upgraded designs for the DJ booths themselves.[13] A microphone onstage to announce the bass drop became a must: "Are you readdyyyy . . . here it comes . . . now!"

As Oakenfold looked over the crowd like a giddy authoritarian dictator, his performance truly magical in more way than one, it became evident that not only was EDM's young fan base growing and loyal, it would continue to grow exponentially in the years to come.

The following week, having just returned from the West Coast to visit the now open House of Blues, John Lyons stopped by my office, plopping down in his favorite chair.

"We need to open an Avalon in L.A.," he proclaimed. "There simply isn't anything like it at all there."

By "anything like it," he was referring to the mega-club experience we were coming close to perfecting.

"You need to get to L.A. and check this place out, it's really perfect," John urged. He handed me a business card with a Vine Street address. The idea had been discussed before and reinforced by John's friend and proclaimed Promoter to the Stars Brent Bolthouse. Upon visiting Avalon, he'd begun pushing the notion even harder.

Any attempt to open an Avalon in L.A. would require starting with a unique location, one that would facilitate an experience for club-goers that couldn't be replicated by any competition. Having worked in a one-time church, converted railcar tunnel, and adapted horse stable, I'd

13 DJ booth design would continue to progress and take on importance, culminating in the 2010 debut of The Cube by Deadmau5 at the Coachella Music Festival, where the DJ booth *itself* became the co-headliner. Deadmau5, aka DJ Joel Zimmerman, had one-upped Oakenfold years earlier, donning an oversized Mickey Mouse-inspired glowing head while performing.

seen first-hand how important this was to sustain nightlife success. It was a factor often overlooked, which helped account for the industry's high attrition rate. If our product could easily be imitated, it would inevitably *invite* competitors into the market. But a historic theater in the heart of Hollywood would be almost impossible to contend with if the alternative was fifteen thousand square feet of traditional retail space.

"With Brent already out there, we have the best promoter in town on our team," John continued. "We just need a manager we can count on . . . and I have just the guy. He'll be here this weekend so we can all talk. He's a golfer, so I set a tee time for us."

Barney Holm, the son of legendary British actor Sir Ian Holm, could best be described as the nightlife version of an English gentleman. Polite and measured in his words, he made me feel like I had known him for years.

As we sat in our golf cart, I checked my watch and looked around; there was no sign of John amongst the carts lining up behind us. Noon approached and still no John. We had no choice but to tee off, or else lose our coveted place in line.

At 12:14, the sound of a revved-up cart engine could be heard as John flew over the hill, bypassing the now eight-deep cart line. He pulled up next to us, balancing a Big Gulp-sized Dunkin' Donuts iced coffee and wearing an oversized Hawaiian-inspired shirt and his signature dark sunglasses. He could have easily been mistaken for the third Blues Brother on his way to a luau.

Parking directly *on* the first tee, John quickly pulled out one of the five clubs in his double king-size Budweiser golf bag.[14] Without any warm-up whatsoever, he stepped up with his 5-iron, placed his *Flintstones*-sized iced latte next to him, and took a mighty swing, drubbing the

---

14 It is not uncommon to see nightclub owners enjoying all sorts of perks, usually gifted to them from liquor distributers as a thank-you or incentive. This could include anything from Jack Daniels visors and Smirnoff scarves to Las Vegas trips, compliments of Heineken. Almost any merchandise I received would be regifted to others, as walking around with the likes of a Captain Morgan logo emblazoned on my shirt always seemed a bit . . . much.

ball a hundred and twenty-five yards and fifteen feet into the surrounding woods, to the collective groan of all waiting their turn.

Somehow the ball had miraculously bounced back onto the edge of the fairway, leaving John a clear shot to the green. Five shots later, all three of us were now standing on the green, and John finally acknowledged Barney: "I need to warm up a little," he said, "but I'm always on my putting. Watch this."

He proceeded to eye his twenty-five-foot putt carefully, stepping away twice to get a better look as the group of four behind us glared. Now poised over what looked like a toothpick in his hands, John took final aim and nailed the putt dead-center, finishing the hole in what John marked as a four.

On the second hole, a short par 3, John delivered a straight-as-an-arrow tee shot—fifty yards past the highly elevated green. With his phone to his ear, he drove beyond the green and down the back of the hill, looking back only to give a quick wave while shouting, "Gotta go."

And with that, Barney Holm became the future general manager of Avalon Hollywood.

Swingers at Roxy. (Photo: Tina Paul)

RuPaul strikes a pose at Roxy. (Photo: Alexis DiBiasio)

Scavullo, Liza, and Issac hold court at Roxy. (Photo: Tina Paul)

Greek Night at Roxy. (Photo: Alexis DiBiasio)

Dance floor chic at Roxy. (Photo: Tina Paul)

With Grandma Mary at Tribeca Grill.

Mickey Rourke and friend at Limelight. (Photo: Tina Paul)

Flava gives a shoutout at Limelight. (Photo: Tina Paul)

Collect all 50 Club Kid trading cards. (Design: Gregory Homs)

Michael Alig and Kids at Limelight. (Photo: Tina Paul)

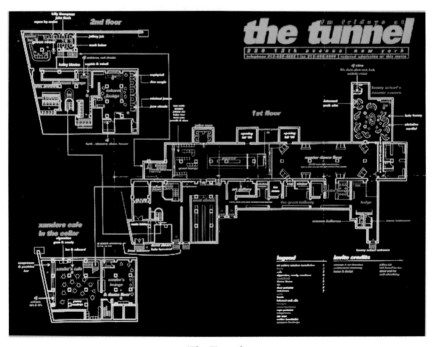

The Tunnel.

Dance floor at Avaland.

Boy George smokin' on the turntables
at Avaland.

Perry Farrell Wow-Lapaloozas
the crowd at Avaland.

Avaland: A World at Night. (Art: Dolphina Jones)

Skrillex waves the white towel at Avalon Hollywood. (Photo: Drew Ressler/rukes.com)

Zedd and Porter Robinson "100% in" at Avalon Hollywood.
(Photo: Drew Ressler/rukes.com)

Moby at Avalon Hollywood. (Photo: Drew Ressler/rukes.com)

Christina leaves her birthday bash at Spider Club.

Black Eyed Peas perform to save the rainforest at Avalon Hollywood.

New Year's Eve at Avalon Hollywood. (Photo: Drew Ressler/rukes.com)

The Godfather of Soul steps it up at Avalon Hollywood.

R.E.M. helps open Avalon Hollywood.

Justin celebrates Grammy Week at Avalon Hollywood.

Spider Club photo shoot.

Bruce greets arrivals for his 50th at Spider Club.

Spider Club.

CALIF🔵RNIA
FOR OBAMA
INVITES YOU TO JOIN US AS WE
MAKE SUPER TUESDAY SUPER

COME JOIN THE POLLSTERS, POLITICOS, INSIDERS, HACKS, AND ALL **THE VOLUNTEERS** WHO HELPED MAKE HISTORY HAPPEN **TO WATCH THE PRIMARY RESULTS** COME IN!

FEBRUARY 5TH, 2008

★ ★ ★ ★ ★ ★ ★ ★ ★ ★

AVALON
HOLLYWOOD
1735 VINE STREET · HOLLYWOOD 90028

★ ★ ★ ★ ★ ★ ★ ★ ★

DOORS OPEN AT 8:30

WE'RE GONNA PARTY LIKE A DEMOCRATIC PARTY

★ ★ 18 AND OVER ONLY ★ ★

RSVP TO **rsvp@obamaca.com** OR FOR MORE INFO GO TO **CA.BarackObama.com**

🔵 Obama'08
CA.BarackObama.com

CREATED IN HOUSE BY VOLUNTEER LABOR

The start of an era.

Dancers at Avalon Hollywood.

Britney takes the stage at Avalon NYC.

The Bush sisters arrive for a girl's night out at Avalon NYC.

Crowds outside Avalon NYC stop traffic on Sixth Avenue.

Avalon NYC entrance.

Awaiting entrance to Avalon Singapore.

Marina Bay Sands opening press conference with Sheldon Adelson and Daniel Boulud.

Avalon Singapore.

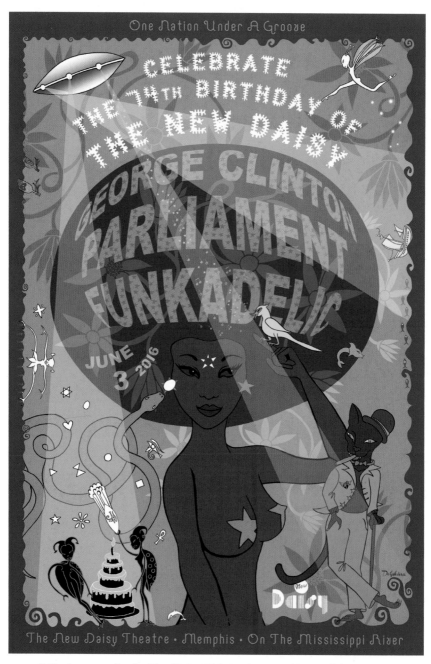

P-Funk returns for the New Daisy 75th Anniversary. (Art: Dolphina Jones)

Mayor Strickland declares May 23 "New Daisy" day in Memphis
with the Stone Temple Pilots.

The New Daisy launches Foo Fighters.

Ben Rector performs opening night at the "new" New Daisy.

CHAPTER 10

LET'S MAKE A DEAL

"The way I see it,
if you want the rainbow,
you gotta put up with the rain."
—Dolly Parton

Leaning anxiously against the window overlooking Beverly Hills, I needed a break from looking at the four sets of documents in front of me, all marked with an overabundance of "Sign Here" stickies. I excused myself to go to the bathroom and, after taking a much-needed sip from the hall water fountain, quickly stepped inside and began dialing.

"Have you sent the money?" I asked one of our investor's assistants, Jean. "I don't see it in the account." She had promised she would check its status and get right back to me. "I'm here at the closing . . . *right now*," I reiterated, trying to maintain some level of cool.

Even if Jean had sent the $300,000, I was going to be $250,000 short. I hadn't heard from my partner, Bruce, in the past six weeks and had found out a few minutes earlier that my other partner, John, wasn't going to be able to come up with his entire share on time to purchase the venue. I was seemingly screwed and needed to rethink matters—*quickly*.

"Money's being wired now," Jean confirmed two minutes later.

"Okay, thanks. I'm going to call you right back with a different account number for where it should be sent. It needs to go directly to the seller and not to me, at this point."

Returning to the conference room, I grabbed one of the documents and again excused myself, with all eyes in the room on me.

"Is there a problem?" asked the venue's current owner, Kay. She might as well have just blurted out, "I knew it," confirming her own worst instincts about the deal.

"Nope, all good. Just had a quick question for Paul. Be back in a moment."

"A little late to be talking to your attorney," Kay said sarcastically.

Back in the hallway, I frantically searched the document for the account information I needed to relay to Jean. "Please email me the wire receipt as soon as the transfer is done," I told her.

Still $250,000 short, I called Bruce's accountant, who, up to that point, had been very difficult to reach. "Hi Fred, this is Steve Adelman from Avalon. I know we said if Bruce sent money next week it would be fine, but I was wondering if he could send it today, as soon as possible."

"What money?" Fred shot back, apparently annoyed by the request.

"His investment money . . . for the club."

"*More* money?" asked Fred, raising the volume of his voice.

"More money? Not sure what you mean by that."

"Are you now asking Mr. Willis for *more* money?"

"No, just the amount we agreed upon."

"I've got to take this call, I will call you back in a minute," said Fred. With that, he hung up.

Leaning anxiously against the window overlooking Beverly Hills, I saw Kay's brother, Bill, heading my way from the meeting room, looking like a thrift-store Marlboro man. He certainly did stick out in a room dominated by corporate suits, if that was his intent.

"We need ya back inside," he said, passing me on his way to the bathroom.

My phone rang. It was Fred calling. "We sent you your money two months ago," he said.

"Two months ago . . . to what account?"

"The one we had on file."

"Please email me that account number as soon as possible. Thanks, Fred." *Two months ago? We hadn't even been able to reach Fred to send any paperwork yet, let alone account information.*

Bill was back, holding his can of Diet Coke. "We need to get this over with now. Kay and I need to go to another meeting at noon."

At that point, I'd had just about enough of "Brother Bill," and my first instinct was to tell him to go fuck himself. This came out as, "Go f—inish your Diet Coke, I'll be there in just a second." *Restrain yourself. Almost to the finish line.*

I had met Bill six months earlier when I'd arrived at Hollywood Boulevard and Vine Street for the first time—a head-to-toe, bright-blue theater directly across from the iconic Capital Records building. It was a stunningly bad choice of not only paint color, but application. Built in 1927, the Spanish Baroque-style building was originally dubbed the Hollywood Playhouse. During the Great Depression it housed government-sponsored theatrical events until the 1940s, when it was renamed the El Capitan Theatre.

Used primarily to host the CBS Radio network, it was the backdrop for Lucille Ball's *My Favorite Husband,* the title of which was not a reference to Lucy's secret double life. She played Liz, a middle-class, happily married, somewhat zany housewife, with Richard Denning playing her husband, George. Each episode would involve a minor crisis caused by one of Liz's off-center ideas, which would end up being solved in the end with Liz saying, "Thanks, George, you're my favorite husband . . . let's have some Jell-O, J-E-L-L-O, the big red letters stand for the Jell-O family." Sound familiar, minus the sponsor plug? After one hundred and twenty-four gelatin-laden episodes, *My Favorite Husband* would, ironically, form the basis for the iconic *I Love Lucy Show,* with Desi Arnaz replacing Richard Denning and birthing the character of *Ricky Ricardo!*

In the 1950s, the El Capitan became a television studio, and the site of Richard Nixon's famous "Checkers" speech. His emotional plea to the country took place on what would later become the Avalon stage. As an homage to this, if someone was heading my way unexpectedly, the code word "checkers" was used by my assistant as a warning. This caused puzzled looks and confusion for the would-be intruder, as she usually resorted to simply shouting out the secret word as they made their way past, leaving me to explain it away, unconvincingly, as "gameboard Tourette's." Interestingly enough, no one ever asked me about the photo of Tricky Dick I had hanging on the wall.

The 1960s brought about a new era for 1735 Vine Street, spurred on by a $400,000 investment by ABC to renovate it into studios for the *Jerry Lewis Show*, aptly renaming it the Jerry Lewis Theatre. Lewis had hosted *The Tonight Show* for two weeks after Jack Paar quit and before Johnny Carson took over, garnishing huge ratings and setting off a bidding war for the talk show host's services. In addition, ABC ponied up an additional $4.5 million just to renovate the stage area to get Lewis to commit to forty shows, making him the highest paid actor at that time to the tune of $8 million. This included what Lewis's demands for a two-story star dressing room, the ground floor of which included a mirrored bar, piano, and plush lounge area. The grand toilet had a wall-mounted phone for him to conduct business while conducting his business.

The second floor was accessed by a spiral staircase, which led to the star's makeup area and a private bedroom with the best Hollywood casting couch money could buy. A new orchestra pit was built, and concrete platforms were poured to support cranes needed for filming. And in what can only be described as an egotistical power move—or a page out of the KISS concert I had seen as a kid—a hydraulic lift was installed for the host's platform, allowing his desk to be raised eight feet above the stage.

The first episode of *The Jerry Lewis Show*, broadcast live on September 21, 1963, was by all accounts a disaster. This was mainly due to the fly system, newly installed for easy set changes, malfunctioning constantly, leaving the proceedings in shambles. Two months later, President Kennedy was assassinated in Dallas, and all television programming was put on delay, preempted by news coverage of the events that followed. Jerry returned in December, but was then canceled thirteen shows into the promised forty. The Alexander the Great desk? It was never used as planned. Whether this was a rethinking of the optics associated with hovering eight feet over an interview subject, or another in a long line of mechanical failures, is hard to say.

In the mid-'60s, the location was renamed the Hollywood Palace and hosted a television variety show of the same name, with the likes of Liberace, Joan Crawford, Bette Davis, Judy Garland, and Diana Ross serving as guest hosts. In the late '70s, the theater was sold and converted into a concert venue, with the name shortened to the Palace. By the early 2000s, it was playing host to mainly punk and heavy metal shows promoted by Paul Tollett, who would later go on to found Coachella.

Now, as I walked to the front of the building, I could make out the architectural details, which by now had been covered by years of reapplied paint. I felt a tap on my shoulder.

"Hey man, do you own this place now?"

Turning around, I came face to face with a man who appeared to be his fifties, although it was difficult to be sure given his long, unwashed beard and makeshift outfit, highlighted by a soiled Beatles t-shirt.

"I do not," I replied, now catching a whiff of his stale odor.

"I've been trying to get the money the owner owes me for twenty years . . . four hundred dollars. Can you help me out, friend?"

Not knowing what to make of my new, down-on-his-luck acquaintance, I offered him $10 and the promise that I would ask the owner about his debt.

Inside, under close inspection, the same original design details I had witnessed outside were everywhere, masked by years of faux construction, renovation, and neglect. Kay had inherited the venue in her divorce, and it was clear that historic preservation was not her top priority. She had recently taken up with a new boyfriend, a bit of a French gigolo right out of central casting for *Dirty Rotten Scoundrels*. The love birds were planning to possibly live on the French Riviera, so she might be open to selling the business—or at least that was the briefing I'd received from John. After exchanging pleasantries, the conversation moved to Kay's future plans, and it became clear that the sale of the business would be funding her new life.

"By the way, as I came in a guy stopped me and said the owner owed him four hundred dollars," I mentioned casually. "Not sure if he's doing that to everyone, so just an FYI."

"Oh, that's just Jesse Lot," smiled Kay. "I pay him seventy-five dollars a week to watch the parking lot and make sure there are no break-ins. The Palace was used for the shooting of *Against All Odds* back in the '80s, and from what I can gather, Jesse worked on set. He supposedly lent James Woods, who was the club owner in the movie, money that he never got paid back. I've told him dozens of time that I'm the owner, not James Woods, but it just doesn't sink in. Poor Jesse . . . too many drugs."

As we discussed a possible deal over lunch at Denny's with Kay's visiting brother, Bill from Montana (who continuously ordered a steady stream of Diet Coke), in tow, we were far from settling on even a range for the selling price. The Palace was doing great, according to Kay, making money hand over fist.

"Bill sure does love his Diet Coke," Kay commented, as I took note of Bill's fifth drink of choice to arrive.

"How much of that stuff can you drink?" I asked.

"I lose count at a six-pack a day," he mumbled through a full mouth of tuna melt. "Better than smoking a pack a day."

I couldn't argue with that, as he ordered one more.

I spent another week in L.A., putting together a list of items needed to determine a price for the business under Brother Bill's not-so-watchful eye. Soon after, we put in an offer that turned into a back-and-forth for over three months. Our plan then became getting Kay to Boston, on our turf, where we would be able to close the deal. When we proposed the trip, Kay indicated that she would be in France for a month, but Brother Bill could come.

Brother Bill's arrival in Boston was marked by below-zero temperatures. As a Montanan, he was quick to point out that this made him feel right at home, having only spent the last two months in L.A. Three cases of Diet Coke waited for him in his room.

"Steve, this is one of the nicest things anyone has ever done for me," he said, awkwardly shaking my hand as we met in the hotel lobby, his voice cracking as he held back tears. "Let's talk some business."

I had come to like Bill by this time, and admired his trait of being a good listener, never interrupting and only speaking cautiously, if at all. I presented our latest proposal, which Bill was very agreeable toward, asking only a few questions regarding timing, and if we actually had the money.

"Bill, I can assure you that we wouldn't be going through all this if we weren't legitimate," I explained for the third time.

"Good, because if we do this, I know Kay plans to move to France, and will need the money," Bill added, also for a third time.

Two weeks later, our attorney completed the papers necessary to close the purchase, sending out a final draft to Kay. One week later I received a call.

"What is this purchase agreement I received?" asked Kay incredulously.

"It's what we negotiated and agreed on with Bill while he was here," I replied, thinking Bill might not have communicated this to her yet. Kay had just returned.

"Bill has no authority to negotiate anything," she shot back.

"No authority? Then what was he doing here?"

"You said it would be a good idea for me to see your clubs in Boston, so Bill went for me. He says thanks again for the Diet Coke."

"Glad he liked it," I replied, gritting my teeth as I held the phone away from my ear, staring at it with a disgusted look. "And what do *you* think of what Bill negotiated and, I may point out again, agreed to?"

"Not nearly enough money," she replied.

I had fallen for one of the oldest of all negotiating ploys, the bait-and-switch:

1. Send Bill and get him to agree on something.
2. Get an attorney to spend time finalizing the deal, pulling us deeper into the negotiation.
3. Find a reason to up the dollar amount last minute.

Classic. At this point, it didn't matter whether this was a pre-conceived plan by Kay, or simply a result of Brother Bill gone rogue; the result was the same.

The deal we had agreed upon with Bill involved paying $1 million up-front, with another $700,000 over the next three years. When hit with a bait-and-switch, one always has to be ready to counter with a cash-is-king offer. In this case, we would offer $1.4 million upfront, period.

If Kay didn't accept within a week and continued to stress a higher price, our final counterproposal would be a short one: best of luck to you. One week later she called back, taking the final offer.

Before going back into the room, I put in a wire transfer to send Bruce's money directly to Kay, which constituted the final funds needed. Once back inside, I was accosted by Kay.

"There is no money in my account."

"It's on its way," I assured. "I know you and Bill need to get to another meeting, so it's best if we sign everything now."

"*Not* until the money arrives," she ordered.

The group sat in silence while Kay checked her account every twenty minutes and I forwarded her wire transfer receipts confirming the money that was on the way. Ninety minutes later she was convinced she had her money, and we proceeded. Kay had her new lease on life in France, and I had my new lease on what would soon be Avalon Hollywood.

Driving back to the Chateau Marmont hotel where I was staying, I passed by the UCLA campus. The pure beauty of the landscaping and pristine buildings combined with another cloudless, seventy-two-degree day had me contemplating: *Why would anyone want to live anywhere else?* Now this paradise was partially mine.

It had been twelve years since I'd arrived in NYC with fifty dollars in my pocket and the promise of a job. Seven years after that, I had worked my way up to becoming a director for four of the city's largest nightclubs during a landmark period in nightlife. Sleeping on couches, borrowing money to get through the week, and late nights at cheap diners on Tenth Avenue were all part of my life for the first few years.

I remember, back then, arriving at Bobby Flay's Mesa Grill on lower Fifth Avenue for one of my first NYC formal dining experiences, having scrounged up what I hoped was enough money. I was met by an overly friendly maître d' who whisked myself and my three friends away to be seated, bypassing the other waiting diners as they looked on.

"My name is Carl," he said, shaking my hand vigorously. "I'm so glad you have decided to dine with us this evening. Only the best table for you and your friends . . . Mr. Adelman." He winked as he pulled out my chair.

I found his behavior odd, but I didn't think much of it for long, overcome by my own ego: *I've made it. This is the kind of treatment a club mogul like myself could get used to.*

After we were fawned over by double the waitstaff that seemed necessary, Carl returned.

"I'm sorry, but Mr. Flay is not here tonight, as I'm sure he would have liked to come out and greet you. He has sent out desserts for everyone, along with some of our finest port, our compliments. Enjoy."

It appeared that being in the nightlife business had its perks, and now I certainly had a place to take a date I needed to impress.

Over the next six months, I returned to see a winking Carl four times; once I met Bobby Flay, who was very gracious.

"Carl, if there is anything I can do for you, just let me know," I said, as he retrieved my coat from behind the host stand.

"Just glad you could make it in, but I really must say, I loved you in *Being John Malkovich*. How many people get a movie named after themselves?"

Huh?

Momentarily stunned, my brain began to connect the dots: *Ultra VIP treatment . . . have been told I look like John Malkovich . . . Carl's comments . . . shit.*

"Not many," I replied, as my date gave me an inquisitive look.

"You act?" she asked as we got into the taxi.

"Apparently, I've been playing a part without knowing it," I quickly replied, changing the subject.

Truth be told, I never fessed up to Carl or the Mesa staff, even taking advantage of the situation when Bobby Flay opened a second restaurant. I looked at it this way: how many people actually get to be someone else for a night, let alone being John Malkovich.

After my long but victorious day in L.A. with Kay, I headed to the restaurant just off the Chateau lobby at around 8:00 PM. With the deal now done, I left messages for my partners: Bruce Willis, Dan Aykroyd, and John Lyons. Usually a hotbed of activity, the entire hotel was quiet, this being the week after the Oscars. Looking around, it was just me, a table of eight across the patio, and another table just being seated.

Handing the waiter the menu while I ordered, I could feel a gaze upon me. Sure enough, it was coming from the adjacent table. Trying not to be too conspicuous, I looked over and recognizing that face instantaneously—*Malkovich*. We looked each other up and down, and I was struck by the fact that I just didn't see it. I looked nothing like this guy.

Over the next few days, our schedules were awkwardly synchronized, dining and lying poolside with no one else in sight. By day two, I began to see the resemblance, and by day three, I found myself avoiding him. *Does my hair look that bad? I need to change it. How did I let myself get that out of shape?*

As I checked out, the front desk person did a double take. "Do you know you look like John Malkovich, and he is also staying here?"

"Been told that before," I said, signing my bill and turning around . . . right into Malkovich.

"I've seen you around here a lot," he said suspiciously. "Do we know each other from somewhere?"

"I don't think so. I have lived in NYC for years, so maybe there? Have you ever been to the Mesa Grill?"

"I have not," he replied, giving me a once-over for what must have been the twentieth time.

"You should try it. I can promise you'll get the best service of your life."

"I'll do that," Malkovich noted, stepping past me to the front of the desk.

As I walked out of the hotel, I felt a sense of relief as I realized how different my life was becoming. I had gone from being John Malkovich to spending a weekend with him, with a few days of constantly staring at myself in a mirror being more than enough.

Deciding to grab lunch before leaving the hotel, I unrolled three sets of large blueprints on my table in the hotel's courtyard, asking the waitress to put my food on the adjoining table.

"What's that for?" she asked, looking over my shoulder.

"Just some plans for a new club."

"Really. I love to go clubbing. Where?"

"In Hollywood. Do you know the Palace on Vine Street?

Not getting an answer, I quickly turned around to see my server looking uncomfortable. I was curious about her response; this was a bit of market research for me.

"Do you know the space?" I asked her again.

"Yup, but I've never been there before . . . and never will."

"I understand. But we're going to do a full renovation, and book . . . "

Putting up her hand to silence me, she uttered softly, "Doesn't matter. That place is haunted."

"I know that the location has had somewhat of a problematic past at times, but—"

Stopping me again in mid-sentence, she said anxiously, "No, man . . . I said *haunted*. As in, ghosts."

The space at 1735 Vine Street had another history, one which conveniently had never come up in conversations with Kay or Brother Bill. Going back to the early 1940s, it had been the location of numerous ghost sightings and attributed activity. There was the invisible jazz pianist heard playing after hours on the second floor; the couple decked out in formalwear, enjoying cocktails in one of the opera boxes; and a man in similar attire who roamed the entire building. On dozens of occasions, there were reports of a ghost sobbing in a locked bathroom stall as well as blood-curdling screams emanating from the balcony, the exact location being marked by a chill in the air and a similar cold spot materializing near the women's bathroom entrance.

A closer look into these happenings revealed an entire cottage industry based around paranormal activity in Hollywood. It seemed like *everywhere* in Tinseltown was haunted, from the landmark Chinese Theatre with its cement hand prints out front, to the Hollywood Sign itself. At the historic Roosevelt Hotel on Hollywood Boulevard, Marilyn Monroe and Montgomery Clift were said to inhabit specific rooms, with reports of Humphrey Bogart and Betty Grable appearing in the lobby. A cold spot in the hotel's Blossom Room, the original location of the Oscars, was said to mark the location where a stylish man from the 1930s takes up residence.

With a large tourist trade driven by celebrity culture, Hollywood had taken it one step further, expanding into the apparition business. Even Aykroyd got into act, attributing his country-style Hollywood Hills home—whose past tenants included Mama Cass Elliot and Natalie Wood—as the inspiration for *Ghostbusters*, with flickering lights and a piano known to play itself as testament.

Originally taken aback by the revelation that we'd just purchased a haunted business, it didn't take long to resolve that I wasn't gonna be afraid of no ghost.

CHAPTER 11

BEYOND THE HOUSE OF PIES

"I love Los Angeles.
I love Hollywood.
They're beautiful.
Everybody's plastic, but I love plastic."
—ANDY WARHOL

In 2003, the city of Hollywood (not to be confused with the "Hollywood" that serves as a moniker for the entertainment industry) fit into the "seen better days" category. It had become widely known for its crime, cheap celebrity trinket shops, and sightseeing destinations, such as the Walk of Fame with its sidewalk-engraved stars ("fame" meaning willing to write a $40,000 check). Few hearty souls ventured into Hollywood after dark, unless they were there to meet their favorite hooker or dealer. It was explained to me that nobody seeking a decent social outing was going to go there in the foreseeable future. Perfect. While others envisioned scenes out of the movie *Escape from L.A.*, I saw something else entirely: opportunity.

I was sure of two things that formed this go-it-alone confidence. Tastemakers (people who had considerable influence over others) actually preferred to venture into unexplored and "dangerous" areas for nightlife; they just needed the right reason to. It gave them a sense of adventure and the feeling of being the "first in." I initially encountered this phenomenon in New York City's Meatpacking District, which was characterized by its "tranny" hookers and their truck-driver companions. Lotus, the first club to set up shop there (with Donald Trump as one of the investors, allowing John Miller to "drop it" as Trump's club for his ladies-man narrative), became an overnight success, leading to the area becoming a nightlife hub.

Mankind has been dancing since the beginning of time, and we aren't about to stop. Growing up, my family's business was in wholesale groceries, and Mel would always tell me: "No matter what happens in the world, people will keep on eating." He just forgot to add, " . . . and dancing."

However, this wasn't the widely held view of Angelenos, who were quick to point out that no one went out dancing in Los Angeles, and they barely ate, for that matter. Only two things mattered: making movies and producing records. There just wasn't time for anything else. Everyone had to look their best and rise early for casting calls (or the potential for one) and spend their time writing lyrics in Laurel Canyon before heading to band practice. It was all about being healthy, and nightclubs were viewed as the opposite.

What a bunch of bullshit that turned out to be.

With this viewpoint being generally accepted, the best entertainment option after midnight, besides a weekly party thrown by Brent Bolthouse and his partner, Jen Rosario, was the House of Pies.

After listening to these well-intended lectures about nightlife in L.A.—and remembering my father's words—my newly informed opinion became: you don't know what you don't know. It seemed ridiculous that, somehow, dancing was reserved for the LGBTQ community, as if straight people in L.A. were strictly governed by the Beaumont town charter.

The venue at 1735 Vine Street had now taken on two new names, one of which was an homage to its haunted history: Spider Club and Avalon Hollywood. I discovered an area being used primarily for storage on the second floor (which I later learned was the purported locale of the ghost jazz pianist, who had yet to make an appearance), and decided to build a subsequent club at the location. Spider Club, a name coined by John's pal and custom-Bentley lender Isaac Tigrett, cofounder of the Hard Rock Cafe and House of Blues, would be first to open, allowing us to take in money as quickly as possible to help pay for the ever-growing renovation budget.

Our design, created by Serge Becker (who'd since split with Eric Goode), featured a motif inspired by Rick's Café (from the movie *Casablanca*). This included custom-designed Moroccan chairs and mirrors, and yards of imported tile. Five immense, beehive-like lighting fixtures, each weighing a thousand pounds, were shipped in from the actual Casablanca and then hoisted by crane into the club's patio area, where they were secured overhead.

Chatting with Jesse in the parking lot one night, I introduced myself as the new owner.

"What about the old owner?" he asked. "Did you talk to him about my money?"

"I wasn't able to, but how about this. What if we up your rate to a hundred and twenty-five dollars until I get a chance to?"

"That would be great," he said. "Thanks, boss. And, oh yeah, someone gave me this for you and said it was urgent." He handed me a business card with the Viper Room logo, a phone number, and "Hal" scratched on the back.

A call the next day revealed that Hal had reached out to me at the behest of the Viper Room owner, whom he couldn't name but instead referred to as "JD." Viper Room, the rock club in West Hollywood, was unfortunately highly recognized for the Halloween-night overdose and death of River Phoenix years earlier, and its owner, Johnny Depp, wasn't a secret by any means. JD was very interested in becoming an investor in our club, and wanted to get more information. When I referred to the non-mystery man as "Johnny," Hal was quick to admonish me. "It's JD, and that's all I can say."

Evidently, the Hollywood version of "not allowed to be seen" was also not allowed to be mentioned. I spoke with Hal on three different occasions, and still he refused to refer to JD by name, leaving me to determine that any potential partner who was off-limits to mention was best not to have as a partner.

One major benefit of being in Hollywood the City was its proximity to Hollywood the Industry. This opened up opportunities not available in New York and Boston, as award shows and their after-parties, film and television locations, product launches, and high-profile music showcases were centered in Los Angeles. With the opening of Avalon Hollywood still six months away, we'd already secured private events, sight unseen, that included the Black Eyed Peas, a "Save the Rainforest" fundraiser, and a BMG Grammys after-party with the Killers, Carlos Santana, and Billy Idol.

When I stopped by to check on the Spider Club's progress, I was shocked to find that the renovation had been completed a week ahead of schedule . . . as a '70s disco. The specialized wall tile had been replaced with shimmering gold lamé fabric, which surrounded a raised fiberglass dance floor with flashing lights right out of *Saturday Night Fever*. The giant beehives had been miraculously transformed into disco balls with light shooting through their ornate design like intricately positioned lasers. The furniture now consisted of oddly futuristic ball chairs and multiple oversized fuchsia, lip-shaped couches.

Utterly confused as to how and why this makeover had taken place, I was thrown off even more by the sight of Ben Stiller, Owen Wilson, and Vince Vaughn dressed as if they'd formed the new Bee Gees.

"You can't be here," a young woman said, motioning for me to step back. We're about to start shooting."

"Shooting?" I asked with a sudden twinge of anger.

"Yes, the scene. Step back over there."

In a rush of remembrance, I asked her the date.

"The twenty-eighth," she replied, now pushing me out of the way.

I remembered that, for the next three days, Spider Club had been rented out to film the movie *Starsky and Hutch*, based on the '70s buddy-cop television show. Looking around with a new lens, I was awestruck by my first encounter with Hollywood filmmaking magic. Stopping construction to allow for the rental now put us behind schedule, but at $15,000 a day it was an interruption we could live with. I only hoped the Moroccan version of Spider Club we'd originally planned would come out nearly as stylish as the temporary Hollywood version.

"Yo, brother, do I know you?" came a voice from one of the disco-clad actors. "Aren't you from Boston, man?"

Getting a closer look at the group's lankiest member, decked out in a fur-trimmed mauve overcoat, matching flat cap, and gold cane, there was no mistaking who it was.

"I am," I said, now remembering the distinct voice.

Heading toward me, Snoop gave me the once-over. "If it ain't the Malkovich-looking motherfucker all in black. You, my nizzle. I remember asking you for some help . . . getting us some more weed. You just ignored us and kept walkin'."

"I thought you didn't want to be bothered. I had some problems with other people who didn't even want to be looked at before going onstage."

"Not looked at? What kind of bizzle shizzle is that?" said Snoop, now being motioned over to the Travolta-esque dance floor. "Man, we're all just God's children and can look at whoever the fuck we want." He adjusted his cap as he walked away, then turned back. "Ain't I the real goddamn Huggy Bear, for shizzle?"

Spider Club was set to be the first membership-only club in Hollywood. Once again, playing on the mentality that defined a hotspot, this sent out the message that only the "chosen few" were allowed. Why there wasn't a long history of private clubs over the years, in a town whose lifeblood was the quest for feeling special, could be explained by Hollywood's longtime approach to nightlife as more of an afterthought than a priority.

The club's staff, led by host Donovan Leitch (son of famed '60s sing-er/songwriter Donovan), had been delivering handmade cards (paid for by the *Starsky and Hutch* rental money) to various "industry types" around Hollywood for weeks. Each consisted of a molded center that was wrapped in leather and individually numbered. After some debate with Gregory, a tactical decision was made to produce them too thick to fit into a wallet, thereby compelling the holder to carry theirs around separately.

This inconvenience was overshadowed by the holder's ability to flash the card at will. I witnessed this in action at dinner one evening, when a young producer sitting at the table next to me pulled the card out of his pocket as if by mistake, then scrambled to put it back. As one of the two actresses across from him rubbed the leather between her thumb and index finger, he asked coolly, "Do you know what that is? Not everyone gets one of these."

Actually, more people received those cards than anyone knew. Lots more. Spider Club had a capacity of three hundred and fifty guests, and we needed two hundred in order to give the place the energy essential for a successful night. To achieve this number, we needed a large enough pool of people, in the thousands. Nine hundred cards were made in three different shades of leather; each shade was numbered 1 through 99, 01 through 099, and 001 through 0099. This would allow all cardholders to have a number under 100 (no one wants to receive an exclusive VIP card with the number 750 on it). If, by coincidence, cardholders compared numbers and they were the same, the hope was that the differing colors would make each person think they'd received the superior card. This actually worked as planned.

With nine hundred cards going out, and the receiver of each card al-lowed to bring up to four guests, we'd attained the critical audience num-ber. This didn't take into account the countless others guaranteed to seek admission without cards. To facilitate this, entry was free for cardhold-ers and their guests, while non-cardholders would pay a cover charge. In reality, this was all one big sleight of hand that would have made even Oakenfold blush.

LAXIOM #9
Find the hidden need.
Like the invention of Post-Its or Reese's Peanut Butter Cups, great entrepreneurial ideas zero in on what a community needs, which oftentimes they themselves aren't yet aware of. To quote Henry Ford, "If I had asked people what they wanted, they would have said faster horses."

Of course, in a place as unpredictable and ego-driven as Hollywood, there is always the chance that things won't go as planned, and the distribution of the now-coveted Spider Club card was no exception.

I now had pages of observations, which would later be used for this book. My friend in L.A., Jamie (owner of the trend-setting clothing store Lost and Found) thought they could be the basis of a TV series. She offered to set up a meeting with, Karen, the head of development at Imagine Entertainment, the company owned by Ron Howard and Brian Grazer.

Three days before the meeting, my computer containing all my notes was stolen, with no backup. Catching an early flight from NY to L.A. and arriving just in time to show up for the meeting at the Imagine offices, I was confident that I had enough of the information in my head to be able to wing it. I was shown to Karen's office through a maze of cubicles. After chatting about some common acquaintances, we had a short discussion about the show concept, after which she stood up and said, "Are you ready?"

Huh?

"I'm always ready," I proclaimed, still not registering why she was standing.

"Okay then, let's go."

Go? Out for an early lunch?

As I entered the brightly lit conference room overlooking Beverly

Hills, I first registered the framed movie posters for *8 Mile*, *A Beautiful Mind*, and *Apollo 13* hanging on the walls. Then I saw the crowd of six people sitting around the table, half of them with notepads already opened. They stood to greet me while I took my assigned seat at the head of the table.

"This is David Nevins, head of television," Karen explained, followed by introductions of the rest of the room. "We're all excited to see what you have for us."

If you are an aspiring television writer, chances are you will toil for years before ever landing a job in the industry, maybe as a staff writer, if you are lucky. Getting your own show idea in the hands of producers involves first getting an agent; as I'd learned, production companies and studios didn't take direct submissions. Getting an agent to rep you is challenging enough. Even if you're talented or lucky enough to get one to agree to represent you, as a newcomer chances are you'll be on the bottom of their priority list, up against other more established clients they can make their fifteen percent commission on. You must complete a pilot script, which the agent will then send around town to sit in a pile with numerous other scripts, waiting to be read at some future date.

When, and if, it is eventually read, most likely by an assistant, it will arrive on their boss's desk accompanied by a set of notes. If the boss likes your idea, maybe you will then be called in for a one-on-one meeting to discuss the script. The chances of this happening are quite low, as your script is competing against dozens of other agent-represented scripts.

Sitting there in the conference room, staring out at my captive audience with nothing in front of me—not even a *small* open notepad—I was becoming acutely aware of my situation. Apparently, I had bypassed the entire process, which just *doesn't happen*, and found myself in front of some the top people in Hollywood. They wanted details, and all I had to deliver were the notes in my head.

Just then, the door popped open, and in bounded Brian Grazer. He quickly shook my hand as I stood with the rest of the group, who all immediately straightened up, looking a bit shell-shocked.

"Is this our man . . . the Spider Club guy?" Brian asked, putting his hand on my shoulder. "Can't wait to see what he has for us. But before you get started, I have a little favor to ask you. How can I get one of those leather membership cards I've heard so much about?"

Before I could answer, Karen leaned over and whispered with a meaningful smile, "Brian *never* attends these types of meetings."

"Do you really want one?" I asked Brian in front of the hushed, puzzled room. The thought that one of the biggest producers in Hollywood thought he needed this seemingly coveted card for entrance was somewhat ludicrous to me. It was all bullshit, for God's sake. From what I knew about him, I didn't see Spider Club as his scene, and quickly determined that he would be out of place amongst the young, less-established Hollywood types. If I was going to do business with him, I certainly didn't want to steer him wrong.

"I don't think you really do," I continued, answering my own question. "Everyone has one, and I don't think it's really for you."

The collective gasp in the room was audible, like the reaction to a morbid plot twist in a movie. Brian gave me a mortified look, then turned to exit the room. *What just happened?* Whispers all around. Not a word to me.

"Anyone have any questions about the show?" I asked my audience, breaking the awkward silence. *Karen is really starting to get fidgety.*

No response . . . and no eye contact. Apparently, the floor was mine, and I was getting quite fidgety myself. I had to do something, so I began: "This show is about a New York City club owner who comes to Hollywood . . . "

I had been in the room less than ten minutes, total. Five minutes into my stream-of-conscious pitch, two people at the end of the table stood and excused themselves. Two minutes later, two more did the same. I was losing my crowd. I needed to pivot.

"Did I tell you about . . . the cat? His name is Whitey, after the Hall

of Fame Yankee pitcher Whitey Ford, and he has a real New York attitude." Nothing. No response. Two more exits. Minutes later, faced with
an empty room, the meeting was adjourned, canceled in real time. Peek-
ing out from the door, I saw no one I recognized. After a few wrong turns,
I guided myself to the exit through the maze of cubicles. My first pitch
ever had been a mitigated disaster.

I sat in my car in the parking lot, contemplating what had just happened. I felt an uneasy feeling in my stomach, like when someone breaks
up with you with no explanation given, but deep down you know what
that reason is. Just then, my phone rang. It was Jamie.

"Congrats, you did it!" she said. "And it was hilarious as you pitched
it."

Huh?

Another call. It was Gregory, on the other line from New York. "How
great . . . it was really funny . . . even better on TV."

"What was?"

"One of your episodes. It ran last night. Didn't you see it?"

Telling Gregory and Jamie I would call them back, I sped home, still
disoriented from the day's events. I checked the TV listings for the latest
Curb episode. "The Larry David Sandwich" was scheduled to run again
that night.

And there it was, just as I had outlined it—the "high holidays tickets"
scene, with the premise being that during Rosh Hashanah and Yom Kip-
pur, the larger synagogues require people outside their congregations to
pay for tickets to attend services. In the episode, Larry is late to the table
and needs to get tickets from a scalper.

Two weeks later, I found myself at dinner with an old friend from
Boston and her husband, Drew, who had a lucrative personal training
business he ran out of his private home gym. The conversation moved
to some of his clients, many of whom were high-profile entertainment
types.

"Did you see that *Curb Your Enthusiasm* episode a few weeks back, the one about the ticket scalper? Wasn't that the best? My client wrote that and sold it for over $20K."

I froze, half a shrimp sticking out of my mouth. Quickly gathering myself, I said, "You don't say . . . tell me more."

Apparently, Drew's client had had my identical idea.

As the conversation continued, the subject quickly moved to another one of his clients he had met with that day—David Nevins. The story making the rounds among movie studios was that a writer pitching his story had gravely insulted Brian Grazer, refusing to allow him admission to a nightclub the writer owned . . . actually telling him he didn't want him there. Since I was in the nightclub business, Drew thought I might know this idiot club guy.

"Doesn't ring a bell," I replied, recounting the room-clearing meeting in my head. "Sounds like a real shmohawk."

Since then, my passion for writing and stories has been put to good use—in nightlife. First as the creator of press releases, which are mini-narratives within themselves, and then through business storytelling while doing investor pitches and press interviews. Incorporating my *Curb* ideas into my answers to reporters, who were unknowingly serving as an audience for my material, became common, earning me an eccentric label by some.

I could understand the labelers' reasoning. When asked what my plans were for the upcoming Avalon, or what the menu at Honey, the adjacent restaurant, would consist of, I would digress into unrelated topics—such as the twenty-year-old tribal elder I had met, or why trapeze artists make bad surgeons (too many callouses), or how being a natural at certain sports is a thing, but being a true unnatural is not.

With the work at Spider Club complete, an event was needed to kick things off. This was accommodated by Bruce Willis, who agreed to hold his birthday party at the club as a sneak-peek opening. Still new to

Hollywood, I watched the frenzy surrounding the night and enjoyed the opportunity to experience Hollywood "culture" firsthand. I soon learned that this new chapter in my life would be one about my ability to adapt. Getting used to perfect weather was one thing; adjusting to just about everything else was something I hadn't expected.

East Meets West

	East Coast	Hollywood
Transportation	Taxi/Uber.	Lease a car you can't come close to affording for appearance, while simultaneously leasing a cheap apartment with no furniture.
Communication	Say what you mean, and mean what you say.	Refer to everyone as either "great," "fabulous," or "amazing." Proceed to call them an "idiot," "asshole," or "pointless" as soon as they walk away—unless they can help you.
Doing Business: Need a Card?	Nope, but it may be helpful in certain situations.	A must, with "President" or "CEO" as your title and "Productions" or "Films" somewhere in the aspiring company's title.
Need Help?	No, I got this.	A status assistant is needed to schedule any meetings

	East Coast	Hollywood
		and to return calls, even if that means once a week. Girlfriends and boyfriends make convenient proxies.
Attire	Dress appropriately for the occasion.	Dress appropriately only for award shows and movie premieres. For all other occasions, dress down as much as possible for "I don't care, I'm a star" maximum effect (ski hats in the middle of the summer are a statement accessory).
Dining Times	Breakfast at 10:00 AM, lunch 2:30 PM, dinner 10:00 PM.	Breakfast before 8:00 AM to avoid any wait, lunch at 1:00 PM, dinner 8:00 PM.
Check the Weather	Every two hours.	Never, no need.
Vacation Spots	South Beach.	Los Angeles.

As an East Coast transplant, at times I felt like a fish out of water. Various people I met wanted to talk about one topic only: themselves. More specifically, they wanted to talk about what they were doing, with an emphasis on what they were *going* to be doing, which, by the time they'd talked themselves out, often didn't seem like much.

I was often sized up to determine one thing: who I knew in the movie industry. Somehow, actor types were able to work a Jedi mind trick into an introduction, to make you name those you're friendly with who could help their acting career. This way of communicating was like learning a new language, which I deemed "Transactionalish," and the person across from me was expecting the same dialogue in return.

It felt like a script everyone had read but me.

THE HOLLYWOOD CONVERSATION

OUTSIDE THE AVALON NIGHTCLUB – DAY

We see STEVE ADELMAN, just arrived in Hollywood,
STANDING NEXT TO HOLLY WOODTYPE, 28,
aspiring actress who has come to pick up her friend from work.
They are in MID-CONVERSATION.

STEVE
Nice to meet you. How's your day going?

HOLLY
(staring at her phone)
My fucking agent is an asshole. He never gets me any work.
What did you say your name was again?

STEVE
I didn't ... Steve.

HOLLY
Steve ... ?

STEVE
Steve Adelman.

HOLLY
Steve Adelman ... how do I know that name?

STEVE
Can't say.

HOLLY
I know I know that name. Are you a producer?

STEVE
In a way . . . but if you mean a movie producer, then no.

HOLLY
In a way? You mean like pornos?

STEVE
No, not like pornos.

HOLLY
Wait . . . you're the guy who directed that Christian Bale movie.

STEVE
Not me. You might have heard my name because
I'm your friend Angela's boss. Here she comes now.
(he motions off-screen)

HOLLY
You're Angela's manager?

STEVE
Not exactly. I'm the owner.

HOLLY
(now looking up from her phone)
You own this place. Wow . . . I heard Bruce Willis is having his birthday
here next week. Can you get me in? I'm sure there'll be a lot of
interesting people to meet. Can you introduce me to him?

STEVE
I'll have to leave that for Angela.

HOLLY
What's your number? Angela told me all sorts of important industry
people are supposed to be hanging out here.
Do you know Bruce's agent, by the way? Do you know Johnny Depp?
I heard he was an investor here.
(Holly continues to talk as we pull away. Steve glances in both
directions, looking for a way out.)

SNAP TO BLACK

A few days before the Spider Club was set to unveil, the receptionist
buzzed my office.

"There's a Mr. Maconti here to see you."

"I don't know a Mr. Maconti. Can you find out what he wants?"

"He says his name is Jackie Maconti and he knows you from New
York."

Stepping outside onto the sidewalk on Vine Street, the mystery man
turned to greet me, engulfing my hand with his bear-sized palm.

"It's been a while . . . almost ten years I think," he said, noticing the
puzzled look on my face. "It's Big Mac."

Stunned, I gazed at the figure in front of me. Gone was the large, almost featureless pumpkin head, replaced by chiseled features. Where there
was once a month-old unkept beard, there was now finely manicured facial hair. His beloved Jets hat was removed, revealing a dark mane cut precisely short enough on the sides and long enough on top to make him look
. . . well, dashing. He must have lost well over 100 pounds, a feat he seemed
all too happy to highlight with his tight Ed Hardy shirt and jeans.

"Big Mac, I don't believe it," I exclaimed, echoing Grandma Mary.
"What the hell are you doing here . . . and what happened to you?" I said,

pointing to all *that*.

"I've been out here now for about a year. Came with Military Mike and Uncle Sal."

"Your uncle is out here with you?"

"Naw, we use to call him Sally Balls, but his sister had her first kid so now we call him Uncle Sal."

"You've got to be the last person I thought I'd see in Hollywood. *Big Mac* . . . who would believe it?"

"I go by Jack Mack now. You know, like Jack Black. Thought it would be good to help people remember my name. When the whole *Sopranos* thing got big, I thought if those guys can make it as actors, then so can I. So, I got serious, eating right, training and shit."

"How are things going?"

"You know, I like it out here. The girls, the beach . . . I mean c'mon. And the people will pay top dollar for everything. They just want to look important. So, even if the acting thing doesn't work out, I'm good. I still keep in touch with Rae and she told me you were here, so I wanted to stop by and say thanks."

"Thanks? For what?" I asked as we began an impromptu stroll down the sidewalk, stopping at the Hollywood Walk of Fame star of Roy Rogers.

"I remember you saying what a character I was. How they should do a movie based on me. How I was great at playing parts. I never forgot that and I think it motivated me to come to L.A." *I did? It did?*

"Here," he said, handing me two Lakers tickets denoted as "floor." "My number is on the back. Let me know if you need anything. I've got a guy who knows a guy whose cousin can get you these any time."

At a loss for words, I watched the newly created Jack Mack turn the corner down Hollywood Boulevard with a pep in his step. I had inadvertently influenced what might be his true calling. One thing was certain—*he* would be just fine in the jungle of Hollywood. A true lion of the transaction-based lifestyle, the lesser creatures of Hollywood were in for a rude awakening.

Now, don't get me wrong, not everyone in Hollywood spoke Trans-actionalish. Joey, the newly hired assistant manager for the soon-to-be-opened Avalon comes to mind. Joey could best be described as the inspiration for the optimistic and kindhearted Ted Lasso character from the Apple TV series of the same name. Going by the name Joey Chicago, when talking to him it became apparent that his identity came from his Midwestern roots, not from defining himself as an actor.

Joey's relationship to his beloved, gritty, tough-as-nails city took on a new meaning when he decided to have it memorialized in a tattoo. Arriving at work with a sense of excitement after finally having his namesake emblazoned across his back, he eagerly took off his shirt for the big reveal.

"How great is that?" he exclaimed.

"What did you tell him you wanted?" I asked, a bit taken aback.

"I told him to give me a tat that represented Chicago. One that everyone would look at and know exactly what it was."

"Well, he did that."

As Joey put his shirt back on with a proud smile, I wasn't about to ruin the moment or dim Joey's Lasso-esque enthusiasm. As I pondered the oversized logo of the '70s pop/rock band Chicago that I had just seen, I thought maybe Joey could make it work, although it did send a different message than I think he intended. The poor guy . . . of all the cities to embrace as your own, why couldn't it at least have been Boston?

The birthday night started with a frenzy as camera crews scurried around to get a shot of Bruce with ex-wife Demi Moore. As I watched the evening unfold, Christian Slater expounded the virtues of being sober and giving up red meat while Kirsten Dunst asked how she could get a leather card, having somehow been overlooked. Hollywood royalty that would never be carded had assembled in the furthest corner. Jack Nicholson held court from a booth with an over-mischievous look on his face, flanked by his apparent partners in crime for the night, Kevin Costner and Joe Pesci.

That's when James Woods walked in.

I thought of Jesse, guarding the parking lot outside, and something inside me needed to know . . . no matter how far-fetched the story was. Grabbing James's attention, I introduced myself, breaking the ice with my tale of the man in the parking lot.

"I need to meet this guy," James replied. "Is he around?"

We went out to the parking lot and Jesse appeared from behind a car in the far corner, looking proud and dapper in a mismatched suit to mark the occasion.

"Jesse," I said, "I know the old owner owed you some money and you wanted to talk to him. I want you to meet my new friend, James."

The two chatted for a few minutes. It seemed like Jesse had been quite a key grip in his day.

"I hope this makes us even, and sorry for the inconvenience," said James, handing Jesse a wad of fifties. Jess held on to the cash like a long-lost pet.

"Did you know the guy?" I asked James as we walked back toward the club.

"Maybe," he replied, stepping into the crowd already singing "Happy Birthday"—including Owen Wilson and Vince Vaughn, who stood with beers in hand at the bar.

Maybe people in Hollywood weren't as self-involved as I thought they were. Maybe people were the same everywhere, and I just needed more time to really find out. Maybe all those maybes didn't even matter at that point.

I was all in, either way.

As I headed out that night, after what many would later describe as the party of the year, I heard a scream from inside Avalon. It was locked up, concealing what was now a demolition site. I grabbed Jesse and unlocked a side door.

"Aaaauugghhhhhhhh!" It came from across the room, this time sounding more like a loud sob as we picked up our pace toward the restrooms.

The women's restroom door was partially ajar, and I could feel a cooling sensation on my forehead, which gave me the chills.

"I'm not sure what we're about to see, but be ready for anything," I uttered, bracing Jesse for what was to come.

He just shrugged, opening the door to reveal . . . two women sitting on the floor.

"Just trying to get into the party," said one. My detective brain kicked in, albeit for just a moment: *A quick inspection of the restroom revealed that both women had tried to enter through a small, unlocked window, where one of them had suffered a cut from a protruding nail. The small amount of blood on the floor made it clear the wound wasn't deep, but undoubtedly painful. Clearly not receiving an invitation, they had spent a significant amount of time looking for an entry point, which garnished my respect for their tenacity.*

Both relieved and disappointed that I hadn't experienced my first Avalon ghost sighting, I asked the women if they were okay. Given their disheveled look, it was apparent things weren't going as planned.

"We're new to town," said the injured one. "We're not sure how these things work yet."

"Well, you're in luck," I said, sensing their frustration. "I'm the owner, and this gentleman works here and would be happy to escort you in."

As all three looked at me, the women with appreciation and Jesse puffing his chest with pride, I felt it was the least I could do for my newfound kindred spirit.

"Just a fish helping another fish swim upstream," I said, heading for the door as Jesse, with a girl on each arm, followed behind into the cool L.A. night.

The launch of Spider Club had gone according to plan, a Halley's Comet in nightlife. Two months later, the opening of Avalon Hollywood would be a nightlife earthquake.

CHAPTER 12

ALPHABETICAL ORDER

"Any problem in the world can be solved by dancing."
—JAMES BROWN

Ever since my time in NYC, I knew when Prince, or, as he was known for a few years, "Indecipherable Glyph," was going to call. Not due to some intuition, but based on his "people" calling my office and the receptionist relaying the message to me: "Prince's people called and said he's going to call your cell in the next five to forty-five minutes."

Not having a designated time for him left me vulnerable to picking up unknown calls during this window, but . . . you just have to be available to take a call from Prince. Two hours and an annoying solicitation from AT&T later, I was talking not with Prince himself, but with someone who claimed to be his new representative. "He" (apparently updated to "Glyph") was interested in finding out more about the club opening. Might even do an impromptu show.

This immediately struck me as what I called the "Hollywood Hustle," which entailed dropping a celebrity name to get access to a number of things, including restaurant reservations, movie premiere tickets, and in this case, VIP nightclub treatment. The hustle portion came when the dropped-name celebrity was a no-show, leaving only the hanger-on entourage who had already evoked their names to get the perks.

"[Celebrity name] is so sorry they couldn't make it, but says thanks so much for taking care of us." *Screw you.*

If He *were* to attend, continued the Rep, He would need the following to happen:

No one could know He was coming in advance.

A private seating area for twenty would need to be provided where He could not be seen, surrounded by security, with no one sitting within at least twelve feet of Him on either side.

He would bring his own champagne but would need a private waitress, who was not to look Him in the eye.

Prince had now entered rare mega-star status, the result of which was He could be neither mentioned *nor* looked at.

His requests were going to be logistically challenging given the expected full house, so I had one condition of my own: I needed proof of body. Not the promise of Him, nor the promise of a sure-to-turn-up group of twelve. Sounding displeased, Rep promised to get back in touch. Oh, and one more thing—He wouldn't know anything for sure until the day of. *Great.*

This put me in a tough situation. If I instructed the staff to block off a seated area and He didn't turn up, I'd be left with a pissed-off waitstaff who would be out the money they could have made serving those same tables, to the tune of $300 each. To make matters worse, other guests left standing, who also considered themselves celebrities, would be irate that they'd been restricted from sitting down with no explanation given (due to our vow of silence to Him). On the other hand, having Him at the Avalon opening would be very good for business, since a rare sighting of the Purple One in public would be hot fodder for the tabloids and the worldwide press. I rationalized that even those relegated to standing-room only could appreciate that.

Now, if He showed up and actually wanted to perform, well . . . that would involve a load-in of equipment, and then we'd somehow need to come up with a way to sound check while moving the existing DJ set-up currently occupying the stage. To complicate matters, I wasn't even certain that Rep was legitimate, and to sound a false alarm would make me look like an amateur in front of the newly hired staff.

We settled on this plan: we would hold an area until midnight, and if He hadn't arrived by then, we would start seating other people there. Six additional security and another sound man would be brought in to move and set up equipment, just in case.

After over two years of planning, construction, and press releases, the opening of Avalon Hollywood had become a much-anticipated event. Not just because it was the first nightclub of its size to open in Hollywood in over forty years, but also because it had the same type of appeal as getting a front-row seat to an unnatural disaster, or a staged version of an eight-car highway pileup.

In late 2003, Los Angeles did not have any established mega-clubs. The closest thing to it was a string of adjoining clubs in "Boystown," a five-block area in West Hollywood that served as the epicenter of gay nightlife. As such, I referred to the crowd that was to attend as "clubber-neckers." For me, the night was my indigo bunting.

While waiting for a doctor's appointment several years earlier in NYC, I'd grabbed a nature magazine and read a story about a bird watcher who had spent his adult life in pursuit of a rare bird called an indigo bunting. For the protagonist to come across this bird, which he considered a perfect specimen, all the conditions had to be just right: temperature, visibility, time of day and year, along with some luck. I was called into the examination room before finding out if he'd ever made contact with his singular obsession, but the idea of searching for that perfect outcome stuck with me and rang true. I related the search for the Indigo Bunting to my quest for the perfect nightlife experience, and was determined that the opening of Avalon Hollywood would be that elusive night.[15]

Around 7:00 AM on the day of the opening, I checked my phone to find my voicemail full. Thirty calls since 11:00 PM. *Did someone get into an accident? Was one of the clubs in Boston raided? Did Mel suffer a heart attack?* As I listened to the messages, I realized these calls were about something of greater importance to those involved, having far-reaching implications and a profound impact on self-esteems, personal lives, and careers: tonight's VIP guest list.

"Christina is coming tonight and needs to be escorted in by at least three people ..." *Escort was not a position we staffed for.*

"Ashton needs a secluded booth and will be there with ten people ..." *No booth fit more than six people.*

"Pink wants to have the menu sent to her ... she will be with six people and needs eight bottles of free Dom ..." *There were no printed menus, or Dom, for that matter.*

Following a strict chain of command, these urgent messages were left by will-work-for-business-cards personal or agent assistants. *How did they even get this number?* These low-on-the-totem-polers needed to make this happen; moving up to the next rung depended on it.

I have never quite come to terms with this feeling of entitlement, but I understand its origin. Having certain people in a club is a magnet to draw others. A sighting of Prince (who at this point I had yet to hear back from) gets a lot of people excited. Somehow, word of his possible appearance had now spread to just about everyone.

I often sorted out these somewhat nonsensical requests by assigning them to my deputized assistant. The war-room session between underlings involved clever negotiation, cunning, and most of all ass-kissing, the

---

15 Indigo bunting was not the actual name of the bird in the article, as I could not recall it. The reference comes from an actual bird-watching expedition I took, during which our guide was in search of the indigo bunting, deeming sightings of it extremely rare.

majority of the puckering coming from our end. Cameron cannot be seen seated next to Lindsay. It cannot get out that Brad will be there. This was serious business, and continued on for hours. Running over an hour late and with 8:00 PM approaching fast, I walked out of my house feeling like I was grabbing an umbrella before heading out into a hurricane.

I unfolded myself from the prom-ready white limo—not my first choice of transportation with my car out of service, but the best available last minute—and there it was. My first red carpet. *Variety*, the *Hollywood Reporter*, *E News*, *Entertainment Tonight*, they were all there, waiting for their next victim. *Who are you expecting tonight? Is Justin coming? Do you know with whom? How do you see the future of Hollywood? Reaallly?*

I could barely manage to process any of these deep and profound questions, as my mind was elsewhere. *This is your moment. You are the toast of the town. Focus.* Standing there with the dazed look of a lost toddler, I knew something that none of the hundred or so people outside did—not the paparazzi, gossip reporters, gawkers, camera people, PR assistants, gofer assistants, Kate, Drew, or Mila. I knew that I was about to *become* toast, and that it would be broadcast in front of a national audience. My fifteen Hollywood minutes were counting down fast.

At that exact moment, the lobby carpeting was being loaded inside through a back-alley door. A gaggle of bartenders were huddled together, awaiting my instruction, as the only liquor delivered to serve the incoming guests was twenty-four bottles of cheap vodka. For Barney Holm, this was no relaxing day at the links; he was pleading his case to the furniture guy's wife, who had instructions not to unload her two trucks until final payment had been made. And our much-hyped celebrity opera boxes? They didn't exist.

Fifteen years of savings *and* my bar mitzvah money were on the line. But on the other hand, the beautiful unpainted, white-primer club interior was sure to be a big hit, if only for its glistening effect. Who needs paint, anyway?

With grim reality punching me in the face, a left hook landed just at the right time, clearing my head. I was not about to let myself go down for the count. Leaning up against the building in my corner, I excused myself from the proceedings, heading for a little-used exit door. Once inside, the scene of staff running in every direction left the impression of an imminent attack. I took a few steps into the lobby, and then stopped in my tracks; apparently, the glue adhesive for the carpet had not yet dried, and I was stuck like a rat in a trap. The scurrying staff was too crazed to even acknowledge me, and I was left to fend for myself. Not wanting to come across as the village idiot, I pretended to urgently check my phone.

One thing I could always depend on was that, during any opening, almost nothing goes as planned. In "daylife," things are governed by a basic set of principles. If you have a day job, you are expected to show up on time and, in most cases, dress a certain way, with an accepted level of hygiene. Most likely, your workday has a degree of structure to it: lunch for a certain amount of time, at a specific time, a calendar of meetings, perhaps. You have your own customized workspace, and hopefully you interact with your colleagues in a civil manner.

If your day begins at 9:00 PM and you throw alcohol, drugs, second jobs, and half-naked people into the mix, those principles go to hell pretty quickly. In nightlife, the workplace is defined by arriving late with an elaborate excuse and wearing whatever sells, which is usually next to nothing. There is a universal dress code for the bar staff, the conventional version for women being: men like boobs. For men: I'm available to *like* your boobs. This is all based on the common nightlife knowledge that people prefer to buy their drinks with the value-added proposition of flirting, however economically driven that may be.

Classic nightlife punctuality excuses include: "My grandfather passed away today" (for the fifth time?); "I *have* been here, you just didn't see me" (we have timecards, you know); and "There was a huge car accident on the way to work, thank God I'm alive" (don't you live four blocks away and walk to work?).

So, why not just fire the person? The answer is, sometimes you do, but over time you wouldn't have anyone left to hire. Nightlife is dominated by Type B's working long, odd hours without the luxury of stable pay, which is not for everyone. Most nightlife meetings start twenty to thirty minutes late, with the attendees looking as if they just came from a night in the emergency room. Again, how is this tolerated? The main reason is that the staff was most likely working the night prior, until 4:00 AM. That's seven hours of hustling on their feet, so a little "fatigue compassion" is sometimes needed before they hit the field again for tonight's back-to-back game. Like ingredients for a Bloody Mary, there are those times when daylife and nightlife don't mix quite right, but you still drink up. No use tossing out perfectly good Grey Goose.

Nightlife is also plagued by the "Bigfoot" of its realm: storage, mainly for sound equipment, lighting, and alcohol (generally referred to as "back of house"). Ask a bar or nightclub owner what they lack most in their life, and the answer won't be spending time with their family—it will be additional storage space. This, combined with the necessity to make every square foot available to sell drinks and admissions, makes office and work space an afterthought. It's simple math: two thousand people in your club is better than seventeen hundred.

Nightclubs, bars, and concert venues are restricted by their legal capacity, or the number of people the fire department deems legal to enter and exit the building safely. This number is a function of square footage, exit doors, and impediments within the space, such as columns and bars. Basically it comes down to, if there were a fire, God forbid, how many people can get out quickly and safely?

Smart club owners do whatever they can to get to their maximum legal capacity, as it determines their earnings potential. Many times, this can lead to payoffs to look the other way or get the necessary approval from building inspectors. Ever seen the office at your neighborhood bar, a nightclub, or any live music venue? Its most likely jammed into an out-of-the-way room, with liquor boxes serving as shelves. The reason is that the owner had no choice, if he wants to increase his chances to be successful.

Nightclub owner offices are often portrayed in movies and on television as grand spaces overlooking the club itself. Take *Scarface*, for example. If Tony was making his money legally, instead of meeting with Frank and Manny in his decked-out-to-the-max office, they would be meeting in a converted janitorial closet.

By now, my Chuck Taylors were permanently stuck to the carpet adhesive, and I needed to find an immediate way out. Reaching down, I was able to untie them and pull my feet out to a point where I was actually standing on top of my shoes. From there, I made a standing broad jump to an area where it appeared that the glue had yet to be applied. Two rabbit hops later, I was back on safe ground.

I slid over to the bar area and saw that, sure enough, there were twenty or so bottles on a shelf that held over sixty. The two other large bars were completely empty, all being manned by an army of bar staff who looked justifiably dumbfounded.

With Barney nowhere in sight, it was all hands on deck.

"Where's Julio?" I asked no one in particular and anyone who would answer. Julio was the person every club owner needs as a necessity, a "can do it all." Need the air conditioning repaired? See Julio. Roof leaking? Julio. Need lights fixed? You guessed it. Never with a complaint, and always with a smile.

"I think he's helping the carpet guys," answered half the group, pointing in unison to where I had just come from.

"What are we going to do?" one of the bartenders asked anxiously. "We open in twenty minutes."

"Whatever we have to," I replied, giving the bar squad an impromptu and hopefully inspirational thumbs-up.

Arriving back in the lobby, I was now blocked by an enormous roll of carpet that had just been pulled out, ready to be laid down. This would be accomplished by pushing it over the glued area until it adhered. Problem is, this process usually took four hours. I spotted Julio, puzzled by the pair of shoes bonded to the lobby floor, in a full Spanish discussion apparently

revolving around theories about how they got there. I motioned to him
to stop what he was doing.

"Boss, we have to get this carpet down now if we are going to open,"
he said.

"I know, and we will. First things first. Come with me."

Descending down the newly resurfaced concrete stairs leading to the
storage office, I focused on each shoeless step so I wouldn't fall on my ass.
I emptied the safe of its cash and handed it to Julio, who took off to the
liquor store in his truck. By California law, you cannot sell retail liquor in
a licensed venue and can only purchase it through a registered wholesaler.
But this was an emergency, where "do whatever you have to" and "do it
now, ask for forgiveness later" both applied.

Back upstairs, I peeked through the cashier's window. It appeared that
all was going somewhat according to plan outside. My phone rang—it was
Jenn, our Brooklyn-born, Jewish mother-of-four publicist. I picked up.

"Where the hell are you?" she asked.

"I got stuck inside with a few last-minute things. Back out there in a
minute, bubby." I knew the chance of this happening was on par with the
prophet Elijah arriving as an uninvited guest.

Barney appeared. "Been trying to reach you," he said. From the look
on his face, there was no time to spare. "They aren't going to take the furniture off the truck unless they get a check. What do you want me to tell
them?" I could tell he was at his wit's end, and in no shape to step into a
last-minute curtailed negotiation.

"Let me talk to them. Where are they?"

"Over there, standing in the VIP area where the furniture is supposed
to be."

"They" was a Roseanne Barr doppelganger who, as I approached, began waving yellow pieces of paper at me. "I need these paid before I can
unload," she said.

You may be wondering: why was the furniture being delivered an
hour before the club opened? Well, in nightlife, *everything* always comes

down to the last second, like some kind of self-destructive Code of the Hills. No one moves unless they *need* to, and in most cases, that means the *need* to get paid. I explained that demanding payment C.O.D. was something I needed to know weeks in advance. How about partial payment in cash now, and the rest first thing next week? "Roseanne" begrudgingly agreed. As I ran back to the office, I suddenly realized: *We don't have any cash. I just gave it all to Julio.*

Doing a nimble pirouette at the end of the dance floor, I headed back toward Roseanne to work on a Plan B. When the words "no cash" came out of my mouth, she began heading toward the door.

I need a plan . . . now.

"Are you a Justin Timberlake fan?" I blurted out.

Roseanne turned around. "A what?"

"Justin Timberlake. You know, NSYNC, *Cry Me a River*. Are you a fan?"

"Why are you asking me that?" Roseanne replied, started toward the door again. "I don't know who that is."

Shit.

"Do you have kids? I'm sure they would know." *She's still walking.* "He'll be here tonight, and your kids can come if they like. It would be a real big deal for them."

Stopping, Rosanne turned around again. "What is this place, anyway?"

"This is the Avalon nightclub. Tonight is our grand opening. A lot of celebrities will be here. You could come if you like. Your kids and husband as well."

Roseanne pulled out her phone. "Have you ever heard of Justeen Timberlakes?" she asked someone on the other end of the line.

"Ask them if they know who Cameron Diaz is, and would they like to meet her too?"

"Apparently yes," she replied, holding the phone away from her ear.

"Well, they're gonna need a place to sit."

Julio had returned from his bootleg mission, and was now loading in cases of vodka, tequila, and champagne. We were T minus ten minutes and counting. I motioned to the carpet guys to unroll the carpet.

"*Atornillar los zapatos*," I shouted. "*Ir sobre ellos.*"

And without hesitation, that's exactly what they did—they rolled the carpet right over my Chuck Taylors.

It was now 8:55, and the pre-festivities outside had concluded. I grabbed Barney and instructed him to hold the doors for fifteen minutes, then open.

"But the carpet still isn't dry," he said.

"I'll figure something out," I replied. *With people trampling over it, it won't be going anywhere.* It was more of a hope than a belief.

At that moment, Julio reappeared. "Boss, the guns aren't working."

Soda guns work on a system of syrup combined with water, the end result being what I would consider barely passable 7 Up or cranberry juice. It costs a club about seventy percent less than using bottled soda or juices. This savings comes with its drawbacks: the lines can get clogged with syrup, which blocks the water from mixing in or throws off the calibration of water added, resulting in watered-down liquid mixed into your iced-down drink. If you ask for just a Coke in almost any club, you'll notice that the taste is off. That's because you're drinking the result of two-month-old syrup and tap water mixed through a plastic tube.

"Not working . . . at all?"

"*Muerto*, and no time to fix them."

We stood staring at each other, evoking Murphy's Law, until Julio took a dollar bill out of his pocket.

"*Donde hay voluntad hay una camino.*"

I just stood there, puzzled.

"*La maquina expendedora.*"

The vending machine. Gotta love Julio.

"Get three hundred one-dollar bills from the bartenders' change for now," I motioned, catching on.

After negotiating the dollar bills from two bartenders who were not about to give them up easily, Julio made his way to the employee soda vending machine downstairs.

Barney was calling. "We've got too many people here waiting to get in. LAPD just showed up and are threatening to close us if we can't control the crowd . . . and Jenn is melting down."

"Buy ten minutes."

Back in the lobby, the carpet was down, and my Jimmy Hoffa sneakers were gone for good (years later, when replacing the carpet, someone would make a baffling discovery). Grabbing our head of security, Thick Rick (the West Coast version of The Mountain), I instructed him to gather all his people. Minutes later, fifteen large men and two not-so-large women were walking randomly around the lobby, like a conductor-less marching band.

The lobby itself looked like a looted English estate, with its bare white walls and lone chandelier. Spotting the lack of overhead lighting, which had yet to be rehung due to the still-wet primer, Rick and I began plugging in whatever we could. One good thing about white is that it reflects light, and three minutes later, we had a glowing blue-and-purple effect. I ran back to check on the bars and was met with the sight of an impromptu assembly loading three hundred cans of soda into coolers. We were as ready as we would ever be.

"Open doors," I instructed Barney two minutes later.

Immediately, the anticipated attack began. In this case it was a Black Friday assault, but instead of "thirty percent off everything" it was an hour of free alcohol. The appeal and frantic passion surrounding open bars has always amazed me. Giving away free drinks is a Nightclub 101 tactic for getting people to arrive early.

The idea is, by giving someone a certain number of free drinks (say two) in an allotted time frame, the cost to the club is around $6, including the two cups. The bartenders are instructed to pack those drinks with ice and serve them in smaller, designated cups. Now, you've spent $6 to get someone there earlier than they would have otherwise arrived, and they have already begun their drinking for the night. If they buy two additional drinks in the next hour at $10 per drink, the venue will net $14. Subtract the open bar cost of $6, and you've got $8 of additional profit during what would normally be the slowest period of the night. With eight hundred people, that's $6,400 net income. If you do this forty times a year, that's $256,000 of "found" money. Not too shabby.

This would all work as planned, if not for the reality of nightlife. People try to order five drinks at a time. They complain about the drinks being too small until the bartender is forced to give them another shot of alcohol in an effort to move them away from the bar as the angry mob behind them demands service.

Of course, if someone behind them sees this, they'll lodge the same complaint, starting a chain reaction that screws up the schematics entirely. Those same people who line up for open bars could, if money and quality of life are a determining factor, just buy a bottle of quality vodka at the store, mix it with fresh juice and maybe even a muddle if they want to be fancy, and have a few drinks at home before they arrive. It would certainly be cheaper and less stressful. Of course, I'm not going to tell them that.

As the stampede swarmed toward the bars, the other group of people arriving sauntered in through an entrance marked "VIP." These were the celebrities and others deemed "guest list-worthy," with one of their main reasons for attending being to be seen. As the "general" crowd (termed the GA for General Admission) rushed toward the booze free-for-all, the celebrities and their entourages went through a much different process.

Make no mistake, this "elite" group was expecting the same thing as the GA group who arrived for the first hour: everything for free, just with a more personal touch. Ushered into a specially designated VIP area, they sucked down the same free drinks (but in glassware) as their unwashed counterparts, smugly observing the battlefield just feet away.

The VIP entrance consisted of a set of eight ropes and stanchions leading to a fifty-foot entry alley under a Baroque-style awning. On the left of the alley was the building itself; to the right, a closely guarded high iron fence with a "for those in the know" sliding gate. This gate was to be used for one sole purpose: to allow the A-list celebrities to enter and exit, thereby avoiding the denoted B and C groups forced to wait behind the ropes until recognized and granted entry.

The alphabetical grading system was calculated by a complex series of factors, the main one being relevance. The grading process itself started with a general hierarchy, consisting of:

A-List
Rock Stars

Movie Stars

Top Pro Athletes

B-List
Executive Producers

Models and Designers

Television Stars

C-List
Producers

Comedians

Pro Athletes

Reality Show Stars

Porn Stars

Other: Musicians, Restaurant Owners and Chefs, Stylists, etc.

To complicate matters, the overlap between groups was a gray area, with status open to interpretation. Larry David and Seth MacFarlane were considered A-list, while Macaulay Culkin (whose latest film, *Party Monster*, had just been released with him playing the lead character—Michael

Alig) was a C. Within the groups were even more specific grades of de-marcation. For example, Mick Jagger was an A+ (NFU), meaning No-Fuck-Up, kid glove treatment.

The A+'s were almost always referred to by first name only: Jack, Will, Shaq, Gwen. When you got down to the C's, they were referred to by association: the slutty one from *Big Brother*, a producer on *Batman*. Apparently, an A+ could not be seen waiting in line with an A, who of course could not be seen with the B's and C's. Within the B through C groups, there were B's who couldn't be seen with C's, C's who thought they were B's, and self-delusional C's who categorized themselves as A's and expected a perfunctory welcome through the St. Peter's entrance.

When the VIP list for the night was complete and sent to the front door, it determined not only who would enter through the VIP entrance, but in what order. This Egocentric Dewey Decimal System was left with the gatekeeper or, as you know him or her, the doorman. We had a good one at Avalon Hollywood, a sort of niche Proust in the nightlife world who, at birth, was given the name Fabrizio, and was now known simply as Fab. As such, he was destined for the job.

Becoming Fab, in both the figurative and literal sense, was not some-thing that happened overnight. It took years of working the doors at Oscar parties and movie premieres, where he became increasingly recog-nized. He was a student of the subtleties needed to operate amongst the narcissistically inclined. Taking his position just inside the velvet ropes, he was flanked by his trusted door security team, who existed to enforce his creed. *You're not entering tonight. I can only do four of your six guests.*

If any of his proclamations were not followed, if you lingered at the door negotiating or tried to brush past with your six guests, you were stepping into security territory. Door security are often versions of six-foot-two gym fanatics who, by a simple nod of their head, can intimidate a would-be violator into quick reconsideration. Their battle stance is one of hands crossed below the waist, head cocked slightly to the left, with a blank stare off into the distance. If you ask them for help—"Is this the guest list line?" "Where do I go to pick up tickets?"—they will break form only to point matter-of-factly, and then return to character.

At times, Fab's job required him to take initiative. Truth is, due to his knowledge of the players, he really didn't need to depend on the list, using it more as a means to *deny* VIP entry to the B's and C's (and occasionally an A). Whenever he actually inquired if the group in question waiting outside the ropes was on the list, it was the pre-planned kiss of death, with the rehearsed reply from the person holding the clipboard being: "I don't see their name here." When the group was informed of their rejection and told that they needed to enter through the GA entrance, this added insult to injury that was socially unbearable.

"I know I'm on the list, I called this morning," the group's incensed leader would demand, giving a nervous, reassuring look to his friends. "Let me see it, there must be some mistake."

And, most likely, he was right. But when Fab made the split-second decision to "re-interpret" the list, he usually had a good reason. If a pro athlete appeared with six male friends who were clearly on the verge of being out of control, that was a problem. If a notoriously obnoxious producer, to the point of being shunned, had somehow talked his way onto the list during the day, that was also a problem. This resulted in threats of violence with punches sometimes being thrown, leading to security stepping in to restore order.

Fab made it a rule to never throw a punch or grab anyone, and understood one thing better than most, which set him apart. Knowing who to let in is one thing; making sure they have a great time after they enter is another. As a social mixologist, Fab was keenly aware of who was inside the VIP area at all times. An Owen Wilson combined with a Vince Vaughn could make for a great party, but throw in a Scott Baio and his ten friends, and you could have a completely different recipe.

At around 11:00 PM, after a long day of finalizing plans, claiming territory, and satisfying special requests, it would inevitably happen—the dreaded "random walk-up." A not-to-be-let-in celeb would show up at the VIP entrance, very much wanting to be let in. The "nots" fell into two basic categories: your one-hundred-percent nots (or "never nots") and your fifty-fifty nots ("maybe nots"). The fifty-fifty caused the most pain and suffering, as their appearance at the door would usually cause an impromptu behind-the-scenes debate.

Hugh Hefner was one such person. Having a seventy-eight-year-old running, or technically staggering, around the VIP area with three made-to-order TV girlfriends did not go over well with Lynne, who held the coveted job of VIP manager. On a daily basis leading up to the opening, Lynne had threatened to resign if anything was done to affect the status that both she and the club were hoping to attain. She was the one responsible for making sure those who entered were "taken care of," which mostly translated into fielding requests for more free drinks.

On the other hand, Hef *was* Hef, so how about a little old-school respect? This heated, pro football draft day debate usually went on for ten minutes until a decision was made. Poor Hef—could I really leave him hanging, subjecting him to the whims of first-born millennials after all that *Playboy* had done for me growing up?

To complicate matters, Hef's "assistant" was complaining that he had reached out to the club, to Aykroyd personally, who had agreed and apparently forgotten to put Hef and the femmebots on the list, along with two private bodyguards, Hef's publicist, and an additional plus-three. This break in protocol was causing a near meltdown for my assistant, who was under strict orders not to take any calls from Hef's assistant, a fifty-plus, bit-too-greasy Dicky-Doo who was both reviled and tolerated.[16] His mode of operating was based on a very simple quid pro quo: do this for me and I'll get you a Golden Ticket . . . an invite to the Mansion.

The official line was that you needed to be one of the "girls" or a

---

16 "Dicky-Doo" was coined by my sister in Memphis. It technically translates as a male whose lower stomach region protrudes a greater distance from his body then his penis. As in: *When Bud looked down and was unable to see his ankles, he realized he had become a chartered member in the Royal Order of the Dicky-Doo.*

personal friend of Hef's to get invited. The underling reality was that the majority of the invitations were getting pimped out by Dicky to distinct demographics: men like himself who had something to trade, or new-to-Hollywood actresses who saw these parties as a way to find an agent, meet Jack Nicholson, or advance their careers in numerous ways.

I appeared outside like the second coming of the Great Gazoo. There was Dicky, front and center outside the rope. Calling my name, for God's sake, as if we were long-lost college roomies. *Your main man?* Dicky was implicating me in front of everyone, which in turn was causing guilt by association. *Can't just walk to the front ropes and expose myself further.*

It was at that moment that I switched to my alternative form of communication: the hand gesture. This primitive yet affective way of delivering information was something I was starting to master, though I was still in my advanced grasshopper stage. Assertive and commanding, its only flaw was its potential for misinterpretation.

In this line of work, where the backdrop can be filled with louder-than-humanly-acceptable noise that makes a simple verbal exchange impossible, "talk to the hand," as the phrase goes, can be a matter of practicality. But, like all great orators come to understand, the devil is in the details. Nuance and timing are key.

Raising my hand high from where I stood without looking up, I responded by putting up my index finger. Now, here's the critical part—I kept both my finger and my hand still, moving only slightly back and forth at the wrist. Not moving the wrist would give the indication of "number one" as if I had just won the Super Bowl. Moving the finger side to side would have sent the message "no, no, gotta stop that." Next, non-verbal acknowledgment comes into play. Look up for a split-second, as if the huddle you're involved in is of grave concern. Then smile, looking slightly pained, but not too pained.

All of this translated to:

Kindly wait one minute while I sort out an issue that doesn't involve you. We are the hottest spot in town and everyone wants to get in, but I will personally take care of you. You are good enough, smart enough, and, dog-gone it, people pretend they like you.

Done, transmission received by Dicky, indicated by a mouthed "okay" and a head nod.

I had bought another five to seven minutes.

LAXIOM #10
The Steve Leave
(develop body language to manage your time).
When I've determined that a meeting needs to wrap up, I give a cordial smile and extend my hand. If that doesn't work, I've been known to just turn and leave. You would be surprised at the amount of time you can save in a day just by eliminating rambling.

Jumping back into the four-person scrum, all sides had drawn their lines in the sand. Lynne was holding her job over the situation, while the hostess who would have to recalibrate the seating chart also fell into the "nay" category. Fab and the assistant were in as a "yes," one being a little more sensitive to Hollywood tradition and the other just wanting the whole mishigas to be done.

I weighed in, making it clear that I understood both sides of the coin. Time was of the essence, and moving them away from the rope was the first priority. Having Hef's entourage blocking those of a more vaulted distinction could ruin us forever. This got the attention of Lynne, who reluctantly nodded in agreement. *Good start. But how, and to where?*

"We will bring the entire group in at one time, *but* have them shielded by security," I said, trying the idea on for size. This way, other guests would not be able to determine who was entering, and the scene of seven people surrounded by another eight staff members could serve as a PR vehicle. Who is that . . . Fall Out Boy? The cast of *Arrested Development*? The assistant would need to accompany the caravan on the side. In the event that a clubber-necker inquired, she could simply nod her head "no" and raise her hand, palm facing the inquisitor: *Don't ask, these people are too important and need to be whisked upstairs before the spell is broken and they turn into pumpkins.*

Fifteen minutes later, the same sequence of events would be replicated when Leonardo DiCaprio showed up outside the ropes with his posse, six guys looking just off the set of an early Guy Ritchie movie and notorious for their unruly behavior.

With Hef, Leo, and their entourages now tucked away safely inside under the watchful eye of security, it was just me, Thick Rick, and Fab outside. That's when I spotted Roseanne rounding the corner at full speed, with what appeared to be a youth soccer team in tow.

"Made it," she said, catching her breath. "This is my husband, Jake, and our three kids, Lilly, Jennifer, and Bennet. And those are my two nieces, Gwen and Norah."

Oh, oh. This is more than I bargained for.

"Welcome," I said, shaking Jake's hand. "Thanks for coming."

"Where is he, where is he? Inside there?" Lilly and Jennifer were shrieking, their eyes affixed to the front doors.

"Yup," I assured them, fielding "what the fuck" looks from the two next to me. "Give me a moment."

Stepping back to ponder the situation, I had what I would call a "Grinch moment." You know, when Cindy-Lou comes downstairs and discovers the Grinch in her family's living room. I needed a story fast, but unlike the Grinch, simple lying wasn't going to cut it. How was I going to let five underage, excited-as-Christmas-Eve kids into a nightclub to meet someone who had no idea they were coming?

Taking Fab aside, I whispered, "This is a special needs family who are here to see their favorite singer, Justin Timberlake. Is he inside yet?"

Now, I felt really bad saying this. I justified it as being true in a sense, and quickly committed to finding a way to redeem myself at a later date.

"He just got here ten minutes ago," Fab replied. "They sat him stage left."

I then found Thick Rick. "Is there a place this special group can sit?" I asked him. "It really needs to be stage left," I added, insinuating that their special need had something to do with the location (again, true-*ish*). "And it is technically their furniture."

This got a rise of pride out of Roseanne, who was still trying to figure out exactly what all of this was. "So, what happens inside?" she asked.

"You're about to find out."

And with that, Rick came out with one of the hostesses, who whisked the group inside just as Hef was on his way out, looking exhausted.

"You okay, Hef?" I asked.

Hef just smiled and gave me a pained wave. One of his bodyguards gathered him into his arms and carted him away, like a passed-out bride being carried across the threshold on her wedding night.

Heading back across the lobby, I stopped just long enough to bounce up and down on the carpet before making my way through the now-packed crowd. I took in the scene of exuberance as over two thousand people mingled and danced (yes, actually danced) to the mash-up of DJ AM. I thought back to how, almost three years earlier, I'd seen this place for the first time and envisioned something that was now right there in front of me, alive and breathing. The feeling of accomplishment was overwhelming.

Regardless of which door they had entered from, or how they'd been superficially graded at the door, everyone was brought together under a mesmerizing light show and dance floor. A's through D's, Dicky-Doos, glyphs, Hollywood types, NFU's, reps, totem polers, free-beers, dopplegangers, randoms, fifty-fifty nots, posses, Beaumont rebels, and, one could imagine, resident ghosts—they all preened, strutted, and dirty danced as one. For tonight, nightlife was the King of Hollywood, with all in attendance part of the royal court.

Ten minutes later, at 11:58, three black town cars pulled up and out popped Prince's Rep, who immediately began asking for me at the door. I made my way back outside one last time, determined to catch the bullshit artist in mid-con. As the new guy in town, this was my litmus test, and no Hollywood slickster was going to pull one over on me. As expected, a group of ten or so people were waiting at the door. Rep was in full conversation with Fab, who pointed toward me as I charged out.

"Bro, thanks so much for taking care of us," said Rep.

I barely heard him through the ringing in my ears, picking up speed as I approached my tormenting matador. He stepped aside as I semi-lunged forward.

And then I saw Him—Prince, calmly waiting. He took a step back to avoid being run over by someone twice his size.

"You okay, man?" He asked, barely audible. "Good to see you."

I blinked, overwhelmed with surprise. "Yeah," I said. "It's been a Hollywood kind of night. Glad you could make it."

With cases of champagne in tow, the ultimate A+ NFU disappeared inside, but not before looking back over his shoulder to do a double-take at my socked feet, giving me an approving hand gesture.

The cumulative experience of the night did not fulfill my quest for perfection; it felt more like we had just (barely) gotten through it. The indigo bunting would have to wait. In the end, Jenn was able to make an intro to Justin, who was more than happy to sign Roseanne's family's posters. Roseanne found me thirty minutes later to say thanks, and ended up discounting the furniture twenty-five percent with sixty days to pay. Prince never played that night, but months later he returned to do one of the best shows I've ever seen.

A week later, I wrote to the Goodwill offering the venue for free if they wanted to do any fundraising, and donated $1,000 in the name of Avalon. No one ever mentioned or asked why I had spent the night in my socks, and Prince was the only one who seemed to notice. That night was a reminder that, in nightlife, you never know what or whom is coming around the corner, so best be prepared—even if that means having an extra pair of Chucks nearby.

CHAPTER 13

BUILD IT AND THEY WILL COME (OR SO THE STORY GOES)

"It's all in the mind."
—GEORGE HARRISON

W hen Starbucks started expanding across the country, their stated vision was "a store on every corner." Yes, demographic research was done on how many potential coffee drinkers were within walking distance, and their habits. And yes, there was wisdom in not allowing your competitors into the market by buying up real estate. After a while, however, neighborhoods began to figure out Starbucks' takeover plan, circulating petitions to prevent them from opening new locations. Starbucks had gone from neighborhood darling to evil empire in a matter of a few short years.

During the same period, Starbucks' per-store sales began to decline. As latte enthusiasm continued to drop, corporate heads identified the problem, which was already understood by store employees: customers were buying less and less into the Starbucks story. Same (exact) stores, same helpful staff, same coffee, only now even more convenient to purchase. What had changed?

Perception.

Being a boutique coffee maker out of Seattle had formed the basis of their brand. Seattle was perceived as the perfect place to produce great coffee, based on an odd mixture of its rainy climate and reputation as a hipster mecca. I mean, all those drunk rockers need rock star coffee the day after, right?

At first, communities were thrilled when their hometowns were chosen for Starbucks locations. But then something happened.

"Coffeeistas," the initial consumers to be sold on the brand, began complaining: "Wait a minute, if we're drinking the finest beans hand-picked by personal friends of Kurt Cobain and ground under the watchful eye of Dave Grohl, how can that be happening in a thousand places at once?" Once the Starbucks brand came into question, the Coffeeistas moved on, buying into new stories of competitors that Starbucks themselves had created.

Whether it's coffee, fashion, cosmetics, or nightlife, people aren't only buying an espresso, a dress, eyeliner, or beer. They're buying the story behind it.

With Michael Bloomberg taking over as mayor, the climate in NYC nightlife changed dramatically overnight. Mega-clubs were shut down and nightlife was dominated by lounges, driven by the concept of "bottle service," the ultimate massaging of the male ego. These reimagined bars were laid out as simple open spaces without a defined dance floor, allowing guests to view each other—a key element. Full bottles of vodka, whiskey, and champagne were available beginning at $350 a pop. Upon ordering one or three, four sequined-mini-skirt servers would deliver it to your table, each carrying a large, custom-lit sparkler. The more bottles you ordered, the longer this procession went on, the idea being that others in the room would take note and be overly impressed with the show.

This is what nightlife had come to in the world's greatest city after dark? My ten years of work gone up in smoke, with nothing remaining? I couldn't stand to let it go on.

With Boston and L.A. needing less day-to-day attention (or so I had convinced myself), at the first outward sign of my latent Yertle Syndrome, I wanted back in.

Finding real estate in NYC can be a daunting task, multiplied by a hundred when looking for a nightclub location. Neighborhoods all have varying and often complicated zoning restrictions, making it all but impossible to obtain the necessary licenses to operate legally. If you can find an area that *is* properly zoned, the actual licensing process can take well over a year, with no guarantees. This doesn't take into account the inevitable elderly person in the neighborhood who makes it their life's work to fight you every step of the way, with nothing but time on their hands to do so.

While all of this is going on, you'll be paying rent to the tune of $80,000 per month, along with attorney and license fees. The prospect of risking over $500,000 just to get to the point where construction can begin, quickly led me to an alternative plan of attack. To avoid this risk, with its potential for financial disaster, was to search for the nightlife holy grail: a location that is properly zoned, with a liquor and dance license intact. And I knew right where to look.

Since being shut down, Limelight had made a feeble attempt to reopen, operated by the landlord and his cousin. That lasted less than three months, and since that time, the location had remained vacant. After some prolonged negotiation, I hammered out an agreement for the property, with a six-month timeline for opening.

The day after signing the lease, I received a call. "Is this Mr. Adelman, the person who just signed a lease on Twentieth Street? Just calling to let you know you are never going to open that location back up as a nightclub."

"Who is this?"

"I'm a member of the community board, and that's all you need to know."

Community boards in NYC were starting to wield increasingly more influence over businesses in their designated neighborhoods. They usually consisted of eight to ten members who had been voted in by the other members. The majority of the boards had been self-appointed decades ago with a mission statement of protecting their community interests, at a time when little formal attention was being paid to neighborhood issues.

The Flatiron Community Board, which I now fell under, had become one of the most powerful over the last decade, coinciding with the accelerated development of Chelsea. Absent of any residential living for decades, the area was now a hotspot for condo developers. With condos came more retail to serve those new tenants, starting a perpetual cycle.

Community boards had no official standing—that is to say, they did not determine licenses nor grant any other official approvals themselves. Their power came from their recommendations. If they didn't want you there, they would exert political pressure (often via high-profile members) on those who granted licenses to influence their decisions. In the case of Limelight, the location was still number-one on their hit list due to its sordid history. Removing blight was at the top of the board's agenda, and Chelsea condo owners shouted and screamed about one thing: their property values.

Thousands of club-goers taking over parking, drinking on the street, and pissing on their cars was their worst-case scenario. What the condo owners never mentioned was that it happened to be Limelight that first set up shop in a neighborhood where, at the time, no one wanted to *be*, let alone live. It was our club that first introduced thousands to the neighborhood, which spurred other businesses, and then developers, to follow. Now, it had become a case of biting the hand that fed you.

I can understand not wanting the chaos of a large club in one's neighborhood. But the fact remained: the new fancy, condo-owning community board members had moved there *knowing* the club was there. You can't move to South Florida and then bitch about the humidity in August. I'll take that back; you *can*, but you shouldn't think people are obligated to listen to you. I had factored in the community board as an entity to be dealt with, but I had not factored threats into the equation.

One month later, I was at the monthly Flatiron meeting with my attorney, Donald, who had attended dozens of such meetings in the past. His advice was to be humble and take the abuse with a smile, which I was willing to do. But I felt that bringing along some moral support might help the situation.

Walking into the meeting room on the second floor of a renovated brownstone, it became clear that this was no ragtag group. They had their own affluently furnished offices, dominated by a common area now set up to replicate a Senate hearing. Ten chairs were equally positioned behind a long table, facing out over a smaller table with two chairs, behind which there was seating for around a hundred people. We took our seats in the back of the room and waited as the room filled up with affluent interest-seekers. An agenda was taped up, with us being third on the list. After sitting through hearings for a new barista parlor and a yoga studio, it was our turn.

I made the call to my extended defense team. As we took our seats behind the testimony table, it became obvious that we were the main show. As the purpose of our being there was formally announced, boos began to emanate from the peanut gallery, followed by outcries.

"This cannot happen."

"It will destroy the neighborhood . . . again."

As the designated chairman called for order, a group of over two dozen began filing in, taking their places around the room. My stakeholders in the situation were not condo owners, but employees who had lost their jobs due to the Giuliani crackdown and were excited about getting back to work, doing what they loved. This consisted of drag queens, Club Kids, dancers, DJs, and their friends living nearby, and they had waited years for this opportunity.

"We've gotten rid of these people twice already," said a board member who bore an uncanny resemblance to Janet Reno.

Big mistake.

"Who are you calling *these people*, honey?" the leader of the drag

contingent shot back from across the room, trace-snapping a large "Z"
into the air. At over six feet tall and dressed for work to the hilt, she was
quite an imposing and fabulous sight.

This caught the board lady by surprise. She immediately froze.

"Wellll . . . cat got your tongue?" continued the spokesqueen, followed by what sounded like a distorted cat hissing sound.

"What I meant was, people coming out at all hours of the night and
destroying the neighborhood," came a feeble reply.

Do yourself a favor and just shut up.

"Does this neighborhood look destroyed to you? I didn't think
so. I've been coming to this neighborhood long before you moved in,
sweetheart, and let me tell you, *these people* made this neighborhood."
She pointed dramatically to her sisters in the room, one by one, who acknowledged her by blowing a kiss.

This brought about a cheer from the entire contingent, followed by
Club Kids revealing items they had deemed appropriate for the occasion,
including a blow-up sex doll with the words "Blow Me" painted on it and
a sign that read, "Don't Fuck with Me—I Know Where you Live. It Used
to Be My Rent-Controlled Apt."

"We *are* the neighborhood," one of them chimed in, looking more
than a little out of place in his cut-off Daisy Dukes and t-shirt, accentuated by a dozen golden chains and a Three Musketeer hat.

This brought even louder cheers from the crowd.

"We need to hear directly from Mr. Adelman on this matter," said
one of the inquisitors, grabbing the microphone from her bitch-slapped
colleague.

Tapping the microphone while seated, I proceeded to make my case
in John Dean-like fashion. "First, thanks for inviting me here to discuss
how we might all work together to improve the Flatiron District. I do realize that there have been problems in the past that led to your concerns,
of which I am very sensitive to. But no matter what happens here today,
this project is going to move forward regardless of what your opinions

are, as you have no authority to stop it. The question we need to answer is, are we going to work in opposition as we move forward, or can we find a better way?"

"Mr. Adelman, we have many tools at our disposal to block this, including the courts."

"That may be true, but the same money that would be spent on baseless lawsuits could be spent on additional security or paying people to clean up the streets after we close. If your goal is indeed to put me out of business before I open, then you are simply creating a path for another 'me' to come forward. What you really need to do is decide if I'm the best 'me.'"

This facilitated another back-and-forth exchange, in which the board members were crushed at every turn. The "nightlife alliance" would fight to the end.

LAXIOM #11
Don't be afraid of some ass-grabbing.
Some view "pulling ideas out of their ass" as a last-minute, impromptu, and sometimes desperate response. I trust it as experience meeting creativity with some urgency thrown in, making it the perfect mix for productive results.

The community board voted 12–0, opposing the opening of the club. This would have ended things, had it not been for the fact that the location already had its necessary licenses. Using every trick in their privileged book, the board technically opposed the liquor license being transferred to me (or any other me). The community board opposition was duly noted, but a legal reason was still required for the license not to be transferred (such as the transferee being a convicted felon). Weeks later, the New York State Liquor Authority approved the transfer, given its grail immunity.

Nightlife: 1
The Man: 0

The challenge the beleaguered location now faced was its new "story."

The owners of NYC's lounges, which included Lotus, Bungalow 8, and Moomba, had sold club-goers on the mega-club closings with a "good riddance" mentality. "Who wants to go to a club with all those people you don't know, many of whom are not like you?" they said. "You need to be *only* with people as elite as yourself." It was nightlife political propaganda, pushing an "us vs. them" mentality.

Before, the "us" group would pay $20 for the cover charge and $6 for a beer. Now they were required to pay $500 for the privilege to sit at a table with five of their friends and be forced to pay for two bottles of alcohol at $350 each. This, for the honor of being surrounded exclusively by others in their "us" group. The new version of a nightclub was a place where the price of entry was an insecurity deep enough that it could be monetized.

I did understand this new incarnation and money-making initiative. After all, being successful in the nightlife business is not an easy proposition. Let me clarify—being profitable over time is all-consuming, and anything but a given. Known for its high attrition rate, opening a nightclub, bar, or live music venue is one thing; *staying* open is quite another. Think of what it would be like to have to reinvent your job or business on a weekly basis, coming to work every Monday knowing you had to develop a new marketing plan and urgently revamp your product. This is the task facing major nightlife businesses.

The process of constantly having to book the next DJ or band, and come up with new events to draw in customers, can be grueling and stressful, with the possibility that a few bad weeks could put you in dire straits. Out of approximately 125 nightclubs that operate legally in NYC on an annual basis, the average shelf life is less than two years. Under original owners Ian Schrager and Steve Rubell, Studio 54 lasted less than three years, even with all the press and celebrity lore chronicling the likes of Cher, Andy Warhol, Michael Jackson, Elton John, and Diana Ross.[17]

Another major attrition factor is the cost of actually operating. Beyond

17 In 1981, one year after closing, Studio 54 reopened under new owner Mark Fleischman, but it was never embraced like the original (see: *Hangover 2*).

the price tag of securing a location, the amount paid for insurance can be crippling, leading to many venues being underinsured. This is a recipe for disaster if you have to pay out for an incident, be it a slip and fall or patron fights where the venue is blamed in some manner—and it always is, resulting in a settlement. *I guess it was my fault that we served you beer in a bottle instead of a plastic cup, tempting you to break it over the guy's head who was hitting on your girlfriend.* In addition to insurance, constant repairs and tax rates on alcohol can quickly cut into margins.

Major cities have the highest rate of nightclub closings due to the number of inexperienced would-be operators from outside the industry, usually driven by vanity or ego. They come to places like NYC because, as everyone knows, if you can make it there, you can make it anywhere. I mean, how hard can it be? Find a location; hire an interior designer who will listen to my (more often bad than not) ideas, along with some sexy bartenders; book some DJs and bands; sit back and count the money.

For decades, Hollywood, and more recently social media, have glamorized nightlife, at times portraying clubs as alluring enclaves for celebrity clientele with exclusive entrance policies and depraved all-night parties. Owners who are new to the business soon come to find that running a venue is not for the narcissistic. It involves wearing the multiple hats of entrepreneur, deal-maker, ringmaster, guidance counselor, and music soothsayer, to name just a few. The long hours spent interacting with people in different states of drunkenness, sexual frustration, self-denial, depression, euphoria, and just about every other human condition wears on you, over time.

This dynamic has led to some spectacularly flawed NYC clubs. Like the Big Kahuna, the surfer-themed tidal wave just north of SoHo designed to reach out to the Wall Street crowd. And Kaos, the cold spot of the early '90s that featured a replica of a plane crashing into its one-story roof, in an apparent attempt to allure those who have witnessed disasters.[18]

---

18 These clubs, and ones like them, were to nightlife as the movie *Hook* was to the film industry— they just shouldn't have happened.

In 2019, nightclubs and bars accounted for over $27 billion in revenue in the U.S. alone, while concert ticket revenue reached $8 billion, employing well over 650,000 people. The high-profile nightlife rise in Las Vegas over the last decade has widened accessibility and exposure to dance music and extravagant nightclub experiences, with over twenty million people visiting a casino nightclub or bar in 2019. Put succinctly, nightlife as an industry is big business, in spite of its attrition and unique challenges.

Most people's first work experience in nightlife is via bartending, which comes with the perk of having your days free. Thousands of college students take advantage of this opportunity annually as a way to support themselves. By learning how to make drinks and operate a point of sale, they now have a skill that can be used at any time in their lives as an income generator. Others move beyond bartending to become a manager, and some even move up the industry ranks to become partners in a business. Then, years after first being introduced to nightlife, they finally have their own business . . . which, on average will close in less than two years. A sad ending to an otherwise happy story.

Nightlife has always been characterized by a follow-the-leader mentality, an ongoing need to experience and be a part of whatever has been determined as the next big thing. This goes for club owners as well as patrons. With lounges in NYC now in vogue, the music of choice had moved solely to a version of the mash-up, with club-going EDM enthusiasts held in contempt by the "us" group. They were portrayed as unwashed, Ecstasy-taking ravers, dressed in an unacceptable manner and listening to unsuitable music.

A strategy was now needed to reverse the last three years and bring club-goers back together. It would need to involve word of mouth, with the story being both easy to understand and communicate, creating a place for everyone in nightlife society. This led to our battle cry: "For the People."

The press would also be needed to push our message, and the history of Limelight still had to be factored in. For starters, both the press and club-goers shared an affinity for the word "new." Limelight had been around for twenty years, and most every New Yorker of age (and countless underage) had been there, done that.

The structure itself had been given landmark status as a church, meaning I couldn't alter the exterior beyond what amounted to paint and lighting. Inside, the foot-thick stone walls were impractical to rip down, leaving limited design options. A major concern was that if we invited people to the new Limelight space and not enough work had been done to alter it significantly, word on the street would be, "They just added some paint—same ol' place I've already been to a dozen times." The often-employed nightlife renovation plan of "smoke and mirrors" was not going to work here.

Instead of focusing on redesign and tearing out walls (which would also invite inspections), we would need to concentrate on *orientation*. The entrance would now be made into an exit. Where you once paid admissions would now become an added room. The DJ booth would become a VIP seating area. By re-orienting the space, we would be able to create a new feel for the venue and generate that "wow" factor.

With the design plans complete, I set out to complete our story. I drafted my thoughts in an initial press release, which began as follows:

PRESS RELEASE
Welcome to a World at Night
The Return of the Mega-Club: Avalon to open in NYC

New York City, (August 15) – On September 10th, the mega-club returns to New York City with the debut of Avalon at 220 West Twentieth Street. Recognizing that NYC nightclubs over the decades have been incubators for creativity and an escape mechanism for millions worldwide, the opening of Avalon NYC will mark the start of a new era for nightlife in the City That Never Sleeps. Celebrating diversity and offering something for everyone, it will feature an ultra-modern design, state-of-the-art visual and sound experience, four dance floors, and ten rooms for exploration, including a "club within a club," the Spider Club. On a nightly basis, Avalon will host a lineup of top international DJs, including Tiësto, Carl Cox, Sasha, and John Digweed, making it NYC's home for the best dance music on the planet.

Now that I felt we had something to tell the press, we needed to reach out to them, which was usually done with the help of a broker: the publicist. A nightlife PR person functions as the middleman between the club and the journalist/editor, ensuring that stories are not only printed, but done so with maximum flattery. This process mainly involves trading favors with a mutually beneficial outcome, or, as I've come to call it, the "here comes the *but*" or the "*but I*":

I'll write a story about your client . . . **but** *I'll need an interview with your other client.*

I'll give you an exclusive on my client . . . **but** *I'll need a feature on my other client.*

The bigger the publicist and the writer (based on their publication), the bigger the *buts*. If a publicist has multiple in-demand clients, they have *but* leverage. To get the story you want comes down to *but* versus *but*, and it's best to be swinging around the biggest one.

The problem with having a publicist with the biggest *buts* is that they also have the most high-profile clients . . . and you run the risk of getting lost in the shuffle. Not to mention their high fee of $10,000 to $15,000 per month, with agreements requiring a minimum of $30,000 per commitment. After talking to multiple big-*but* publicists, I felt it better to bring in a young upstart to work in-house at half the cost, armed with the "*and if*," a close relative of the "*but I*":

I need a positive feature for the new club . . . **and if** *you're able to come down, I'll have a $500 tab set up for you at the bar . . .* **and if** *you ever want to see a show, just let me know, and I'll have tickets waiting for you at the door.*

Entertainment writers are swamped with sales pitches every day. Getting one of them on the phone is not easy . . . but if a nightclub is involved, the chances increase dramatically. No if, ands, or buts about it.

Naming the club Avalon, with Avalons already established in Boston and Hollywood, was debated for weeks. NYC was known as the place where brands were *created*, not where they expanded. Also, the concept of a nightclub chain was something Clubistas might not stand for. Walking a fine line and with the Starbucks story ingrained in my psyche, it was decided that we would create a third Avalon, based on the following:

1. Avalon was an established brand, which could help eliminate the stigma of an unstable location. No one wants to invest time in a place that's going to close a few months after it opens.

2. As the third location, we would not yet be perceived as an evil empire.

3. We had built up a relationship with DJ agents who could now sell their clients on playing three of the biggest markets in the U.S., with the consistency of dealing with just one group.

Avalon NYC opened to great fanfare, with over five thousand people clamoring to gain entry. The NYPD to shut down Sixth Avenue for six blocks in an attempt at crowd control. The club quickly gained a celebrity following, with the likes of Britney Spears and Jared Leto attending in the weeks to come. Britney returned months later to perform a blindfolded, risqué striptease performance that drew attention worldwide, cheered on by President George W. Bush's daughters, Jenna and Barbara, a slew of Secret Service agents, and, oddly enough (but typical for NYC nightlife), Kid Rock.

Wanting to make amends with the community board, Avalon hosted a black-tie political fundraiser for the Democratic National Party, with Howard Dean as the keynote speaker. Flatiron board members mingled with familiar faces from my nightlife Alliance—who had turned black tie into "creative tie"—and with Dem elites such as Al Franken and Whoopi Goldberg, all bound together for their dislike of the current president. A new mutual respect appeared to be forming while standing on common ground.

What the neighborhood policing group was not aware of was that Howard's appearance was an homage to the days of Limelight. After he took the stage and gave his career-defining (and somewhat ending) awkward "Yeaahhh!" call to arms, the Alliance erupted in cheers, having seen this before. The board members were surprised and delighted, impressed by their political enthusiasm.[19] Howard, now playing to the crowd, repeated, "Yeaahhh Avalon!" This defined a new era for the church and put Howard Dean in the same vaulted category as Edith Fore and Gary Coleman in its annals of history.

Nightlife: 2

The Man: 0

Within two years it was clear that our story had landed, but with unintended consequences. The "return of the mega-club" had worked so well that it not only attracted customers and a resurgence in nightlife, but also drew follow-the-leader club owners from around the world wanting to cash in on the opportunity. Didn't they understand that this whole thing was just about perception?

After three years, other venues like Crobar, Mansion, and Pacha had opened, saturating the market. The cost to open these clubs from the ground up was astronomical, and with competition being what it was, they needed immediate customers, at any cost. One-hour open bars turned into three-hour ones. Getting in without paying a cover charge became the norm.

Our story had sold *too* well, to the point that there now seemed to be a branded club on every corner, making NYC nightlife a battle of attrition. Although our location set us apart, the one thing we couldn't compete with was *free*.

We would need to win this war by continually reimagining our brand

---

19 Which later made its way into pop culture as the "I Have a Scream" speech. The original translation was "Yeehawww!," later updated after clarification by Dean himself.

to stay ahead of the competition, and not fall into the trap of "giving the house away" to temporarily survive. As the hard reality of my Yertle Syndrome finally sunk in, this battle would become harder to win while keeping plates spinning in Boston and Hollywood.

By 2007, a new nightlife concept had come into vogue: the social restaurant. Until then, restaurants and clubs had never really worked in unison. Most people simply liked to eat at one place, and then move elsewhere to spend the rest of their night. *How much can you really trust nightclub food anyway?* Dining in one expansive, over-the-top designed space until 3:00 AM brought the "us" and "them" groups together in one spot.

The "us" group had also embraced DJs like Tiësto and Calvin Harris who had begun producing songs of their own, many of which became Top 40 radio hits and gave them "us" credibility. Picking up where Oakenfold left off, these same radio hits were seen as sell-outs by some of the EDM crowd, who moved on to other, more underground artists such as Skrillex and Diplo, which expanded the market for DJs even further. DJs of all kinds were now in high demand.

The fact that some were now pop stars, making them acceptable to the "us" crowd, was a nightlife paradigm change in perception only. The "us" group could now associate a name with a song that the DJ would play once during the night, amounting to ten minutes out of three hours. They played the same set they always had for the other 170 minutes. This shift meant that "us" and "them" crowds now had a rallying force: the Superstar DJ.

One night I visited Tao way up on Fifty-Eighth Street (at Madison), having been invited by one of its owners. I passed through the ornate entrance, scanning the crowd. Recognizing some Clubistas, each rising up and motioning me to join them at their tables, I gestured with a slight wave that I was fine, but thanks. With a smile, they went back to checking their phones. After all, they needed to be ready for the next big thing and be the first ones there to experience it.

It was with that hand wave that I said goodbye.

PART III
2008–2021

Avalon Singapore, New Daisy Theatre

CHAPTER 14

LEARNING TO BOW

"An American shoe designer decides to open a store in Singapore to take advantage of the retail boom there. To save on costs, he has his new shoe designs manufactured locally. Four months later, he receives his order of two thousand pairs, and upon opening the boxes discovers there is an issue. He immediately calls the manufacturer.

'There must be a mistake,' he says. 'All the pairs of shoes you sent me have two left shoes.'

'Oh, you didn't specify over the phone. The price for one left and one right is substantially more. You could always just order two thousand right shoes to match.'"

—As told to me by my taxi driver, upon my initial arrival in Singapore

W hat do you mean there's a problem?" I asked, clenching my jaw. Awaiting a response, I pressed the phone even tighter to my ear while attempting to swallow what was left of my surprisingly tasty cha siu bun, a local barbecue pork-filled delicacy I had recently discovered. (Technically it's "bao," not "bun," but I had already learned to go with bun since saying "bao" opened me up to further conversation in Cantonese and my limited vocabulary left me with only the option of awkwardly pointing to my bao-bun and uttering, "cha siu." Not quite the expected response when asked, "How is your day going?" in Cantonese.)

It's not that I thought learning the local dialect wasn't important, but I had been in Singapore for only four days, and the local language appeared to be English, or a version of it. Everyone I met spoke it in different intriguing accents but would then veer off into a mysterious dialect, leaving me to deduce how the sentence ended. Often the last word was "lah," serving as what I determined to be a stand-in for "you know what I mean?" or a drawn-out pause—something of that nature.[20] I would have time later to figure out the language thing.

"We can't agree to this and need some revisions," Jack said on the other end of the line.

Stay calm. A few corrected typos, and all will be good.

"Best if I send them to you now," he continued. "They will . . . [mysterious dialect] . . . -lah."

They will what? Be sent? Be minor? Change the entire deal?

I was able to make out the words "ass swoon sign" before Jack hung up.

My phone was dying and I needed to find my charger, fast. That would involve rummaging through my suitcase, which wasn't exactly meticulously packed due to my last-minute rush to the airport for my flight back to Los Angeles. Once located—in the last compartment I checked, of course—the next issue was finding an outlet.

Ass swoon sign?

Initially, I'd been enjoying my time in the Singapore Airlines Gold VIP Lounge at Singapore's Changi Airport. It was considered one of, if not *the* world's best airline, lounge, and airport. It was not a place where hectic carry-on searches appeared to be the norm. No, this serene area was reserved for the crème de la crème of world travelers, which apparently now included me.

My induction into this exclusive club was the result of a one-time perk that came included with my ticket from Los Angeles. This was most likely designed to ease the painful truth that Singapore was on the other side of the world (5:00 PM in L.A. is 7:00 AM the next day in Singapore). In addition, Singapore is Asia's furthest point south, so L.A. to Singapore is the world's longest nonstop flight: eighteen-plus hours directly over the Pacific Ocean. If you took off from Denver, for example, the fastest route would be to fly around the world in the *other direction*, over Europe and the Middle East. With a stopover, most likely in Tokyo or Hong Kong,

20 Known locally as Singlish.

you are looking at over twenty-two hours.

Surrounded by the travel-privileged (who were, in turn, surrounded by a multitude of their plugged-in electronic devices), I soon realized that the dress code strictly adhered to Comme des Garcons and Prada, shoes included, making the overall atmosphere akin to a Paris Fashion Week press room. This made me a bit of an *enfant terrible* in my J Brand jeans and black Chucks, but with the impending journey I thought it best to be a slave to comfort, not fashion.

One could not help noticing the ample plush seating, magazines and newspapers from every conceivable country, seemingly original pop artwork, and the main centerpiece: an elegant complimentary buffet with the aforementioned cha siu bao, laksa (a kind of chicken soup), wonton noodles, dim sum, and perfectly prepared tiny little ribs. All of this (and much more) was served with an impressive array of wine, sake, and beer.

This created a dilemma for me. As hungry as I was, I make it a rule to never eat from buffets (the one exception being the Gold VIP Lounge Buffet at Changi, where I recommend the kaya toast with the Rudolf Furst pinot), and not for reasons you might think. I have no real problem with others touching or breathing down on my soon-to-be food selections. I figure the kitchen staff has already inflicted enough damage, and isn't that what the tempered glass semi-awnings are for? And I'm not overwhelmed by the number of choices, nor swayed by the cleverly promoted bargain price accompanied by the final hook, "All You Can Eat."

For me, it is a matter of principle: if I am going to eat out, I prefer to eat *exactly* what I want, and not settle. A buffet, to me, is like a cuisine arranged marriage. I want to be free to choose my own true love, thank you very much. I'm not about to do a buffet pre-walk-by to see if what I want is included. If I'm going to do that, I might as well just use the menu and avoid any line. If I indeed want lamp-heated prime rib, a salad topped off with cherry tomatoes, and two-week-exposed Italian dressing, I'd prefer to just order them and do away with the other white noise options.

LAXIOM #12
The Buffet Paradox.
Having an abundance of choices when making a decision can often cloud the best choice. The first step should be taking the time to determine exactly what you want, and then immediately eliminating options that cannot achieve that outcome. When clothes shopping, for example, I know precisely what I'm looking for when I arrive at a store, an efficiency that makes me a favorite amongst the sales staff.

With every outlet now in use in the lounge, I was directed to the men's spa area, which was just what it sounds like, but unexpected in an airport: avant-garde full-length mirrors, a dry sauna, and private marble showers with six-hundred-thread-count terry cloth towels and robes (both embroidered with "SA" for Singapore Airlines, which seemed like a coincidence—karma, we'll say—that I couldn't pass up). As luck would have it, I found the only place left to plug in my now-dead phone—the single handicap stall, leaving me with my moral dilemma of the day. With my biggest deal ever potentially at stake, I locked myself in with the self-justification that it would only be for a minute for two.

Immediately, my plan ran up against its first challenge: I needed my Singaporean power adaptor, which of course was in my bag, which of course was on the couch I had been occupying as a way of saving my seat. *Ass swoon?* The clock was ticking, and my flight was leaving in ninety minutes. Contorting myself into a yet-to-be-defined yoga pose, I was able to monitor, while seated, the comings and goings of others through their majority Prada footwear. *Is that gabardine?*

With my foot patrol indicating that the coast was clear, I slid myself under the door while keeping it locked, then bounced to my feet to make a quick beeline to my couch area. Without slowing down, I grabbed my outsider messenger bag and headed straight back to the spa, only to find what appeared to be actor Ken Watanabe and his young son (in Prada Kids) peering into my locked office stall and pulling at the door. *Think fast.*

"Han-dee-capped," was all I could come up with, pointing to the de-noted sign.

This was miraculously met with a short bow, without a word spoken. As luck would have it, a vacancy opened up just then.

Back inside the stall with a ten percent charge now showing, I checked for additional calls. Nothing. Only a text—"sent." *What? Sent where?* I needed to check my email, and therein lay my second challenge: I didn't have the Wi-Fi password, which meant I was back on foot patrol. As I returned a second time, the stall two doors down opened and out came Ken and son.

"Baaag," I said, looking up from the terrazzo floor in mid-shimmy, pointing with my exposed arm. Another smiling bow and they were off. This language thing was going to be easier than I thought.

An email and attachment with the heading: "Revised Final Contract" had indeed been sent minutes earlier with the instructions: "Please return as soon possible signed" (*ass swoon sign*). A moment later, staring at the document version of *The Game of Thrones'* Red Wedding, I began to feel faint while somehow containing a rare profanity-laced rant. Apparently, the Korean translation for "signed contract" was "negotiation starting point."

"Heading back to the hotel now," I typed furiously. "We need to meet."

Grabbing my bags and cutting into the line to grab an extra bun to go, I passed Ken and son in the buffet line.

"Seems like you're just always one step ahead us-lah," Ken said intriguingly.

I had just *finished* a marathon negotiation session with Jack and his partner, Bill, at the hotel I was now rushing back to. This in itself was unexpected, given that I had gotten on the plane in Los Angeles four days ago with what I thought was *already* a finished agreement in hand. I'd thought of this trip as a get-to-know-each-other, followed by a kumbaya with my new partners.

While taking off from LAX, I'd begun my flight ritual of replicating my office desk on the allotted fold-out tray. This tray appeared to be only slightly smaller than my actual desk, with the added features of indented pen, paperclip, and cup holders. As I commenced, making sure that the allotted stacks of folders designated for my left and right were in place, Jia-Xin the flight attendant appeared in my private pod with a smaller tray, this one carrying full champagne glasses. She placed a glass in its designated place on my desk-tray. This was how I'd imagined it was like to fly Pan Am in the late 1960s.

The "Singapore Girl," a heavily criticized nickname given to the female attendants, had become widely recognized by travelers, who associated it with the airline's brand. Dressed in kebayas of different colors denoting seniority, my first impression of the attendants was that they represented a sense of nationalistic pride, rather than a reinforcement of a cultural stereotype, most likely due to my nightlife lens. *Why can't I get my staff to look that professional?*

After an elegant four-course meal, I attempted to prepare my mini-cabin for sleep, which involved fiddling with multiple levers as if operating a crane. I woke in the middle of the night and careened from pod to pod toward the restroom, only to be met by a pajama-ed figure awaiting his turn.

"I'm Bootie," he proclaimed, extending his hand. "How are you enjoying the flight?"

"So far, so good. And you?"

"I love this flight every time I fly it," he smiled back.

"How often is that?"

"Twice a week. I'm the pilot."

The pilot? Didn't know pilots wore silk sleepwear on the job.

To ease the obvious look of panic on my face, Bootie went on to explain that he was indeed the pilot of this flight—one of a team of six. Due to its duration, the flight was piloted in shifts, three at a time. Bootie had just ended his shift and liked to take a brisk walk around the plane before retiring for his extended nap. *In his pajamas?*

"Usually everyone is asleep," he assured me before stepping inside the restroom.

I'll admit, in this instance it was nice to put a face to the job, and helped me sleep better.

Departing the plane in Singapore at 5:30 AM left me with the same feeling I'd had moving out of my first apartment. My pod had served me well, it'd had its moment, and now it was time to move on. Walking into the terminal, the first thing that struck me was how new and pristine *everything* appeared to be—including, apparently, the air conditioning units, which had me reaching into my bag to find my designated sleeping sweatshirt.

Outside I was hit by a tropical humidity wave that demanded immediate removal of the sweatshirt, as sweat began pouring out of everywhere. At the hotel, eating became first order. I quickly passed (as a matter of principle) on the featured Continental Breakfast Buffet, instead opting for my first authentic Singaporean breakfast, carrot cake. Expecting to be eating a sanctioned dessert before 9:00 AM for the first time, I found myself instead looking down at what was my first lesson in literal translation: chunks of a mystery cake combined with egg, all smothered in a brown sauce. I'd really had my heart set on some cream cheese frosting.

"Is this carrot cake?" I asked, grabbing the waiter's arm. I received a single affirmative nod. Starving, I dug in and was glad I did.

Now, in the lobby, I met with a group of suited mystery men who had fully assembled alongside Jack-n-Bill. After some introductory bowing, we quickly moved to a conference room. As we sat staring at each other, apparently waiting for someone to start the conversation, a post-adrenaline-induced delirium began to creep in that grew stronger by the minute, causing a sudden need to put my head down on the table. I fought my battle against unconsciousness, suddenly jolted upright by everyone standing in unison and leaving me as the only one seated.

I stood up quickly, and as the assembled men orchestrated a group bow, I awkwardly returned the favor, bowing a second time as a way of thanking them for their grandiose welcome, though it seemed a bit much. This was met not with smiles all around, but mortification. *Why is no one making eye contact?* As their collective gaze went over my right shoulder, a small man I had never seen before and who had not been at any of the prior negotiations passed by, seating himself at the other end of the long table. The group simultaneously followed his lead, as did I.

A month earlier, the original terms I had negotiated with Jack-n-Bill in a series of phone calls and a dinner meeting in L.A. were straightforward: I would be in full control of operating the venue. This would include hiring staff, some of whom I would by bringing from L.A., designing the venue, and being responsible for day-to-day operations. Basically, this was *my* baby, and that eliminated one of the biggest challenges these types of projects face: too many cooks in the kitchen. Don't get me wrong, collaboration is the name of the game. Constructive input is critical, as making million-dollar decisions in a fishbowl is ill-advised. Non-constructive input is where problems come in.

Almost everyone surrounding a nightclub project seems to instantly morph into a nightlife expert, especially when it comes to investors. Raising money for a venue project is never easy. As the old adage goes, "It's easier to raise $20 million then $2 million." At around $5 million and above, you are dealing with professional investors and institutions such as banks. Below that, it's strictly individuals, and you never really know

---

LAXIOM #13
Proximity Delusion.
Just because you have some second-hand experience, or have read about a subject extensively, does not make you an expert. I liken Proximity Delusion to someone buying NBA season tickets on the floor . . . and then feeling that they are ready to coach the team.

what you are getting. I'll get to that in a moment.

My process for raising money involved always being the first one to invest, taking the initial risk. This put me in a position where my money was worth more, and justifiably so. It takes months to find a location, put together a business plan, and come up with a winning concept, all with the risk that your efforts will never see the light of day. When all this is complete, you're off to find partners with a very short time frame for a courtship and honeymoon, increasing the chances of a divorce somewhere down the line.

The Singapore project was different than this in many ways, and anything but typical. First, the pure scope of $30 million made financing complicated, and involved multiple entities: the Singapore government, private investors from Korea, and the Sands Group, the majority owners of the Marina Bay Sands Resort and Casino (referred to as MBS—not affiliated in any way with the Prince of Saudi Arabia).

The Sands Group founder, Sheldon Adelson, had been developing MBS for years. He'd hired famed Israeli architect Moshe Safdie as its designer, and designated one of Safdie's two floating "Crystal Pavilions" as a nightlife location, with the world's largest Louis Vuitton store going into the other. The Pavilions were seventy-thousand-square-foot glass structures built from the ground up *in* the actual Marina Bay, adjacent to the casino itself and accessible only by large boardwalks extending over the water.

The building process for these engineering marvels involved laying giant pylons to form its base, then connecting them with concrete, with all of this happening below water level. Next, the water was removed to create a giant crater that supported the above-water structure, and you were off and running after almost two years of around- the-clock construction.

Bill, one of the on-site construction managers for the entire resort, saw an insider opportunity. He contacted his longtime friend, Jack from Korea, and together they formed a plan to obtain the lease for the Crystal

Pavilion nightlife venue. Problem was, Jack-n-Bill had never operated a nightclub before, so obtaining the lease was dependent on not only finding an experienced nightclub operator, but securing a recognized brand as well. You could say they were fighting an uphill battle—and that's where I came in.

With Avalon now tapped by Jack-n-Bill as the first U.S. nightclub brand ever to open in Asia as part of MBS, a meeting was set up in L.A.[21] As we discussed their proposal over steaks and seventy-year-old waiters at Musso and Frank's, I couldn't help but be taken by the romanticism of the whole idea. I'd never had the opportunity to visit Southeast Asia, and I saw this as a perhaps once-in-a-lifetime opportunity, a chance to journey to a far-off, exotic land. They needed an answer the next day. The quote "If not now, when? If not us, who?" dominated my stream of consciousness, and I focused my sights on what I now deemed as more an adventure than business opportunity, with one stipulation: I could commit five years max to the undertaking.[22]

Casinos, whether in Las Vegas, Macau, or Singapore, were by this time running a pretty similar model with respect to both dining and entertainment. This started with the era of the celebrity chef and was based on bringing in known brands, such as Gordon Ramsay or Bobby Flay, who had already spent time building their name. The concept was that guests would get to experience these restaurants they'd heard of while visiting the casino property . . . automatic value added. This also applies to live entertainment. Major casinos give residencies to performers who have decades of name recognition, such as Celine Dion and Elton John. The model had only recently begun to be applied to nightclubs.

21 Jack-n-Bill were originally introduced to me by an ex-employee from New York, Greg Gumo, who was then living in Singapore. In a bizarre and morbid confluence of events, like Michael Alig, in 2015 Gumo was also convicted of murder, resulting from the drowning death of a woman in Japan.

22 This quote has famously been attributed to Robert Kennedy, but its true origin is Rabbi Hillel circa 110 BCE. My reference is somewhat less scholarly, being a skit from *Saturday Night Live* featuring Will Forte.

The attitude of Vegas casino owners towards nightclubs began changing in the early 2000s, with the opening of the Brent Bolthouse-promoted Body English at the Hard Rock Casino and the Bank at the Bellagio, managed by ex-Lansdowne employees. By successfully charging a $25 cover charge, $15 and up for a drink, $350 for a full bottle of alcohol, and an additional $50 per-person booth charge (which amounted to basically charging a customer to sit down), these venues began to demonstrate that nightclubs could not only outperform the casino's gaming floor on a per-square-foot basis, but become a destination for additional guests, greatly increasing hotel room, food, and beverage spending.

As a group of three at the end of the table began an impromptu huddle with the late-arriving attendee, I had the distinct feeling of walking into a movie theater halfway through the feature, missing something that others already understood.

"Mr. Minh has a few questions," said Jack.

Not knowing if he was awaiting a response, I determined that it was best to remain silent.

"There is no indication of who signs the checks," he continued after a long pause.

"That would be me, as you know," I said.

Another huddle ensued, this time with two others coming around the back, crouching down to put them in earshot.

"Mr. Minh finds this unacceptable," said Jack.

"Which part?"

"Mr. Minh needs to sign the checks."

"Who *is* Mr. Minh again?"

"He is the investor, with his brother."

While it was good to move beyond just "Korean investor" and put a face to a name, this demand raised a red flag. In the world of nightlife, when an investment partner wants to be involved in any manner of the day-to-day business—be that signing checks, hiring staff, or approving what bands are booked—I knew all too well that it could only mean one thing: he was a "*That* Guy."

That Guy is a common nightlife figure. His basic profile usually consists of being an outsider in high school, constantly being shunned by the cool kids, with the same pattern repeating itself in college. He's a little too insecure, or unjustifiably overconfident, or perhaps nerdy. Somewhere along the line he makes enough money, or has additional cash available, to invest in something—with that something being an ill-conceived social revenge motive when it comes to nightclubs. A look-at-me-now to all those girls who ignored him in the past and all the boys who never picked him in gym class. It's a deep-seated male issue. To prove the point, over the years I have neither seen nor met a single female investor in a nightclub, making Marlo Thomas the only *That* Girl I've still ever heard of.

In every venue I had opened, with the exception of Avalon Hollywood, at least one *That* Guy was involved. I knew it going in, and took full responsibility for it. Finding investors for those projects inevitably led to a pool of *That* Guys, each of varying degrees. When someone started throwing in having a girl he knew being hired as a manager (probably one who wouldn't date him in high school) or demanding five complimentary bottles of champagne every night he was at the club, that was where I drew the line.

It was not uncommon for *That* Guy to be eventually barred from the club, due to his inability to stop himself from yelling, "Don't you know me? I own this place!" as he berates a newly hired staff member or tries to walk in with a group of twelve for the tenth time, none of whom were thinking of paying the cover charge.

Just to get to a *That* Guy you thought you could contain, you had to sift through multiple others. Some didn't even qualify as *That* Guys, as their purpose for meeting as a potential investor was to inform their revenge targets, "I'm thinking of investing in this club, what do you think?" He hoped that this alone would elevate him to cool guy status, without ever having the money to actually invest.

I needed to determine where Mr. Minh fell on the *That* Guy spectrum.

As I contemplated my next move, the group rose again in unison, followed by another group bow. *Was this some sort of intimidation tactic?* As I turned again, *another* man entered the room, walking past me to take a seat next to Mr. Minh.

As everyone sat down, Mr. Minh finally spoke, looking directly at me as he addressed the room. "This is Mr. Minh, my older brother."

The mood in the room suddenly changed; everyone sat up a bit straighter and more attentive. *Who's in charge here? Am I now dealing with two* That *Guys?*

"Which Mr. Minh wants to sign the checks?" I asked, trying to sort matters out.

Another huddle ensued, apparently to bring the new-other Mr. Minh up to speed.

"Maegsi," said Jack, which apparently meant the later arriving one.

"Can I ask why, after months negotiating our agreement, this change is coming out of the blue?"

"This morning was the first time Maegsi and Mini saw the agreement. Now they are here to complete the *definitive agreement.*"

Mini? The what?

"They always sign the checks for all their businesses," Jack continued.

This gave me the inside information I needed to determine which *That* Guy argument I needed, having over a dozen to choose from. I explained that I understood how Maegsi (which, I learned, translated to "Maxi") and Mini felt. But, in this business, checks were written at all hours and were needed immediately—for emergencies at two in the morning or to pay staff working on commission, for example. (This fell into the true-*ish* category, but I had refined this speech to a point where I always included it.)

"It wouldn't be responsible to make these payments in cash, because that would open up the business to theft," I went on. "It's in your best interest not to be signing the checks, as it would slow the business down. After all, I have money invested, too, so we're on the same team here."

Blank looks. The Brothers Minh were a tough crowd.

"I'll tell you what," I said, "I'll meet with Jack once a week and we can review in detail what is going on financially. But, as we agreed, it's best that I sign all the checks."

Mini and Maxi both got up to leave the room, as I alone bowed as they exited. Five minutes later, they both returned to the bows of everyone, including myself. *Got it, bow during entrance. No bow during exit.*

"Okay," said Maxi, again taking his seat.

We proceeded to rehash other major parts of what had already been negotiated with Jack-n-Bill. The original investment commitment of $12 million was reduced to $10 million, leaving me $2 million short with construction planned to begin in two months. It had originally been agreed that investor payback would be on the same schedule as my own, but that was changed to a preferred schedule that paid the Minhs the majority of the money first.[23]

Three hours later, Maxi proclaimed calmly, "Now, we celebrate." This was met by clapping and an awkward version of high-fiving.

The biggest nightclub deal ever was done—again—and hopefully for the last time.

Jack handed me a business card with an address and told me to meet him there at 10:00 PM. Starving, I didn't know if I could wait that long for dinner but was too tired at that point to do anything but check in at my hotel again and get some rest. Arriving by taxi to an out-of-the-way (and, by first appearances, substandard) Holiday Inn, I rechecked the address. Then I spotted Jack out front, smoking.

"Let's eat," I said, somewhat revitalized.

"Of course," said Jack, leading me through the lobby and stopping at a set of large doors.

---

23 The final negotiated document title was indeed changed from "Agreement" to "Definitive Agreement." For the weeks that followed, I kept expecting a call from Jack voiding its terms until the "Ultimate Definitive Agreement" could be negotiated. Fortunately, that call never came.

A woman who appeared to be in her late fifties stepped outside.

"Maegsi Minh," said Jack.

"Ha." She smiled after checking her slip of paper. "Follow me-lah."

She then led us inside, down what seemed like an endless hallway with doors on either side. Three rights and a left turn later, we stopped.

"Give my best to Maegsi-lah," she said, heading back down the maze.

"Jack, what is this place?" I asked, my eyes darting around for the nearest EXIT sign.

"This, my friend, is a KTV . . . a very special one."

Stepping through the door, I imagined that this was what the first U.S. Marine entering Saddam's palace must have felt like. The room itself was rectangular, with ornate drapes covering three walls. The fourth wall appeared to be designed to replicate the sportsbook at MBS, with over a dozen screens playing music videos. There were two pool tables, three bars, and more than a dozen leather couches. *Holiday Inns in Asia are sure different.* There were over twenty people inside, but as I continued to search, no food.

"Jack, is there a way to get something to eat?"

He motioned to the back of the room, already holding drinks in both hands. As I navigated through the darkness, I had my sights sets on finding the way to the restaurant, but instead came upon a large table with giant platters of shrimp, something looking like chicken satay, and other unidentifiable oddities. A buffet. It had now been sixteen hours of only eating three buns, a piece of carrot cake, and kaya toast, but, holding true, I could wait a few more.

I had driven by numerous KTVs (standing for Karaoke Television) over the course of the last few days. They were easy to spot. Designated by neon signs with names like FunTime or K-Star, they consisted of a room or multiple rooms with a traditional karaoke machine and a bar. You paid $15, and away you sang. It was basically the same experience you had at a karaoke bar in the U.S. As I sat down, I soon realized this was not that.

"Drink . . . Martell, the best." It was Mini, handing me one of his two drinks as he chugged the other.

Next, it was Maxi's turn. He sat on my other side and also handed me one of his two drinks. "Drink . . . Martell, the best," he slurred. "Drink all now-lah." He nudged my hand to my face until I took a sip.

"You big U.S. boss," Maxi sputtered. "Can I take a photo?"

This was getting weird. Looking toward the door, I could see guests streaming in until the room held over fifty people, all men. They began taking seats. There were now five people on my crowded couch.

Door Lady then reappeared, this time followed by some sort of Miss Singapore pageant procession, each girl dressed in a different style of gown. They paraded around the room to the sound of uproarious clapping.

"What is happening?" I asked Maxi, pointing to the line of over three dozen contestants.

"Just pick one," he said, interrupting his discussion with the judge next to him.

"What do they win?" *And . . . is there a talent portion to this?*

"Just pick one."

Around the room the judges voted, none seeming to agree on who the winner should be.

Then Door Lady pointed at me. As the whole room awaited my decision, I pointed to a random participant, drawing more awkward high fives from Maxi and Mini and still more clapping from the other judges.

With the voting finished, I felt it was time to head toward the door. As I stood up, both Mini and Maxi put a hand on my shoulders.

"You need to wait here. For the girl."

My pick as winner was heading toward me, smiling. *She must have won.*

"What can I get you?" she asked, stopping to bow in front of me.

The gesture of wanting to show gratitude to the judge who selected her as the winner seemed sweet, but I couldn't accept.

"Nothing at all. I'm happy for you that you won."

This was met by a puzzled look.

"Then we can just sit-lah," she said.

Both Mini and Maxi also had their "picks" come over to say thanks. *What a polite country.*

Sitting in awkward silence on the couch, I began to survey the room. Every judge was now sitting with his pick, some of whom they apparently already knew quite well.

"Having fun?" asked Jack, walking by hand-in-hand with his pick.

"Jack, what is up with all this?"

"I told you, this is a special place," he replied, flashing a Cheshire smile as he stumbled away.

"It is time for the competition to begin," Jack announced, taking his place at the front of the room. He handed the microphone over to Mini.

Now what? So, there is a talent portion after all.

As the array of screens all synced up to a single video, Mini began to transform himself, first ripping off his half-buttoned, sweat-and-Martell-stained white shirt and pulling his tie over his head. After hiking up his pants to just under the crease between his doughy stomach and waist, he waited intensely.

"I wanna hold 'em like they do in Texas, plays," he belted out, right on cue. "Fold 'em, let 'em hit me, raise it baby, stay . . ." Mini was now stepping up his performance to mimic the moves of Lady Gaga on the screens behind him.

"Can't read, no he can't read my pokaaaa face," he sang off-key, turning the mic to the now cheering crowd, this time upping his game to include perfectly replicated facial expressions. *How long had he been practicing this?*

Next up was Maxi, who delivered a stunning interpretation of "My Way," followed by a member of the negotiation team's rendition of "You Give Love a Bad Name" that included mock pistol play. As the mic passed around the room and headed toward me, I was suddenly overcome with dread. I had not sung in public since Friday night services twenty years ago, let alone practiced a choreographed dance routine.

"*Sangsa, sangsa*," the crowd chanted, urging me to stand.

"*Gamsa*, I'm very honored," I replied, now being pulled up by both Maxi and Mini.

"To celebrate our new business, I would like to invite my new partners to join me," I said. This was met with shouts of "Maegsi-lah" as I now held up the two barely functioning Minhs, throwing my arms around them for support.

As the Backstreet Boys' "I Want It That Way" blared, they took on the roles of AJ and Kevin, which I'd been hoping for, leaving me in the Howie support role. Our encore of "Hey Ya" turned out to be the show-stopper, with a flash mob "shakin' it like a Polaroid picture" in perfect unison as I stuck to my best Big Boi impression.

Turning around to see Mini passed out on the floor, empty glass still in hand, and Maxi well on his way to joining him, it hit me where I really was ... the ultimate *That* Guy Convention. I was now partners with a different type of *That* Guy, one I had never encountered before. Panicked, I grabbed someone's drink from the table in front of me, finishing it to the delight of my Miss KTV, who spoke as much English as I did Cantonese. It was later explained to me that her job was to get me to buy as much alcohol as possible, receiving a percentage of what I bought as commission.

Stumbling over multiple *That* Guys, I made my way to the exit, but not before I hand-signaled to order five bottles of Martell and put them on Maxi and Mini's tab. Only the best for my new partners, and the least I could do to thank them for a great day-lah.

On my flight back to L.A., I Googled "Minh brothers Seoul Korea" to get more information on the mysterious duo. This came up on page four of my search:

Negotiating with Koreans
Koreans are renowned as skillful negotiators. Still, they put a strong emphasis on developing a personal relationship, and this investment in up-front relationship-building will be one of your most powerful bargaining

chips. Without a high level of comfort with the other party, things may go nowhere; but with a feeling of camaraderie and trust, things can go far.

Because of this relationship-based nature of business, an introduction is a must for starters, and the higher the status of the introducer, the better. The first meetings are "get to know you" meetings and generally involve higher-level participants as part of the relationship-building. The nitty-gritty of the work to come will be left to mid- and lower-level managers.

During the early stages, socializing after hours will be critical. If the emotional comfort level is good, and the venture seems in their interest, only then will the Korean side decide to move forward in trying to work together. A long, drawn-out process follows for haggling. Keep in mind that proceedings must still be polite, and nobody should suffer any sort of public embarrassment, even with mild criticism.

Giving concessions too soon or showing any impatience will be seen as signs of weakness and taken advantage of. Remember, Koreans take a shrewd approach to negotiating. They are prepared to wait patiently until a frustrated "opponent" gives in. If your negotiators are not the patient, gentle-but-firm type, you may want to rethink your choice of negotiators. Likewise, if you are not prepared to engage in negotiations for as long as it takes, you may want to rethink your plans altogether.

Clear communication during these meetings is essential. It behooves you to have your own interpreter and to get the meeting notes down in writing and get them agreed to. Remember that the simple act of interpretation adds time, so prepare for this. Trying to shorten the time and expenses of using an interpreter, however, can, in the end, add much more of both through the problems created by miscommunication.

Korea is a group-oriented society. This means that getting the internal buy-in from a large number of people will add to the time. Highlighting the ways your proposal benefits their country, as well as their company, is seen as favorable to the group. On the other hand, in light of your highly personal relationship, they can manipulate the context to make it seem like you are undermining the group harmony. Don't give up—they admire people who are tenacious.

The contract should be considered more of a memorandum of understanding, because there will be more negotiating after the contract is signed. Consequently, it goes without saying that you should never make all your concessions before the contract is signed.

Be diplomatic, always. Be patient, always. But always be a clever poker player.

I had always prided myself on being fully prepared for business encounters of any kind, from weekly staff meetings to intense lease negotiations. What I never fully considered was that, until now, these had all taken place under the umbrella of *one* business culture. The Brothers Minh weren't unethical or underhanded, but were acting in a manner that followed their national ethos. It was up to *me* to develop an understanding of this, if I had any chance of survival in Singapore, one of the most diverse places to do business in the world. I quickly put together my list:

Negotiating with:
Singaporeans
Malaysians
Chinese
Japanese
Indonesians
Indians
Vietnamese
Thai

I had a lot of reading to do, and notes to take, before returning. Next time, I would be ready . . . or so I thought-lah.

CHAPTER 15

THE MONEY SHOT

"I did things for the excitement, the dare,
that fact that it was new, not for the money.
And too many times I was the first,
not the beneficiary."
—GRACE JONES

The one piece of advice I've most valued over the years was given to me by Maurice Brahms: "The more you are in the public eye, the riskier your life becomes. There is always a person, who was denied entrance to your club at some time or sees you as flaunting yourself and thinks: I'm gonna get that asshole. Best just to be invisible."

It's no coincidence that the high-profile owners of Studio 54—and subsequently Maurice as owner of Xenon, Peter Gatien, and others over the years—have ended up in prison.

With this is in mind, I always made a focused effort to stay behind the scenes. In the early years, this was easy; no one had any interest in pulling me out from behind the curtain. With a degree of success came a degree of interest, with the press placing me front and center in the story. This created a dilemma, where on one side anything you can do to promote your product is good for business, and on the flip side there are a lot of people out there who hate nightclub owners, or the sensationalized pop culture *image* of one.

LAXIOM #14
Some quick dos and don'ts
when personally promoting your business.
Do: Be humble and never use the word "I" (it's "we").
Don't: Mention money.
Do: Focus on the benefits for the community, jobs, revitalizing a downtrodden area, and attracting other businesses to the area. The consumer spending-generated (aka high tide) floats all boats.
Don't: Talk about any of your past successes. They should be self-evident.
Do: Under-promise and over-deliver.
Don't: Ever say you're "changing the market" or "reinventing" how things are currently being done. Let your actions do the talking.

A few years back, I received a text regarding the Tao Group, owners of the restaurant/club Tao at the Venetian in Las Vegas. It contained an article purporting how Tao Vegas was the highest-grossing nightclub in the world, with supporting quotes from two of the owners, whom I knew, having gotten their start promoting high school parties at Limelight and Tunnel. If that text had come from Maurice, it would have no doubt also included the message: don't let this be you.

As I moved my life to Singapore, I had thus taken a vow of anonymity, especially given the country's reputation as a no-nonsense, stringent society (to clarify, you do not get caned in Singapore for dropping gum on the street). Detouring into the nearest airport bookstore to pick up an *International Herald Tribune*, I couldn't help but notice its contrast to the bookstore I had browsed in L.A. before boarding my flight to Singapore.

The Singaporean version had an overwhelming theme of anything business-related: biographies of business leaders and entrepreneurs, magazines such as *Fortune* and *The Economist* in multiple languages, and how-to-books relating to business software and accounting principles. There were no tabloids, romance novels, or fiction titles in sight; these were replaced by high-end lifestyle magazines with titles like *The Peak* and *Upgrade*. Business leaders such as Bill Gates, Jeff Bezos, and Jack Ma were the stars, with covers sporting the Kardashians or Justin Bieber nowhere to be found.

In my travels, I'd always found that airport bookstores were key indicators of what a city, or country in this case, valued. Books on the art of slow-cooked barbecue are nowhere to be seen in De Gaulle Airport, but you can find little else in Memphis. In Singapore's case, a premium was put on business—more specifically, becoming rich.

Heading to the taxi stand, I recognized a few passengers from my flight, easily identifiable from their Tom Ford neck pillows, as one of the twenty or so drivers sitting on their car trunks excitedly motioned me in their direction. Sweltering in the thick pre-dawn air, I happily jumped into one of the taxis. As I caught a view of my disheveled self in the driver's rearview mirror and a porcelain Lucky Cat bobblehead on his dashboard, I eased back and dozed off.

LAXIOM #15
Sock thickness matters.
Warm, cozy socks are great for international flying, but when your destination is 100 degrees with ninety percent humidity, they make your day very uncomfortable. Wool versus cotton versus wool/cotton blends also need to be figured into the equation.

"Excuse me-lah, sir," came a voice from the front of the cab, jolting me out of my half-sleep. "I just want to say it's an honor to have you in my taxi. I'm a big fan."

Huh?

"Ah ... *xie xie*," I replied. (I had been practicing my Chinese, as almost all Singaporeans spoke two languages: Singlish and usually Mandarin Chinese, with Malay, Korean, Bahasa, and Vietnamese also prevalent.)

"I'm a big fan and think you're a genius."

Rubbing my eyes, I tried to focus. "Very funny, I bet you say that to all the exhausted expats," I replied, believing I had caught on to the joke.

"We are very honored to have you in our country. Marina Bay Sands is a great place. I don't get many Americans in my taxi, especially one so rich. So to have you is a real stroke of luck."

As we drove on, passing immaculately arranged palm trees that seemed to serve as a floral military welcome to the country, my overly complimentary driver maintained a constant backseat stare through his rearview mirror.

"My name is Steve," I uttered, in an attempt to ease my uneasiness.

"I know your name," he laughed. "Everyone here does-lah. I'm Suan."

"How do you know my name? I've only been to Singapore a handful of times."

"Oh, I follow everything you do. My two children are big fans."

I then began to piece together a probable explanation for my new-found fame. The Marina Bay Sands project, as a whole, was a very big deal for the entire country. Avalon was a well-known nightclub brand, so his children must be club-goers. There had been two articles in the *Straits Times*, Singapore's national newspaper, regarding Avalon's arrival, and they did mention my name, with one including a small stock photo of myself . . . and this was a small country.

"How old are your children, Suan?"

"Twenty and twenty-two," he replied. *Makes sense.* "I think what you do is very innovative. You have actually changed the world."

Seems a bit much . . . but okay.

Suan was now on his phone in an animated conversation, barely able to keep an eye on the road.

"It's my daughter, Lillian, can you say hi to her? She doesn't believe me you are here-lah?" asked Suan, passing me back his phone.

"Is it really you-lah?" said a voice on the phone. "I can't believe it."

"It's really me, nice to talk to you," I replied, handing the phone back to Suan while Lillian continued on, now in an animated conversation with her brother who was apparently standing next to her.

Crossing the ultra-modern bridge leading to the city center, the three large towers of MBS appeared, creating the illusion of a giant Stonehenge emerging through the dense haze. A sense of pride began to well up in me. The thought of being recognized on the other side of the world for my work felt good. Being the first nightclub brand from the U.S. to open anywhere in Asia was not only being accepted, but people appeared very excited about it. This could be a country where I was a revered business leader, extolling my wisdom through books and speaking engagements. Anonymity would have to take a back seat, the country was calling . . . no, demanding, that I take my place front and center as the "club king" of Asia. I was ready for my coronation.

Pulling up to the entrance, Suan quickly got out to open my door. As I stepped out slowly, he handed me his phone, along with a large gold Sharpie.

"Could you please sign my phone, it would really mean a lot," Suan asked. *Wow, already signing autographs.* "Only iPhone for us. Samsung no good-lah . . . cheap."

"Sure, but only if I can keep the Sharpie," I replied, smiling. I was going to need this in the future and wanted to be prepared. The signing of a phone must have been a Singaporean thing.

Taking the time to practice my soon-to-be-in-demand autograph, I made sure to get every swoop and curve right as Suan looked on anxiously.

"There you go," I said, returning his now-treasured souvenir, which he maneuvered through his fingers like a magic stone.

A strange, puzzled look came over his face as he examined my perfectly formed signature on the back cover of the phone.

"This is very strange," he said, looking up. "I'm not sure how to make this out."

Grabbing the phone from his hand, I was more than happy to show him. "This part here says 'Best,' while this is 'Steve,' and this, 'A-d-e-l-man' makes Adelman. 'Best, Steve Adelman.'"

"Steve Abelmen?" asked my admirer, snatching his phone "Who is that? I thought you were Steve Jobs." With that, he began rubbing the phone with his shirt sleeve in an attempt to remove the permanent ink, but to no avail. Shaking the phone out the window and yelling something in Mandarin, which I could only make out as "waste of space guy," he sped away, keeping my anonymity intact.

I can see how Suan fell for a case of mistaken identity, as all bald, dressed in black, bespectacled Americans do look somewhat alike. Given that this was my second case of mistaken identity, maybe it was just time to change my look.

It had been almost a year since my strange encounter with the Minh brothers, and a lot had happened. Not unexpectedly, a lot of it was unexpected. Building the most elaborate nightclub ever, at a total cost of over $30 million, was proving to be more insane than ambitious. Large water leaks constantly halted work until new engineering solutions could be found. The twenty-four thousand square feet of glass needed to enclose the structure kept on cracking, predating new custom panes to be made and delivered from Malaysia. This put the project severely over budget.

With updated construction plans calling for a larger subterranean space, Jack, Bill, and the Minh brothers made a deal with a second nightclub, Pangaea in NYC, to inhabit the newly expanded level, while Avalon would be housed on the second and third levels.

After two months, a no-holds-barred fight broke out between Jack-n-Bill and the Pangaea owner, Michael Ault. Jack-n-Bill came to view Ault as erratic and a liability based on his behavior in the bi-weekly Skype construction meetings. When they approached me to determine if Ault had a drug or alcohol problem—an odd question, given that I had just recently met him—their question seemed part of an agenda to take over Pangaea for *themselves*. Realizing that Avalon could be next on their list, and that the whole project from the beginning might be an intricate plan for them to command control over both locations, I immediately shut down the inquiry.

Two weeks later, as I boarded my flight to L.A., Jack-n-Bill terminated Ault's contract. Ault, who was not about to go anywhere, struck back. Within days, a mysterious affidavit appeared, orchestrated by Ault's partner and sometimes-lawyer. It alleged that Jack-n-Bill had acted obscenely in front of a waitress, who was now threatening litigation eighteen months later. Ault and his partner threatened to release the information to the Singapore press, implicating not only the accused pair, but by association, the Minh brothers as investors.

The whole matter playing out publicly was something that the Sands Group desperately needed to avoid. After winning a prolonged international bidding process to develop MBS, any whiff of scandal this early in the process was not going to play well and could potentially jeopardize the hundreds of millions in funds they were receiving from the Singaporean government. To avoid any public "loss of face," the Sands Group applied an ethics clause in the Pangaea lease to terminate it. Jack-n-Bill and the Minhs were out. I was livid.

This left both Avalon and Pangaea without investors in the middle of construction, with government pressure to complete the project under the agreed-upon timetable. To worsen matters, Ault was convinced that I had orchestrated his firing in a coup attempt to take over Pangaea, causing a rift that would last for years. First the firing of Ault, then the subsequent fallout, seemed to bury the project in its tracks. I needed money and a new construction team, and I needed them fast.

One week later, I was back on a plane to Singapore. After a month of wrangling, I was able to put together a group of investors while hiring the same construction group responsible for building the one hundred retail spaces inside the MBS shopping mall, raising over $10 million in a series of frantic meetings and conference calls.

Without the necessary time to vet the new investor group properly, I had inadvertently assembled an unrivaled international team of *That Guys*, all from different countries currently doing business in Singapore, and each bringing their own business ethos to the table.

The Chinese *That* Guy seemed set on doing whatever he could, by any means necessary, to wrestle away control of the company's finances, including trying to install his own accounting department. The two Indian *That* Guys contracted proximity delusion almost immediately, pushing to have their cousin hired as a manager based on his credentials of running a janitorial service for other nightclubs in Singapore—which, they determined, gave him a unique understanding of the market. Their constant complaint of me "not being from around here" was a thinly veiled scheme that could only lead them down the same rabbit hole as Jack-n-Bill. Finally, the Hong Kong *That* Guy and his wife were convinced by the other two groups that a theft ring would develop, if they were not allowed to install their own personnel.[24]

Mind you, all of these demands happened *after* agreements had been signed that stipulated, down to the last detail, how the business would be operated, and included the necessary *That* Guy clause I had honed for years.

The launch of Avalon Singapore was scheduled as a two-day weekend celebration, to coincide with Formula 1 and a worldwide audience. F1 racing was one of the biggest spectator sports in Southeast Asia, along with European soccer, the NBA, and ping pong.

F1 Singapore is unique in nature, and often compared to the most famous F1 annual race of all: Monte Carlo. Roaring through the center of the city, it is by far Singapore's biggest event. As teams from Ferrari, Renault, and Red Bull raced around hairpin turns, going from zero to sixty miles per hour in two seconds and reaching top speeds of over two hundred miles per hour, the sound could be heard miles away. Upfront and close, it was like experiencing roaring T-Rexes from *Jurassic Park*.

Given the number of party people taking over the country, at the MBS Convention Center two hundred yards away from Avalon, the

---

24 His wife could not be described as a *That* Girl, since she would show up at investor meetings more to keep an eye on her husband than anything else, giving the impression that she held the family purse strings.

newly assembled Singapore team created Avalon at Large, a music festival taking place during the same weekend. It featured an eclectic lineup headlined by Ludacris, the Chemical Brothers, Sander van Doorn, and many others, with over 15,000 advance tickets sold. It would be a weekend to remember—or perhaps, best to forget.

Friday began with a preview night hosted by the F1 teams. The greatest drivers in the world, including Lewis Hamilton, Sebastian Vettel, and Jenson Button, along with their crews, drank and sprayed countless bottles of Dom Perignon with guests who appeared to be taking the night off from a *Vogue* fashion spread. Across the way, Avalon at Large was sold out, the convention center packed to a point of ripping at the seams. Day One was a hit.

Unavailable to make the weekend trip to Singapore, Mr. Turnover was never more needed than on Day Two. The problems started with a phone call from the production manager explaining that the "wall of sound" for Kruder and Dorfmeister, the headline DJ duo to perform at Avalon, had been held up in customs and would be late to arrive. The setup included over two dozen speakers linked together to form a twenty-by-thirty-five-foot backdrop, giving the effect of being at a Metallica concert and requiring a crew of over a dozen to assemble.

Over at the festival, a communication mistake left us a dozen tables short to fulfill our VIP reservations. The problem was, we had already rented every usable table we could get our hands on, amounting to five hundred in total, for the likes of Richard Branson, family members of the Sultan of Brunei, and Chef Daniel Boulud.

This left us with no choice but to temporarily "borrow" items from the MBS hotel lobby, which itself was jammed full of guests. If a group got up to leave, assigned VIP crew members would quickly remove their tables and chairs, while others were dispensed to run interference with lobby staff. All in all, over twenty hotel vignettes were removed before unsuspecting MBS staff realized they were missing.

In the chaos of the evening, they continued to serve standing guests

from the hotel lobby bar without the time to determine what had occurred. When they returned to work the following evening, everything
was neatly in place, leaving the feeling for many that they somehow imagined the entire incident.

The DJs finally took the stage at Avalon after 2:00 AM, to a chorus
of boos from the exasperated crowd—a first-time experience for me, and
hopefully the last. Far from finding the indigo bunting that night, Avalon
had laid a giant egg.

Avalon Singapore eventually found its footing. With EDM dominat-
ing nightclubs worldwide, the movement that Avalon Boston was instru-
mental in creating had turned into a phenomenon, with Las Vegas being
ground zero. In the extravagant mega-clubs XS and Hakkasan, DJs such
as Calvin Harris and Zedd were paid over $500,000 a night to perform,
drawing crowds of over four thousand revelers.[25] The same DJs began
making weekly appearances in Singapore, awed by the uniqueness of the
space itself and the John-installed sound system and elaborate lighting.

As DJ Steve Aoki began his set, I took my usual place for the night at
the end of the immense, twelve-station main bar. A twenty-year nightly
tradition was about to commence.

The classic nightlife portrayal of the bartender in pop culture as being both a soother of woes and an innate psychologist has played out
in scenes on television and in movies for decades, with *Cheers* probably the most recognizable example. In the show, pulling up to the bar
to be greeted by Woody gave fictional customers a sense of comfort, as
the famed theme song emphasized: "You want to go where people know
people are all the same . . ." This ease allowed them to confide in Woody,
whose small-town manner endeared him to the whole country. In some
episodes, it was the owner, Sam, who played the role of trained listener, at

---

25 By 2019, the Sin City EDM phenomenon had become an inundated market as an
   overabundance of opulent venues competed for the same audience. As attendance decreased,
   the ship that had set sail over a decade earlier hit shallow ground, highlighted by the fast-track
   collapse of the Kaos nightclub at the newly re-launched Palms Casino Resort that led to a $28
   million loss for its owners.

times doling out advice.

Since the Boston opening of Avalon, I had spent well over 2,500 nights with late-night revelers viewing me as their Sam and de facto ringleader. With the added enhancement of more than just a few beers, every night more customers than Sam dealt with in an entire season of *Cheers* were willing to confide in me about just about anything. There probably isn't a break-up or work or family situation I've not heard of first hand.

LAXIOM #16
The silent sounding board.
When confronted with another's venting or frustration, just listen; advice or a response isn't necessary. Just hearing themselves verbalize the issue will trigger the necessary action.

Similar to airport bookstores, if you wanted to understand people in a certain geographic area, just listen to what is being talked about in nightclubs. In New York, the main topic was being able to afford the city and climb the ladder in your chosen field. In L.A., it was about landing your next job in the industry. In Boston, it was sports. In Singapore, it was money.

In scenes that belonged in the movie *Crazy Rich Asians* (which was filmed in Singapore), common-theme stories were spilled as I listened, which was always difficult given the volume of background music and chatter (a challenge Sam never had to deal with). One impromptu psych session was with Jasmine, a young woman who told me her father was about to cut her off. Her friends circled her, sharing in her horror, clearly on her payroll. At age thirty-two, how was she supposed to get a job? Indicating her correct age, or at least something close to it, was probably a good place to start.

Avalon-goer Benjamin, on the other hand, had a problem of spending too much money on his potential girlfriend. After finding out she was dating three other people, he wanted to get his iPad and Louis Vuitton bag purchases back and was now formulating a break-in of her apartment.

Then there was Mia, who had been promised a $2,500 monthly salary from her boyfriend, who had so far only come up with half his end. I mean, how's a girl supposed to live? Especially when his best friend is offering $3,000, with $30,000 guaranteed upfront and monthly payments after that?

By 5:00 AM, I would often see these same club-goers drowning their frustrations amongst other party animals in the Ceremony of the Smashed. However, unlike Boston, Hollywood, or New York, the Singapore edition somehow became a scene from *Dirty Dancing*, with the added precision of a military parade. Appearing as if passing out was inevitable due to over-drinking and exertion, the group inexplicably remained in almost perfect dance step, a true testament to the Singaporean daily emphasis on both conformity and resolve.

Another distinctive segment of the Singapore Ceremony were the constant drunken fights that broke out between men over money issues: who was worth more, or who had the most expensive car or watch. On these occasions, assembled group members would pick a side in support. You were either a Patek Philippe or a Rolex man . . . but you couldn't be both.

Traveling in large packs, these skirmishes soon became twelve-person melees. Unlike New York or Boston, where they were broken up to avoid posing a serious risk of injury for combatants and those in their vicinity, in Singapore the men were allowed to fight it out, to the entertainment of security and interested onlookers.

The brawls usually began when one person felt insulted by another, and instead of challenging his tormenter, he would wait until he turned around and then give him a cheap shot to the back of the head—the punching power of a Labrador waking you up in the morning, causing the recipient more anger than damage. With none of the group over five foot four or a hundred and forty pounds, and all of them better at evaluating high-end brands than executing impromptu roundhouse kicks, very few blows were actually landed, beyond some last-minute hair-pulling.

In early 2014, I had been doing some hair-pulling of my own. Unable to keep up my planned schedule of alternating months between being in L.A. and Singapore, I had been back to the U.S. only once in the last two years. The volume of work and time needed to make Avalon Singapore a success meant staying in Asia full-time, with no let-up of my schedule in sight.

LAXIOM #17
Beware of the one-trick pony.
No matter how much I get involved in work, I have always tried not to let it become my life. This comes with the benefit of hopefully avoiding the warning label: "May Cause Regret in the Future."

Singapore had proved to be the adventure I'd hoped for, with its unexpected twists and turns along the way. All told, I had met people from over twenty countries who had migrated to Singapore for economic opportunity, coming from places like Ulaanbaatar, Mongolia, and Vientiane, Laos. After a short while, I mastered Singlish and a bit of Mandarin. With the five-year mark approaching, my adventure had turned into a life decision.

It had been twenty-five years since I'd battled through a snowstorm to reach the Roxy, working tirelessly while sacrificing any semblance of a personal life, let alone a family. With Mel's health declining back in Michigan, I had come to a conclusion: it was time to return to the U.S.

I reached an agreement with the international *That* Guys. They could finally live out their fantasies, and the Avalon name could live on through a monthly $10,000 licensing fee. By 2015, the group couldn't keep up the payment. The ITGs had been engaging in their own brawls for control of the company. Less than a year after my departure, they needed the one thing they valued more than becoming club kings—money.

CHAPTER 16

CULTURE SHOCK

*"If life was fair, Elvis would still be alive,
and all the impersonators would be dead."*
—Johnny Carson

There have been concepts in my life that I've had difficulty grasping. One that had always bothered me was the idea of kosher food being blessed by a rabbi. Standing in a Kroger kosher food section, where the products numbered in the hundreds—a kosher "buffet," oddly enough—the logistics seemed, well, unrealistic. Was a minyan of rabbis standing at the end of the assembly lines, chanting mitzvahs as workers screwed tops on jars of Manischewitz gefilte fish? A Google search only complicated matters; I found that, for any food to be deemed kosher, the rabbi needed to be there when it was produced or slaughtered.

Another one of these mysteries was Tyler Perry, or more specifically, Madea, the character portrayed by Tyler Perry. Now, to be fair, I really hadn't given any of the Madea movies, which numbered a dozen, a fair shake by sitting through an entire one, only catching snippets over the years on television and in movie theater previews. Just hearing that voice, however, triggered the exact tune-out reaction as when I'd encountered Sean Hannity ranting while channel surfing.

Or maybe I had simply spent too much of my life around men in drag, and was experiencing "queen burn-out."

With time on my hands, I was determined to finally resolve these personal mysteries. I peered through the bars of my single, concrete jail cell into what I could see of a dimly lit common area with a blaring television. The irony of listening to what I had come to realize was a Madea movie in which she finds herself in jail was not lost on me.

"Get your things together and follow me, you're leaving," said the corpulent guard. He unlocked the door, sliding the heavy metal with a loud clang. Gathering my unused bed sheet, blanket, and pillow and leaving a toothbrush and small tube of toothpaste behind, I walked past the group of twenty cells on my block, eyes focused straight ahead.

"You gettin' out already?" a saddened voice asked from the darkness.

I never looked back or answered, following apace through a maze of ominous, dimly lit corridors. I retrieved my clothes, and then was shown to the exit.

Standing outside the Shelby County Jail with a lone ex-inmate, waiting for my ride to arrive, I felt an unusual bond with the straggly man next to me as I anticipated the sun about to rise over the Tennessee horizon.

"What were you in for?" I asked. If this had been a movie, I'd be offering him a cigarette, lighting it for him, and then waiting while he took a long drag before speaking.

"Wrecked a car," he said abruptly. "Drove it right into the side of a gas station. Old lady's ride. She's not happy."

"Jesus," I said. "Were you hurt? You look okay."

"Yup, but you should see the gas station," he said, borrowing a cliché with a pained smile.

"You . . . what . . . why are you here?" he asked, turning towards me.

"I have no idea," I replied. "By the way, what time is it?"

"Almost five," he replied, unwrapping a piece of gum and offering me a piece.

I had been in jail almost twenty hours. Like most situations I had faced since coming to Memphis, it left me shaking my head.

In the summer of 2014, I visited the "Bluff City" for the first time in over a decade. This coincided with the city's annual Elvis Week celebration, a thirty-six-year tradition that drew thousands of impersonators from around the world to compete for the vaulted honor of "The King." The pageantry dominated life in Memphis for that week, with a culture all its own full of idiosyncratic traditions—one of which was local businesses leaving out large assortments of donuts for their employees every morning as an homage to Elvis's "heavyset" era.

The competition was spread out across multiple locations, with the gala finals being held at the downtown Orpheum Theater. With Elvises from almost every country descending on the city, including unexpected participants from Vietnam and India and an age group that ranged from ten years old to eighty, this uniquely eclectic gathering was indeed a worldwide cultural phenomenon.

Many King imitators took liberties with their presentations, some intentional, others inherent. There was Elfish, the little person, not to be confused with Elvish, who performed his act with Christmas elf flair. Melvis was either trying to differentiate himself as the Jewish Elvis or perhaps Brooklyn Elvis (it was hard to tell), but there was no mistaking the intent of Pelvis, who took the King's traditional stage moves to another level.

During the final night, Mexico's El Vez performed "Jailhouse Rock" with the intensity of young, skinny Elvis himself. The sight of him shaking his maracas (literally) in a tasseled sombrero, cummerbund, and traditional Spanish red floppy tie struck me as both hilarious and genius. I began to laugh uncontrollably, not at El Vez's expense, but in appreciation of his *distintivo instinto* . . . to the horror of those around me.

Seated in an aisle seat as security appeared by my side, I soon learned that the standing-room-only crowd, consisting of performers and lifelong Elvis fans who had waited all year for this night, didn't see Tijuana's finest as humorously as I did. As almost the only person in the audience not dressed in some sort of Elvis memorabilia, my reaction was apparently interpreted as outsider ridicule. In one quick moment, I was made aware of how seriously this was taken by all involved. Elvis imitators have no problem with being gawked or pointed at, but laughter was the ultimate insult.

"Sir, we are gonna have to ask you to leave?" said one of the ushers, outfitted in what could best be described as a white cape-coat to honor the occasion.

As I walked out amidst icy stares, it was clear that I would never fit into or fully understand Elvis Culture; but I could certainly respect this glorious week of nightlife performers, who would have more than held their own at Avalon.

Occasions such as Elvis Week gave me insight into Memphis's own unique, complex culture. Known as the Home of the Blues, Birthplace of Rock 'n' Roll, and a center of the civil rights movement, Memphis had a unique feel that was exemplified through its food, entertainment, and people, the historic center being downtown on Beale Street.

The area was identified by its three blocks of adjacent clubs and bars, the most notable being B.B. King's Blues Club. Beale Street had long been known as a nightlife destination in the same vein as Bourbon Street in New Orleans, both sharing the perk of allowing alcohol to be consumed outside on the street itself. While the Memphis Tourism Bureau had worked hard to build Beale Street into an international brand for tourists—capitalizing on the over 600,000 annual pilgrimages to Elvis's Graceland home, now itself a sprawling commercial enterprise—the reality for many local residents was quite a different story. For them, Beale Street had become akin to kosher food (without the considerable congregation of associated rabbis, still unconfirmed in my mind at this point)— disingenuous and existing in title only.

These born-and-raised Memphians had stopped frequenting Beale Street by the early 2000s, retaining the occasion only to show out-of-town guests a slice of their city, with often disappointing results. On-street drinking, once a positive, had turned into a city issue, as visitors became accustomed to buying drinks from to-go windows and then loitering for hours, never entering one of the street's dozen-plus sit down locations.

This dynamic brought an onset of violent incidents, branding the area with a reputation of being unsafe. With the crowd on Saturday night, by far the street's busiest, being predominantly black, a racial divide had formed, with Beale Street regarded by many as being for a black audience only.

I was introduced to Beale Street by the manager of the NBA's Memphis Grizzlies, who my sister had come to know as an attorney for two of their players. The Grizzlies' games took place at the FedExForum, which lined the street's southern-most side. With issues on Beale Street affecting their fans, an improved situation would help ticket sales and alleviate any aversion to the neighborhood, as well as offer a pre- and post-game entertainment option. The situation was something I had seen before, combining the problems we'd faced in Hollywood circa 2003 and the one-stop-shopping potential of Lansdowne Street.

The history of Beale Street nightlife was as rich and diverse as Memphis itself. Dating back to the 1920s, when its nightclubs formed the basis for the street's carnival-like atmosphere, it had drawn a mix of gamblers, prostitutes, pick-pockets, club-goers, and local politicians out for a night on the town. It served as a career launching pad for musicians and other more nefarious characters such as Machine Gun Kelly, who hawked whiskey from a back alley before progressing to big-time crime. One club, the Monarch, became known as "The Castle for Missing Men," where the bodies of shooting victims and dead gamblers could easily be disposed of by the undertaker who shared a back alley. From the 1920s to the 1940s, Beale Street hosted the likes of B.B. King, Muddy Waters, and Louis Armstrong along with other blues and jazz legends, cementing its legacy in pop culture.[26]

---

26 A youthful B.B. King was originally billed as the "Beale Street Blues Boy."

With my only sister and nephew already in Memphis, helping the once-iconic Beale Street return to relevance seemed a challenge worth pursuing. The east end of the street had long been marked as a particular problem area, so it was there that I would start.

Multiple adjacent buildings were marked for the initial Beale development plan, most importantly 380 Beale Street. A troubled nightclub location most recently named Plush, it was originally built by Muhammad Ali as his namesake movie theater. Its sordid past included drug dealing, prostitution, and multiple shootings, which might have been overlooked in the 1920s, but in 2013 the city closed the location for good, proclaiming it a public nuisance.

The other building on my list was the New Daisy Theatre, a live music venue best known by Memphians either as "the first place I ever saw a show, while in high school," or by older members of the black community as the first place they'd seen a movie. One thing everyone could agree on was its subpar bathroom conditions. While the New Daisy had served as a rite of passage for underage patrons, as the only venue of its type in Memphis it also hosted legitimate shows for the likes of Nirvana, Oasis, and Smashing Pumpkins in the early '90s. By the time competition arrived it had long gone out of favor, with little upkeep being done on the space for an entire decade. By 2015, the literal smell of despair emanated from its worn, two-decades-old carpets.

While inquiring around town about these desired properties, it became evident that Memphis had a way of doing business all its own, unlike anything I had experienced in either the U.S. or Asia. To begin with, all business deals appeared to come with peculiar conditions. At 380 Beale, one was the request that the wood patio and all copper wiring be taken out and given to its owner, George Miller, who had won the property in a disputed poker game decades earlier.

Another stipulation at the New Daisy was that the owner's son needed to stay on with the business. This was a potential stumbling block. Every national concert promoter I had spoken to about becoming the venue's booking partner had a condition of their own: that Mike Glenn, the owner of the New Daisy since the early '90s, not be allowed in the building. Apparently, Glenn, who wore an oversized beige suit with a prop cigar and could best be described as the guy in a mafia movie you knew was going to be wacked first, had made quite a reputation for himself over the years.

Just like acquiring the New Daisy lease had its unique challenges, its renovation would follow suit. While filming a 2003 television special, local-boy-done-well Justin Timberlake had left behind a large, intricate theatrical set of Beale Street facades, which had since served as the backdrop of the stage. The set protruded more than twelve feet out of the backstage wall, and took up valuable stage space that incoming acts would require. It needed to be ripped out.

As anyone who has ever done demolition can attest to, you often cannot tell what you'll find until you start whacking away. This was certainly the case here. Before long, we discovered not the usual support beam hidden within the installation, but an entire dwelling—someone had been *living* there for quite some time. What had started as a stage expansion job had turned into an apartment razing.

The current resident of the faux Beale Street facade was a man named Clement, the building's jack-of-all-trades who had used his access to secretly occupy a second-floor storefront for years, creating a multi-room walk-up. After making arrangements for him to relocate, I determined that he was exactly what the new business needed: a Memphis Julio.

Since being converted in the 1980s to an event space mainly to host boxing matches, the New Daisy had never operated with a functioning bar, nor adequate plumbing. This added to the infamous history of its bathrooms, as a stench would build up most nights to accompany the grungy fixtures.

What was identified as the "bar" was actually three display cases pushed together with a makeshift wooden top and then covered with cheap black fabric, allowing two people to serve from behind. To rectify this situation, the entire floor would need to be ripped out to make way for new copper piping, facilitating nine new bar stations and eliminating part of the bad-dream bathroom problem forever, especially in the ladies' room.

Without question, the most important room in any nightclub is the women's bathroom. With the lighting level needed to apply makeup, every blemish of the room is on display, and this makes a lasting impact on the female customer experience. Get it wrong, and you'll have hell to pay. Most men, on the other hand, could care less about the condition and design of their private space, content to take care of business in almost total darkness and happy if there is a partition between stalls.

Considering the life changes I had made moving from New York to Boston, and then Boston to L.A., and then L.A. to Singapore, I thought I was prepared for my time in good ol' Memphis. I was mistaken. While Boston had seemed small compared to NYC, Memphis was not really a city at all, with the persona of a large small town. As such, everyone knew everyone else's name and business.

Long-standing families had dominated Memphis for decades, leaving third and fourth generations of sons (and very few daughters) in charge of area real estate holdings and financial companies. They'd adopted a history rewrite, portraying themselves as self-made men and sweeping under the carpet the "old money" they'd been handed to get ahead. This left Memphis with an underlying desire to maintain the status quo, so as not to disrupt its "good ol' boy" network.[27]

Any significant changes proposed for Beale Street were aggressively pushed back on by the business owners entrenched there for decades. This group had formed a Merchants Association with a sole purpose that appeared to be protecting the interests of its members, who could bully the other members into submission. While attending my first Merchants meeting as a way of introducing myself, I was surprised to see Glenn

27 This part of Memphis culture was portrayed in the March 18, 2021, *Vanity Fair* article by Abigail Tracy titled "A Private Jet of Rich Trumpers Wanted to 'Stop the Steal' – But They Don't Want You to Read This."

already seated at the conference table, quickly leading me to assume that he had some emeritus involvement.

Listening to the group members talk over each other gave me a deeper insight into what might lay ahead. Loitering had become a city safety issue, but for the Beale Street clubs and bars it had become a by-product of their survival. It was simply easier to serve drinks via the to-go windows than to reinvent their entertainment offerings, which had not changed since Bon Jovi and Fleetwood Mac topped the record charts.

I saw an opportunity to celebrate Beale Street's history of blues music, and move Memphis nightlife beyond just milking Elvis's legacy. But others saw this as a radical departure from the ways things had always been done, evoking the rallying cry I had heard before: "You don't know how things work . . . you're not from around here." Which was exactly the point. So much for new perspectives.

When I did have the opportunity to speak at the meeting, I suggested that an overall beautification of the street be considered as a way to increase community involvement, including flower boxes lining its center and art installations by local muralists to refresh many of the buildings in disrepair. This was met with hostile responses for the sake of being hostile, not in opposition to the initiatives. It wasn't my view that others in the room were opposed to . . . it was *me*.

LAXIOM #18
Prepare for the most discerning, and others will follow.
Aim for whom you see as the most astute segment of your customer base. Make them happy, and you'll be off and running. But if your watermark is "it will be good enough," spoiler alert: it never is.

The New Daisy re-opened in the fall of 2015, with a week of shows highlighted by an audience-pleasing performance by Ben Rector. I adjusted my usual Avalon operations to better fit the Memphis audience, with a greater focus on live shows and a bi-monthly dance night to appeal to the city's smaller EDM market.

Returning to the venue the morning after a sold-out show for local rapper-made-good Yo Gotti, I arrived to find it padlocked, accompanied by a notice from the state tax authorities. We had been open for all of two weeks. I would come to find out later that day that our friend, Mike Glenn, had not been keeping current on his sales tax, a detail that appeared to have slipped his mind when selling the business.

Now, here you would be justified in saying, "It's up to you to find this out beforehand, not just take Glenn's word for it. Are you a shmohawk or what?"

Truth is, I *did* spend weeks looking up every tax, violation, and legal notice available to me, hiring a well-regarded local attorney to lead the process and leave no stone unturned. There were a few past violations for underage drinking in the early 2000s, a lawsuit that was well past its statute of limitations . . . the usual stuff. But nothing regarding past taxes.

My first call was to our attorney, who I assumed had missed a huge rock that rolled into the New Daisy front doors and was now blocking my entry. He knew nothing and instructed to me to go directly to the offices of the Tennessee Department of Revenue located thirty minutes away. Upon my arrival to the generic government office, I was shown to a generic conference room. Twenty minutes later, a woman identifying herself as the manager sat down and began to show me a list of unpaid taxes amounting to $22,000.

"These need to be paid before I can take the locks off the building," she informed me.

"We had no idea these were outstanding," I pleaded. "We looked at all the online records we could."

"Well, sometimes these"—she held up the mailed tax notices—"don't make it into our system, especially ones as old as these. Will that be check or credit card?"

"There's a show tonight we need to be open for. How quickly after these are paid will the locks be removed?

"Hard to say," she responded, generically.

"Of all the days to have this happen . . . the night of Disturbed," I mumbled under my breath.

"Sorry you are disturbed, but I'm just doing my job," she shot back.

"Tonight's band is called Disturbed," I explained (the heavy metal band had sold out in less than two hours). "But actually, so am I. Why didn't you just call us and let us know this was going on before locking us out?"

"We tried many times."

"Tried many times? What number did you call?" She then handed me one of the mailed notices and pointed to Mike Glenn's number, which was directly under his mailing address. "This one."

Jesus Christ, they know the business was sold. It's been all over the newspapers and TV.

"Why didn't you just call the New Daisy?"

"We called the number we had on file."

The rest of my day was spent reviewing amounts due while trying to calm down a panicked staff waiting outside along with an SBD TM, who made both *Spinal Tap* and Real Ian look like Joey Chicago. Finally, checks were cut and the locks were removed, but not before an hour-long liquor inventory check by agents who seemed set on carrying out a "fuck you" before exiting.

So irate was our attorney that he helped me draft a letter to the editor of the *Commercial Appeal*, the area's largest and longest-running newspaper. The letter's purpose was to draw attention to the fact that well over $500,000 had been spent just to restore the New Daisy—a much-needed overhaul for a landmark on the beleaguered Beale—along with bringing in top live acts and events good for the development of downtown Memphis as a whole.

The letter was supported by the New Daisy's landlord, the Downtown Memphis Commission, which was also caught off-guard by the situation and those trying to attract outside money (as well as millennials) to populate a wide range of new residential construction projects. Just a single phone call to the New Daisy could have avoided the entire fiasco. Was this the way to deal with out-of-town investors who were trying to improve the city?

Waking up at 5:00 AM (I didn't leave the Disturbed show until 1:00 AM) after an exhausting and anything but generic day, I sat in bed recalling the dream I'd just had:

I'm back in the Avalon Hollywood parking lot, recounting an actual conversation I'd had with Jesse and his new boss, Glen, an ex-actor who claimed to be a stand-in for Bo Duke, one of the lead characters on the early '80s TV show Dukes of Hazzard. *He was recounting an episode where he had to drive the famous 1969 Dodge Charger named the General Lee. Then I saw the General Lee go flying overhead, landing twenty feet from us, followed by what appeared to be a Keystone Cops car.*

I laid back down in thought. *It must be related to the events of the last twenty-four hours.* Bolting back up minutes later as if revived by an over-charged defibrillator, it came to me. *Oh my God . . . I've just been Boss Hogged!*

For the club's first six months of shows, I was plagued with situations that ate into my day in the form of distractions. Mike Glenn had made it his mission to appear outside the front door of the venue in full regalia, greeting customers as if he were the VIP doorman emeritus. This provoked the ire of our concert booking partner, Live Nation, which had made it clear that any sighting of Glenn would be deemed an act of bad faith.

To integrate the project locally—which I had been advised was a necessity to overcome any city obstacles, such as inspections and license renewals—I had taken on what was available in the Memphis investor pool, leading to the inevitable group of *That* Guys. One Memphis *That* Guy made it a point to show up for sold-out shows, demanding entry for himself and numerous guests even though he'd been repeatedly warned against it. He'd then throw a temper tantrum, not because he hadn't received tickets, but because he had to wait for the manager, Daniel, to bring them out. Another *That* Guy took it upon himself to become a drunken security vigilante, annoyingly pointing out customers he was convinced had snuck in through a side door.

Our guests and staff presented more of the same. A woman exiting a show under the influence claimed that one of the security staff had bit off part of her finger, showing her hand, covered with a blood-soaked napkin, as proof. Returning the same night to search for the missing appendage, she later determined that it was her boyfriend who had performed the deed, stashing the half-finger in her car before driving off.

Staff members were constantly at odds over matters such as the stealing of pre-assigned parking spots, leading to constant animated confrontations. Before the hip-hop artist 6lack's show, a stagehand was seen lying around inside instead of loading in band equipment. He was told to go home without pay by the production manager, Rory. The same stagehand, who was scheduled to work later that night as a barback, called who he deemed as his superior, a recent bartender-turned-bar manager, who then threatened a bartender walk-out unless the loader/bartender was immediately reinstated.

When I interceded as owner, deciding to have the loader/barback come back that night to work and then be removed as a loader going forward, Rory became incensed by this challenge of his authority. In a scene that even Tyler Perry might have deemed overdramatic, he began to dismantle the sound system, piece by piece, and load it into his pickup truck (which, according to the bar manager, was parked in her space).

As Rory huffed and puffed, continuing to load heavy speakers into his Ford F150 with the staff and band looking on in a combination of distain and freak-show fascination, the police were called. They arrived just as Rory was about to drive away with his haul. Seeing the cops down the block, Rory attempted to speed out of the parking lot, traveling all of six feet . . . before he ran out of gas.

Sitting in his truck surrounded by officers, Rory refused to roll down the window, pretending to be on his phone. A hostage negotiation took place, the result of which was the truck being pushed back to the load-out door and the equipment being put back. The only casualty was Rory's mental health and ego.[28]

After a year of working on developing 380 Beale, the main component of the Beale Street upgrade, I had reached an impasse. As demolition commenced, it wasn't a tenant we found hidden in its bowels, but illegal construction that had been masked for years. The club's entire second-floor wrap-around balcony, which had been added as an afterthought, was supported by sub-standard beams, creating a situation where the right amount of weight would cause the entire balcony to collapse. (The beams themselves were salvage beams, purchased second-hand from a metal junk yard. They didn't meet legal safety requirements, and were covered with a façade to avoid detection. For years, club-goers were unknowingly at risk of an imminent disaster.) It was also discovered that, although I had not agreed to give the building's remaining copper wiring away, it had indeed been removed through a little-known unsecured door on the roof.

The cost of renovation had increased by $400,000, and we now needed to build an entire new balcony and completely redo the plumbing and electrical system. At this point, it was not feasible to put that money into a building we were about to rent. For this to make sense, we needed to own it. We submitted an offer at fifteen percent over market value to purchase the property.

After George Miller passed away in 2014, the ownership of 380 Beale Street transferred to a family trust, whose main benefactor was George's ex-wife, now in her seventies. The ex-Mrs. Miller was well-known at the Memphis District Attorney's office. For years before moving out of town,

---

28 I must mention here that I have yet to be in a Memphis parking lot where someone wasn't sitting in their car on the phone. In fact, outside places like Kroger, it often looks like the car chatters outnumber the people inside. When I asked a local Memphian about this practice, he said, "Never really thought about it, but come to think of it, you're right. I guess it's just what we do down here." This left me with more questions than answers.

she would appear there unannounced, with proof of her husband's underhanded dealings, demanding action in an apparent takeover attempt. In a bizarre-for-the-course conference call to try and complete a sale, the family matriarch set a new asking price of $1.2 million—three times its assessed value. In a manner that made Gene look like a choir boy by comparison, she proceeded to berate me to the point that I had to remind her my name was not "goddamn motherfucker" as I made every attempt to explain the reality of the situation.

It was the first and last time I spoke with the widow Miller.

As the development of 380 Beale stalled, I received a call from a reporter at the *Commercial Appeal* claiming that he wanted to discuss its progress. Listening to his questions during our coffee meeting, I learned that Memphis had its own version of the Bambino curse known as the "Pyramid Scheme," which helped explained a lot of my recent encounters. The Great American Pyramid, opened in 1991, was originally built as a 20,000-seat arena on the Mississippi River in Memphis's Pinch District. Envisioned by local entrepreneur John Tigrett (Isaac's father) as a shining symbol of his hometown, the structure played on the city's Egyptian name origin, and was welcomed with the enthusiasm of being the eighth Wonder of the World.[29]

Public financing was tapped to cover half the $65 million price tag, with businessman and part Denver Nuggets owner Sidney Shlenker teaming up with Tigrett to manage construction and develop aspects of the facility. Shlenker, who passed away in 2003, was a man of big, often questionable ideas. Part P.T. Barnum, part Donald Trump, he was best known for arranging the "Battle of the Sexes" tennis match between Bobby Riggs and Billie Jean King at the Houston Astrodome. What he possessed in showmanship was a far second to his ambitious vision. His plans included a 3-D laser production, a massive computerized jukebox, and an in-house radio station, as well as a Hard Rock Café, Grammy Museum,

29 It actually measured as the tenth-tallest pyramid ever built.

College Football Hall of Fame, and private nightclub. He also wanted to build the world's highest-incline elevator and convert the neighboring Mud Island River Park into a $100 million theme park called Rakapolis. During the project's groundbreaking (coined the "Big Dig") in 1989, Shlenker's over-the-top style was on full display when a giant illuminated shovel was lowered from a helicopter as a laser-generated silhouette of a pyramid appeared in the night sky, costing city taxpayers over $400,000.[30]

From the start, the Memphis Pyramid ran into serious problems, both financial and logistical. During an opening night performance by The Judds, the mighty Mississippi flooded into the bathrooms, forcing workers to surround the stage with sandbags to protect the electrical equipment onstage. By this time, the venture was more than $16 million in debt due to construction overruns. There would be no Hard Rock Café, Grammy Museum, private nightclub, or any of the other accoutrements Shlenker had been promoting. Lewis Graham, also of the *Commercial Appeal*, summed up the situation in a 1992 postmortem: "For decades, the city lusted for a tourism boom, for a professional sports franchise, for a recognized symbol of major league status, anything to catapult it to national prominence. Shlenker promised to deliver on that dream. To do it, though, he needed other people's money."

During its short-lived run as an arena, the Pyramid hosted concerts for the likes of Mary J. Blige and Phish. But there was a reason you didn't see any other pyramid-shaped concert venues around, let alone one made of glass and steel: the acoustics were terrible, creating an unmanageable echo. To add insult to injury, in 1993 the Luxor Hotel and Casino opened in Las Vegas, becoming the tallest pyramid in North America and surpassing the Memphis Pyramid by a mere eighteen feet.

In 2001, Memphis was awarded its professional sports franchise, relocating the NBA's Vancouver Grizzlies to town. Considered inadequate

30 The Big Dig was coincidentally the same name given to the infamous Central Artery project in Boston at the same time. The project later became the most expensive highway undertaking ever in the U.S. at a cost *overrun* of over $16 billion.

as an NBA venue, the Pyramid was shuttered just over a decade after opening, when the Grizzlies opted to play at the newly built FedExForum two miles away. The Pyramid went unused for the next decade, until Memphis could finally lay claim to the world's biggest and best . . . Bass Pro Shop.

I asked then Mayor Wharton how the Bass Pro Shop deal had come about. I'd been a fan of the mayor since my arrival, based on his Grandma Mary-like warm demeanor and enthusiasm for positive change. He replied, "Well, in the end, the bar for developing what had become a problem for the city was pretty low. At least it wasn't turned into a parking lot."

What had begun as a defining moment for Memphis, filled with promise, hope, and economic opportunity, had left a Pyramid-shaped scar on the city. As Nashville continued to grow, attracting new development while defining itself as the shining jewel of the Mid-South, the envious Memphis was left behind, its skyline defined by a colossal outdoorsman man-cave.[31]

The name Sidney Shlenker came up frequently as I spoke with *Commercial Appeal* journalist. He drew many parallels between Shlenker and myself, describing Shlenker as the out-of-towner who had rolled in, taken the city's money, and then escaped on the midnight train. Never mind the fact that I had not asked the city for a dime, bearing all the risk with the Memphis *That* Guys to revive an area of Beale Street that had been all but left for naught—or that the New Daisy was already refurbished and operating, receiving rave reviews.

With the Pyramid Scheme hanging palpably over our conversation, it was unlike any press interview I had ever sat for. In NYC and L.A., it was widely accepted that the reason you were in town was to be successful at the highest level, hence the "New York, New York" lyrics. This was the first time I had been asked, albeit indirectly: Why would you come *here*? The only conclusion being drawn was that I must be a "Shlenker," rather

31 The way many Memphians felt about Nashville was eerily similar to how Bostonians felt about NYC.

than a fan of Memphis's rich musical history, potential for development, and lifestyle affordability—not to mention that I had recently gotten engaged and was building a new house. This prevalent attitude toward outsiders certainly wasn't doing Memphis any favors. In fact, it had become self-prophesizing, as top entrepreneurs from around the country continued to bypass Pyramid-scarred Memphis and head to Nashville instead.

LAXIOM #19
The trap of the one-legged man.
Success does not translate from situation to situation, but the elements of success *do* . . . just ask any movie director. Guy Ritchie received a "worst director" nomination for *Swept Away* after his critical acclaim for *Lock, Stock and Two Smoking Barrels* and *Snatch*. By making the *decision* to get involved in *Swept Away*, he became a one-legged man in an ass-kicking contest.

In June of 2019, as I was leaving the house for a Saturday morning walk, two cop cars pulled up. Four officers approached me, indicating that they had a warrant out for my arrest. The charge: theft. Leaving my fiancée shocked and confused and spurring our dog, Milton, to jump into the police car with me out of protective instinct, I was transported to the Shelby County Jail. Upon arrival, no other information about the charge was available, and it wasn't until I returned home at 5:00 AM that I was able to piece together what had transpired.

The story had been the lead-in for all the local nightly news channels, portraying the situation as major breaking news. It involved bounced $20,000 checks from the New Daisy that were never reimbursed. The person making the claim: Mike Glenn.

The reporters then added their own color, stating that the venue had been closed under "mysterious circumstances" (it had been closed temporarily while a fire safety system, state-mandated for all venues built pre-1960, was being installed) and that it had a "history of building code violations" (which was true-*ish*, with dozens of them under the ownership of Glenn and three since 2015—for an EXIT sign light that had burned out).

My sister contacted a prominent defense attorney, who agreed to look over the case. On Monday morning before the court arraignment, I met with Mark at his office, a four-room stand-alone building near the courthouse filled with requisite law journals and stability-indicating leather armchairs. As Mark read Glenn's deposition to me for the first time, he stopped mid-sentence and, in Branfman-like fashion, stated, "This all smells like bullshit." I had seen that look of confidence and defiance before, knowing then that I had indeed found my Ben Branfman.

Glenn's assertion was that I had written him a check for $19,000 owed to him for a New Daisy concert he'd promoted, which had subsequently bounced.

"What this says," explained Mark, "is that you stole Glenn's $19,000 and took off to, say, Cancun with it. Have you been to Cancun lately? I've got to tell you, I've never quite seen anything like this before."

Arriving at the courtroom, I took my seat in the assigned area and watched Mark in discussion with the district attorney and his team of public prosecutors. My second visit to a courtroom was much different than the first. Gone were the highly colorful nightlife ambassadors and large gallery. I was now a defendant, not an observer.

One thing that both proceedings did have in common was the presence of a Michele Adelman, who in this case had signed in at security as Michele Ryland. In a month she would become my wife, sitting ten rows behind me with a supportive but worried look on her face.

Off to the left side of the judge was a small, enclosed benched area. A concealed door behind it opened, and six handcuffed black men were walked in and sat down. These were inmates who had not made bail. After each was introduced to the judge by a jail guard, who bore an uncanny resemblance to Delroy Lindo's character Bo in the movie *Get Shorty*, the judge reviewed their case folders and then asked the same two questions of each:

"Can you make bail?"

"Do you have an attorney?"

The men's stories were heartbreaking, on display for all in the court-room to hear and witness. One had no money and no family, unable to make the $50 bail bond he needed to be released. Another seemed to lack comprehension of his situation, needing assistance to answer the judge's question, while a third didn't know any attorneys or have the means to pay for one. The judge projected compassion for their situations, advising them on potential options for help, but was limited by procedure on next steps. The men were then marched back out the door like a chain gang in their issued orange shirt and pants.

Stunned and disheartened, I pondered the fate of these men whose crimes where at a level where $100 would give them their freedom. See-ing myself as someone with the good fortune of being exposed to a wide range of experiences in my life, nothing had prepared me for this culture shock, opening my eyes to the fact that, by luck of the draw, that could have been me.

"We can go," said Mark, motioning to me from the aisle as I stared at the now-empty bench. "The DA wants some time to look into these charges. He just got the case this morning. Any backup you can provide would be helpful. We've agreed to meet again in two weeks."

Backup in the form of emails and bank records was easy to come by in refuting Glenn's claim. First, eight months earlier a check had been writ-ten by the New Daisy to a small-time promoter named Bowe O'Brien, who Glenn was now claiming as his silent partner. The New Daisy con-troller had instructed O'Brien to wait three days before cashing the check while the online ticket money for his event was sent—an instruction he had ignored, depositing the check immediately.

At the same time, O'Brien had booked another show. I received a call from a confused agent, discovering that O'Brien was trying to move to a larger venue due to unexpectedly high ticket sales, his excuse being that the New Daisy had no lights or sound for shows.

Fuming over O'Brien's attempt to unethically move the show and damage the standing of the New Daisy, O'Brien was then informed that he would be sent fifty percent of his ticket money, with the other half being held back until he corrected the situation with the agent. He remained silent, unable to walk back what he had said for fear of damaging his own future. Whether or not O'Brien had ever spoken to Glenn about any of this remained unknown, but the result was that Glenn had made false statements to the police.

Two weeks later, I was back in a courtroom. After waiting all but five minutes, Mark told me to wait in the lobby. One hour later he informed me that all charges had been dropped. When discussing what to do next with Glenn, he recommended, with Branfman-like candor, that knowing he would spend the rest of his life as Mike Glenn would be remuneration enough. Anything beyond that just wasn't worth the time.

One month after walking out of jail, I was married to Michele on Fourth of July weekend in the small southwestern Michigan town of Three Oaks, just miles from Lake Michigan. If any of those mistrusting spectators of twenty years ago at the Gatien trial came across Michele on Facebook, their theory regarding me being a confidential informant might have been mistakenly confirmed. *Holy shit . . . he was married to her!*

It had been more than forty years since that first dance in a converted-for-the-night high school gym, and now I was fortunate enough to experience my second "first dance" with my wife. The John Hughes types were now adult Judd Apatow types, and my early dreams of running away with Miss Sanderson had been fulfilled in a manner better than I could have ever imagined.

Following long-standing nightlife tradition, our close friends and out-of-shape uncles and aunts used this celebration as a way to pass their out-of-sync dance moves to the next generation, in a perspiration shower of awkward twisting and gyration. A Misty or Mr. and Mrs. J, they were not . . . no matter how they saw themselves. However, this passing of the torch was rejected by Gen Z-ers, the new, social media-savvy breed that was fully able to discern their own dance future. As parents brought back classics like the "Elaine Dance" and "Looking for My Keys," their kids Dougie-d and twerked circles around them.

To bridge the generational divide, Michele's BFF, Becki, had organized a flash mob performance of "Uptown Funk" as part of the festivities. Taking their music cue, twenty-five people of all generations took to the dance floor in what could best be described as the Celebration of the Smashed All-Stars, with the well-planned choreography breaking down into improvised solo routines by the end of the song.

Standing next to my best man, Gregory Homs, I couldn't help but reflect back to when we'd first met. Since that time, I had been headhunted by two murderers, relied on advice from felons and arrested myself, and watched my Nana out-dance an ex-NFL lineman and then mistake her for Danny DeVito. I'd been drunkenly taken for Sherlock Holmes, chastised by a rock icon, ghost-hunted, and hit by a projectile cheeseburger. I'd launched a musical movement, butted heads with Jerry Falwell, served as an equal opportunity employer for little people, rang in the New Year with Matt Damon's mother, leveraged a porn star, almost pancaked Prince, and built the world's most lavish nightclub, all in a day's work.

Grandma Mary had passed away thirteen years earlier, and for the first time, her true age was revealed to the entire public. Claiming to be a perpetual seventy-five, years before her death she had wrapped her Seville-boat around a tree and walked away unscathed. Apparently, she was driving a mere twenty-five miles per hour while hogging two lanes when a fellow motorist sped past her on the shoulder of the road, flipping her the bird. Mary, barely able to see over the dashboard, took this as a friendly wave, returning the gesture as her eyes left the road. The *Bay City Times* report of the incident listed Mary's true age, which her two sons knew would cause her distress. They took to the neighborhood to remove as many newspapers off front porches as they could. Mary was ninety-nine when she died.

With his health declining and the onset of dementia imminent, Mel was unable to attend the ceremony. At the age of eighty-five, he might have lost a step getting around, but not from his welcoming nature. Just imagining him going from guest to guest with his standard greeting, "Hello, I'm Mel, how are you doing today?," made his presence felt.

"This is the best planned wedding I've ever been to," said Michele's impeccable friend, Jill. "It's like a cool club."

Well, I did have the advantage of experience with such things, and although Michele and the wedding planner had done most of the legwork, I was around to ensure that the music, lighting, and ambiance were just right.

Looking around the room at the smiles of those who really mattered, I felt something gently land on my shoulder.

The elusive indigo bunting had appeared.

It didn't happen when, where, or how I had expected, but as nightlife had taught me so well, that's not how life works.

EPILOGUE

In March of 2020, as the COVID-19 virus landed like a live grenade in the laps of the entire planet, for the first time in history nightlife around the world all but ceased to exist. In the U.S. alone, well over 400,000 people lost their jobs, many of whom lived paycheck to paycheck, as the entire $27 billion industry came to a screeching halt.

Many took to social media as pseudo-experts, with doomsday predictions for the end of nightlife as we know it. These "false pundits" fail to realize that nightlife is always on the verge of being a new experience, staying one step ahead and constantly reinventing itself as we anxiously anticipate its next move.

Now, well over two years later, as we work to recover from an unprecedented time, nightlife has begun to not only bounce back, but as social norms are slowly restored, to become an even more valued aspect of everyday life as dance floors, concert venues, and music festivals populate with renewed enthusiasm and energy. Like a significant other taken for granted, only when they are gone do you truly realize how much they are missed.

The details of what nightlife will end up looking like moving forward are something I currently spend my days formulating. As many millennials and others struggle to regain their disposable income, high admission and drink costs in major cities such as Las Vegas will likely need to adjust. Settings that allow people to interact easily will be at a premium as the public seeks to reconnect en masse. Creativity will need to take a front-row seat as many venues move forward with limited funds. The result will be a more inclusive and enjoyable shared experience, something of amplified value in today's world.

What has always motivated me and kept me moving forward is the opportunity to wake up on any given day with an idea, any idea, good or not so good, and turn it into reality—whether it's conceiving a brand that has current social relevance, developing a seen-better-days city block and changing the culture of a city, testing my abilities on the other side of the world, or plotting the future of nightlife itself. No waiting around here. In almost all instances, the feedback is swift and absolute.

Perhaps longtime NYC nightlife personality Amanda Lepore put it best: "People always think that when they grew up, it was better. The people who went to Studio 54 say, 'Oh, this is nothing.' Or 'The Limelight is nothing. In our day it was much better.' But I mean, it's always great . . . to me, you've just got to make it happen. You can't be a downer and say, 'This is nothing like the Roaring Twenties.'"

It is no coincidence that the Roaring Twenties came on the heels of the 1918 influenza pandemic. The 1920s became the age of art deco, jazz, Coco Chanel, *The Great Gatsby*, and Walt Disney. "It was the first truly modern decade," points out retired Marquette University economics historian Gene Smiley. Literary critic Malcolm Cowley captured the era as follows: "Americans . . . chose to live in the pure moment, live gaily on gin and love."

My favorite London mathematician, Hannah Fry, who interestingly studies the statistics behind sex, happiness, and love, sees the numbers stacking up. "The Roaring Twenties were really about being near people," she points out. "We can expect that again."

I have no doubt that the new era of nightlife to be ushered in will define a new Golden Age, the perfect storm of pent-up demand meeting a changing society. Whatever the future of nightlife brings us, one thing is for sure: the next RuPaul, Madonna, Avicii, or Jiggy is out there somewhere, just waiting to be discovered.

ACKNOWLEDGMENTS

Thanks to Gene, Peter, John, and Rich for giving me my big breaks and to all those who took time out of their day to help me in the writing of the manuscript:

Gregory Homs and the team at Wink, for their original concepts and the ability to translate them into business reality. Your constant feedback and ideas were critical not only in shaping the final story but also in providing me with food for thought.

Candy for bringing ideas to vibrant life with your visionary artwork since day one.

Cristen Iris, who took an idea and formed it into something tangible. Without your guidance, technical expertise, vision, and communication, there would be no book.

Jonathan Starke for his command of editing and positive words.

Jeffrey Goldman and the staff at Santa Monica Press for patiently guiding me through the publishing process.

Anthony Haden-Guest, Tina Paul, and Drew Ressler for their efforts and contributions.

Lüüle, editor emeritus, whose love for the written word was contagious.

To Big Mama, Dirt, Pappy, Peg, Steph, Pops, Pat, Sue, Jeff, Chris, and Cousin Fred, thanks for your valued thoughts and perspectives.

Also, Alden, Ernie, Lorno, and Jenn for your help and enthusiasm, and my daily sidekick, Milton, who was always there for a needed distraction.

And, of course, all those too numerous to mention here who I've laughed with over the last thirty years and whose support has made this book possible.